SCIENCE

Authors
Brian Arnold, Hannah Kingston & Emma Poole

CONTENTS

BIOLOGY

Revised

- Life Processes and Cells 4
- Plant and Human Organ Systems 6
- Nutrition and Food Tests 8
- The Digestive System 10
- Heart of the Matter 12
- Blood and Circulatory System 14
- Skeleton, Muscles and Joints 16
- The Lungs and Breathing 18
- Adolescence and the Menstrual Cycle 20
- Reproduction 21
- Drugs, Solvents, Alcohol and Tobacco 22
- Fighting Disease 24
- Photosynthesis 26
- Plant Reproduction 28
- The Carbon and Nitrogen Cycles 30
- Classification 32
- Variation and Selective Breeding 34
- Inheritance and Genetics 36
- Food Chains and Webs 38
- Adaptation and Competition 40
- Exam Questions 42

CHEMISTRY

Revised

- Rocks 44
- The Rock Cycle 46
- Pollution of the Atmosphere 48
- States of Matter 50
- Dissolving 52
- Particle Theory 54
- Atoms and Elements 56
- Metals 58
- Unusual Metals and Non-Metals 60
- Simple Chemical Reactions 62
- Reactivity Series 64

	Revised
Metal Displacement Reactions 66	☐
Acids and Alkalis 68	☐
Making Salts 70	☐
Common Tests and Apparatus 72	☐
Mixtures 74	☐
Separation Techniques 76	☐
Compounds 78	☐
Naming Compounds 80	☐
Balancing Equations 82	☐
Exam Questions 84	☐

PHYSICS

	Revised
Speed 86	☐
Graphs of Motion 88	☐
Forces 90	☐
Friction and Terminal Velocity 92	☐
Moments 94	☐
Pressure 96	☐
Light Rays and Reflection 98	☐
Refraction and Colour 100	☐
Sounds 102	☐
Echoes and Hearing 104	☐
Energy 106	☐
Using Energy Resources 108	☐
Alternative Sources of Energy 110	☐
Heat Transfer 112	☐
Circuit Diagrams and Components 114	☐
Circuits – Current and Voltage 116	☐
Magnetism and Electromagnetism 118	☐
The Solar System and Beyond I 120	☐
The Solar System and Beyond II 122	☐
Exam Questions 124	☐
Answers 126	☐
Index 127	☐

LIFE PROCESSES AND CELLS

Cells are the building blocks of life. All living things are made up of cells. A living thing is called an organism. Plants and animals are organisms. To be alive animals and plants need to have seven characteristics. These are movement, respiration, sensitivity, growth, reproduction, excretion and nutrition.

ANIMAL AND PLANT CELLS

- The cells that make up plants and animals can be seen using a microscope and staining them so they show up more clearly.
- You need to know the differences between them.

They both have:
Nucleus
Cytoplasm
Cell membrane

Only plant cells have:
Cell wall
Vacuole
Chloroplasts

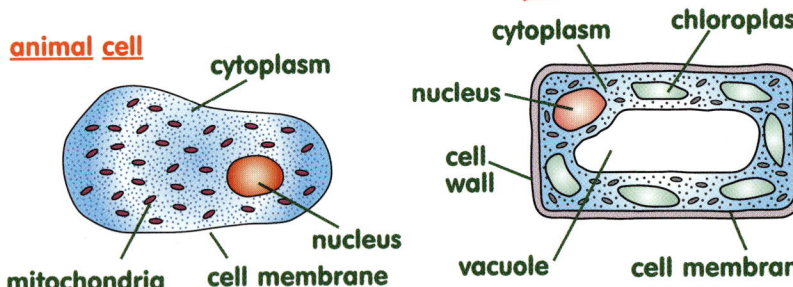

Nucleus – controls the cell. It controls everything the cell does and also contains all the information needed to produce a new living organism.
Cytoplasm – where the chemical reactions take place.
Cell membrane – holds the cell together and controls what passes in and out of the cell.
Cell wall – made of cellulose, which gives a plant cell strength and support.
Vacuole – contains a weak solution of salts and sugar called cell sap.
Chloroplasts – contain a green substance called chlorophyll. This absorbs the Sun's energy so that the plant can make its own food by photosynthesis.
Mitochondria – where respiration takes place in plant and animal cells.

CELL DIVISION

- Animal and plant cells multiply from single cells to entire organisms and they also have to be replaced if they become damaged. This is achieved by a process called mitosis. Mitosis forms cells that are exactly the same as the original cell. For example, if you cut yourself, your skin cells divide by mitosis to replace the lost cells, first into two, then into four and so on.

- Another type of cell division is called meiosis. Meiosis occurs when producing sex cells: sperms and eggs. This type of cell division produces cells that contain only half the information in the original cell. In this way, when a sperm fertilises an egg a full set of information is restored. These cells can then begin to multiply by mitosis.

SPECIAL CELLS

Some cells can change their shape in order to carry out a particular job. It's a bit like a factory where each person has their own job. It's more efficient this way. One cell can't do everything.

SPECIALISED ANIMAL CELLS

- A sperm cell has a tail which enables it to swim towards the egg.

tail

- Red blood cells carry oxygen around the body.
- They have no nucleus.

biconcave discs

cross section

- Nerve cells are shaped like wires to conduct messages around the body.

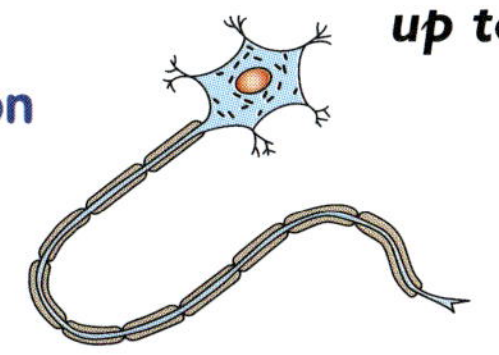

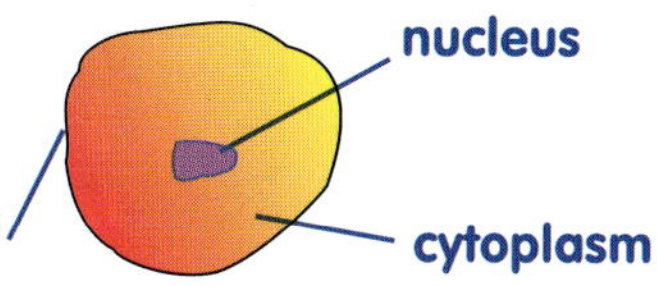

cell membrane — nucleus — cytoplasm

- Egg cells or ova are much larger than sperm. The nucleus contains chromosomes from the mother. In the cytoplasm is yolk, which provides a food store for the developing organism if fertilised.

- Ciliated cells line all air passages into your lungs. They produce mucus, which traps dust and bacteria. Tiny hairs called cilia waft the mucus up to the throat to be swallowed.

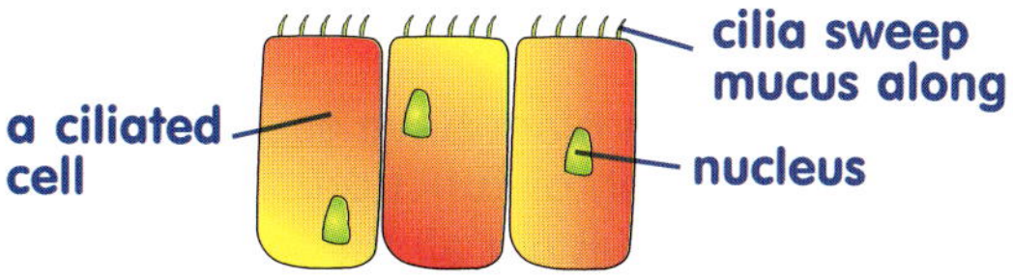

a ciliated cell — cilia sweep mucus along — nucleus

SPECIALISED PLANT CELLS

- Root hair cells are long and thin to absorb water and minerals from the soil.
- They increase the surface area of the roots

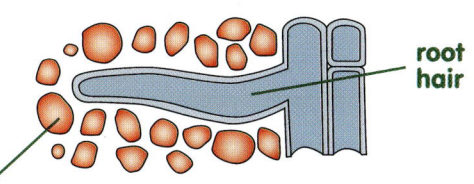
the soil — root hair

- Palisade cells have lots of chloroplasts. They are near the surface of the leaf so they can absorb sunlight for photosynthesis.

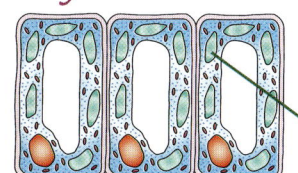
lots of chloroplasts

Examiner's Top Tip
Learn the examples of specialised plant and animal cells. Note that they all have a nucleus, cell membrane and cytoplasm.

CELLS, TISSUES, ORGANS, ORGAN SYSTEMS

- A group of similar cells working together form a tissue.
- An organ is made up of different tissues working together.
- Organs working together make organ systems.
- Cells group together to form tissues and organs until all the cells make up an organism.
- In animals, muscle cells make up muscle tissue; muscle tissue makes up organs such as the heart and blood vessels; and the heart and blood vessels work together to form the circulatory system, pumping blood around the body.

QUICK TEST

1. Name three differences between a plant and an animal cell.
2. What does the cell membrane do?
3. What does the cell wall do?
4. What is a specialised cell?
5. A group of similar cells carrying out the same job are called a _____?
6. Which type of cell division is used for growth and replacement of cells?

1. Plant cell has chloroplasts, cell wall and a vacuole.
2. It controls what passes in and out of the cell.
3. Gives a plant cell extra strength and support.
4. A cell that has changed its shape to do a particular job.
5. Tissue.
6. Mitosis.

PLANT AND HUMAN ORGAN SYSTEMS

PLANT ORGANS

- The plant's basic structure is divided up into five parts.
- The parts of a plant have each adapted to do a particular job or function.
- The plant carries out all the seven life processes.
- Every cell in the plant carries out respiration.

1. THE FLOWER

This contains the male and female sex organs. These make seeds.
The flower is usually brightly coloured to attract insects for pollination.

2. THE STEM

This holds the plant upright.
It contains hollow tubes called xylem and phloem.
Xylem tubes carry water and dissolved minerals from the root to the leaves.
Phloem carries glucose made by the leaf in photosynthesis up and down the plant.

3. THE ROOT

The root's main job is anchoring the plant in the soil.
It also takes up water and minerals from the soil.

4. THE ROOT HAIRS

The actual place where water and minerals are absorbed from the soil.
Root hairs increase the surface area of the root for more efficient absorption.

Examiner's Top Tip
Learn the five parts of a flowering plant and what they are for.

5. THE LEAF

- The leaf is the organ of photosynthesis. It makes all the food for the plant.
- The top layer of the leaf contains the palisade cells. This is where most photosynthesis takes place.
- The palisade cells contain lots of chloroplasts. The chloroplasts contain a pigment called chlorophyll. Chlorophyll absorbs sunlight for photosynthesis.
- On the lower surface of the leaf are tiny holes called stomata.
- The stomata open and close to let carbon dioxide in and water vapour and oxygen out.

HUMAN ORGAN SYSTEMS

- The <u>seven life processes</u> are carried out by different systems in the human body.
- There are <u>nine organ systems</u> in the body.
- The following are covered in detail on other pages in this book.

1) The skeletal system
2) The muscle system
3) The respiratory system
4) The digestive system
5) The circulatory system
6) The reproductive system

The three remaining systems are:

NERVOUS SYSTEM

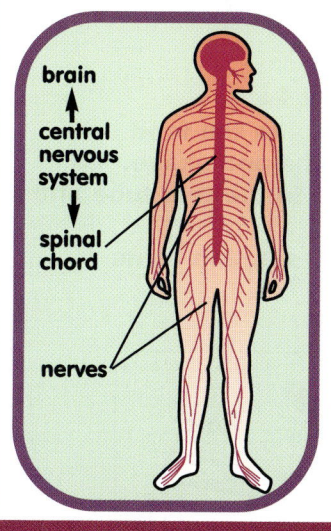

- We have <u>five sense organs</u> that respond to the environment around us.
- They are the <u>nose</u> (smell), <u>eyes</u> (sight), <u>ear</u> (sound), <u>tongue</u> (taste) and <u>skin</u> (touch).
- All the sense organs contain nerves that detect changes in our surroundings.
- The nerves send signals to the brain and spinal cord, which make up the central nervous system.
- The brain or spinal chord responds by sending signals back to instruct our muscles what to do.

THE EXCRETORY SYSTEM

- The main organs of excretion are the kidneys.
- Cells produce waste products which go into the blood, some of which are poisonous.
- The kidneys filter and 'clean' the blood by removing these waste products.
- The poisonous waste is turned into <u>urine</u> and stored in the bladder until ready to be released.
- The kidneys control the amount of water going to the bladder so that if you drink a lot of liquid you produce more urine.

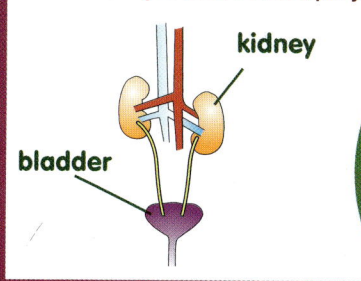

Examiner's Top Tip
Be able to name the nine organ systems of the body and say briefly what they do.

ENDOCRINE SYSTEM

- The endocrine system produces <u>hormones</u> in parts of the body called <u>glands</u>.
- The glands release the hormones into the <u>bloodstream</u> where they are carried to where their action is needed.
- Hormones travel a lot slower than nerve messages but their effects are usually longer lasting.
- Hormones control things like <u>menstruation</u> in women as well as the changes that occur during puberty.

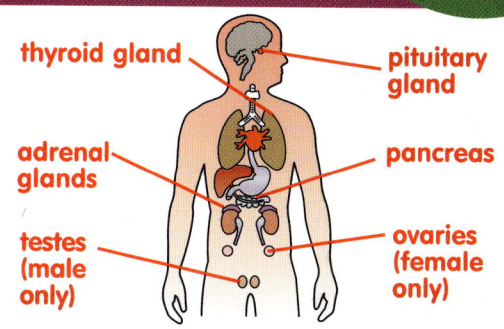

DIABETES

- Diabetes is a disease caused by the pancreas not making enough of the hormone insulin.
- Insulin makes sure that the body cells get enough glucose (from food) for respiration. This keeps the blood sugar level normal.
- Without treatment a diabetic would have high blood sugar levels and feel tired and thirsty because their glucose would remain in the blood and very little would be absorbed by their body cells.

QUICK TEST

1. What is the job of the leaf?
2. Name the part of the plant that keeps it upright.
3. What is the root's main job?
4. What do the palisade cells contain a lot of?
5. What are the tubes called that transport water and minerals to the leaf?
6. Which organ in the body produces the hormone insulin?

1. Photosynthesis. 2. Stem. 3. To anchor the plant. 4. Chloroplasts/chlorophyll. 5. Xylem. 6. The pancreas.

NUTRITION AND FOOD TESTS

CARBOHYDRATES

- Carbohydrates consist of starch and different types of sugar e.g. glucose (the sugar our bodies use for respiration).
- We need carbohydrates to <u>give us energy</u>.
- Starch is actually made up of smaller glucose molecules joined together.

CHEMICAL TEST FOR STARCH
- Add two drops of yellow/brown <u>iodine solution</u> to food solution.
- Solution will turn blue/black if starch is present.

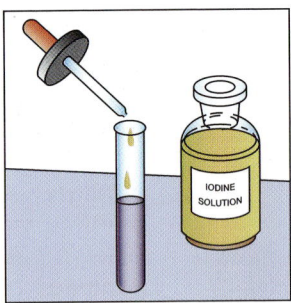

CHEMICAL TEST FOR GLUCOSE
- Add a few drops of <u>Benedict's solution</u> to food solution.
- Heat in a water bath until it boils.
- If glucose is present, an orange/red precipitate will form.

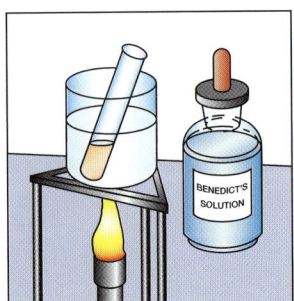

Examiner's Top Tip
Learn the food tests for starch, glucose, protein and fats.

FATS

- Fats are made from fatty acids and glycerol.
- We need fats for a <u>store of energy</u>, to make <u>cell membranes</u> and for <u>warmth</u> (insulation).

CHEMICAL TEST FOR FAT
- Add 2 cm^3 of <u>ethanol</u> to the food solution in a test tube and shake.
- Add 2 cm^3 of <u>water</u> to the test tube and shake again.
- Fat is present if the solution turns <u>cloudy white</u>.

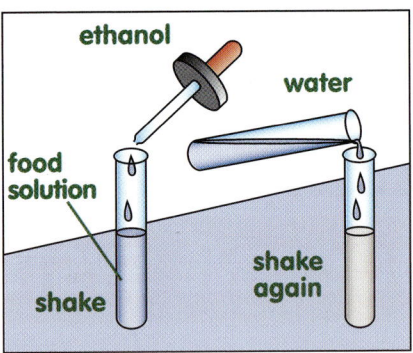

WATER

Water makes up approximately 65% of your body weight.
Water is important because:
- Our blood plasma is mainly water.
- Water is in sweat that cools us down.
- Chemical reactions in our cells take place in water.
- Waste products are removed from our bodies in water.
- Food and drink contain water.

Examiner's Top Tip
Find out examples of foods belonging to each food group.

The nutrition groups are:
- Carbohydrates, proteins, fat, vitamins and minerals, fibre and water.
- A balanced diet is made up of all of the above nutrients.
- There are chemical tests for carbohydrates, proteins and fats.

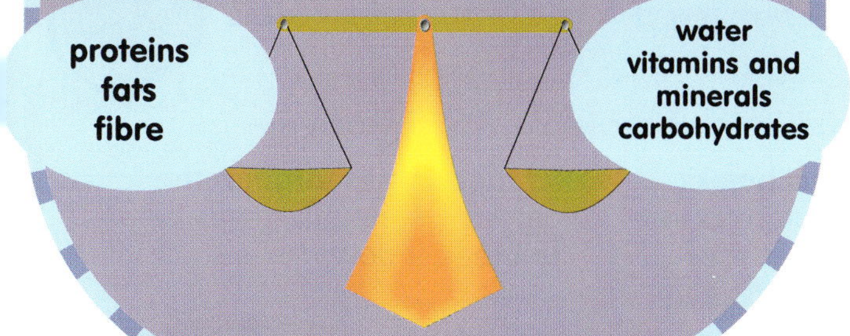

proteins fats fibre

water vitamins and minerals carbohydrates

A balanced diet

PROTEIN

- Your body cells are mostly made of protein.
- Proteins are made up of lots of amino acids.
- We need protein to repair and replace damaged cells and to make new cells during growth.

CHEMICAL TEST FOR PROTEIN (THE BIURET TEST)
- Add some weak copper sulphate to the food solution.
- Carefully add drops of sodium hydroxide to the solution.
- If protein is present, the solution gradually turns purple.

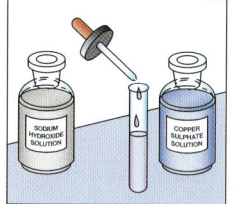

VITAMINS AND MINERALS

We only need these in small amounts, but they are essential for good health. Vitamins and minerals are found in fruit, vegetables and cereals.

Deficiency diseases are caused by a lack of vitamins and minerals.

Vitamin C keeps the skin strong and supple; without it the skin cracks and the gums bleed (called scurvy).

Vitamin D helps the bones harden in children; without it the bones stay soft (a disease called rickets).

We need the mineral iron for making haemoglobin and the mineral calcium for healthy bones and teeth.

FIBRE

- Fibre, or roughage, comes from plants.
- Fibre is not actually digested; it just keeps food moving smoothly through your system.
- Fibre provides something for your gut muscles to push against. It is a bit like squeezing toothpaste through a tube.
- It prevents constipation.

NUTRITIONAL NEEDS

- The amount of energy a person needs from their food depends on:
  - their size
  - how active they are
  - their age.
- Males need more energy than females as they are generally bigger and metabolise faster.
- A person who has an active job needs more energy than, for example, a person who works in an office.
- A growing child needs more energy than a fully grown adult.
- A pregnant woman needs slightly more energy than normal.

QUICK TEST

1. What do we use carbohydrates for?
2. What is the chemical test for starch?
3. What is the chemical test for glucose?
4. What do our bodies need fat for?
5. Why is protein important to our cells?
6. What is the chemical test for protein?
7. Why is fibre important?

Answers (upside down):
1. Energy.
2. Iodine solution; a blue/black colour means starch is present.
3. Benedict's solution and heat; an orange precipitate means glucose is present.
4. Store energy, make cell membranes and insulation.
5. Repair and replace cells, and make new cells for growth.
6. Biuret test; if solution turns purple, protein is present.
7. It helps food move through your system and prevents constipation.

THE DIGESTIVE SYSTEM

- The digestive system is really one long tube called the gut. If it were unravelled it would be about nine metres long!
- Digestion begins with the teeth and ends at the anus.
- It normally takes food 24–48 hours to pass through your digestive system.

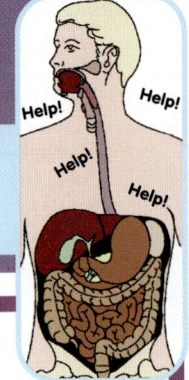

HELP WITH DIGESTION

- Ultimately we need nutrients from our food to keep our bodies healthy.
- Remember: digestion breaks down large food molecules into small molecules so that they can pass into our bloodstream.
- As food passes through the digestive system it needs help to break it down.

ENZYMES SPEED THINGS UP

- Starch, protein and fats are large, insoluble food molecules.
- Even after the teeth have done their bit and the stomach has churned the food up, it is still too big and insoluble to pass into the bloodstream.
- If you look at the diagram of the digestive system on page 11 you will see where the chemicals called enzymes are made.
- Enzymes are specific. There are three main enzymes in your system.

Examiner's Top Tip
Each part of the digestive system has a particular job. Learn the functions of each part and where the enzymes and other helpful secretions are produced.

ENZYME ACTIONS

- a protein molecule is made up of many different amino acids → protease breaks down protein molecules → amino acids
- a starch molecule is made up of many glucose molecules → amylase breaks down carbohydrate molecules → glucose
- a fat molecule is made up of fatty acid and glycerol molecules → lipase breaks down fat molecules → fatty acids, glycerol

- Food molecules are now small enough to be absorbed through the small intestine wall and into the bloodstream to be carried to the cells.

ENZYMES ARE SPECIFIC

- Enzymes work by being a particular shape, so they will only fit and digest a particular food type. Amylase enzymes will only fit and digest carbohydrate food molecules. Different enzymes are different shapes.
- Enzymes are very sensitive to pH levels and temperature. Enzymes work best at a temperature of 37°C, which is of course human body temperature.
- Certain enzymes will only work in alkaline conditions, whilst others prefer acidic conditions.
- Pepsin, a protease enzyme, works in acidic conditions.
- If the temperature or pH level is not right for the enzyme, it changes shape and no longer works. We say the enzyme has been denatured.

ABSORPTION

- The small intestine is where the digested food is absorbed into the blood. The blood then transports digested products around the body.
- The small intestine is well suited to absorption.
- It has a thin lining, a good blood supply and a very large surface area.
- The large surface area is provided by the villi (single = villus) that extend from the inside of the small intestine wall.

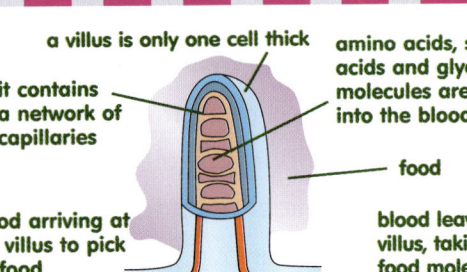

- a villus is only one cell thick
- it contains a network of capillaries
- amino acids, sugars, fatty acids and glycerol molecules are absorbed into the blood capillary
- food
- blood arriving at the villus to pick up food molecules
- blood leaving the villus, taking the food molecules to the rest of the body

DIGESTION

- Digestion is the breaking down of large, insoluble molecules into small, soluble molecules so that they can be absorbed into the bloodstream.
- The large, insoluble molecules are starch, protein and fat.
- This action is speeded up (catalysed) by enzymes.
- Enzymes in the small intestine are found throughout the digestive system.

Examiner's Top Tip
Make sure you can list the organs which food passes through on a complete journey of the digestive system.

Liver produces bile, a green solution that has two functions: – It neutralises stomach acid so that the enzymes in the small intestine can work properly. (Only pepsin likes acid conditions)
– It acts on fats, breaking them up into small droplets. This is called emulsification. Emulsifying fats makes it easier for lipase enzymes to work as they have a larger surface area to work on

6. Large intestine receives any food that has not been absorbed into the blood. Excess water and salts are removed from the food. The remaining solid food is turned into faeces

Rectum where the faeces are stored before they leave the body via the anus

Note: Food does not pass through the pancreas, liver and gall bladder. They are organs that secrete enzymes and bile to help digestion

1. Mouth contains teeth that begin digestion by breaking up food

2. Salivary glands secrete amylase which is a carbohydrase enzyme
– Mucus lubricates the food as it passes down the oesophagus

3. Oesophagus sometimes called the gullet

4. Stomach has muscular walls which churn up the food and mix it with the gastric juices that the stomach produces
– The gastric juices contain protease enzymes and hydrochloric acid
– The hydrochloric acid provides the acidic conditions for a protease enzyme called pepsin to work

Pancreas produces carbohydrase, protease and lipase enzymes

5. Small intestine also produces all three types of enzymes
– This is where digestion is completed and dissolved food is absorbed into the bloodstream
– The inner surface is covered in tiny finger-like projections called villi

THE DIGESTIVE SYSTEM

QUICK TEST

1. What does starch get digested into?
2. What does protein get digested into?
3. What do fats get broken down into?
4. Where in the digestive system does the food get absorbed into the blood stream?
5. At what temperature do enzymes work best?

1. Glucose. 2. Amino acids. 3. Fatty acids and glycerol. 4. Small intestine. 5. 37°C (body temperature).

VEINS

Examiner's Top Tip
Learn the differences between the arteries, veins and capillaries.

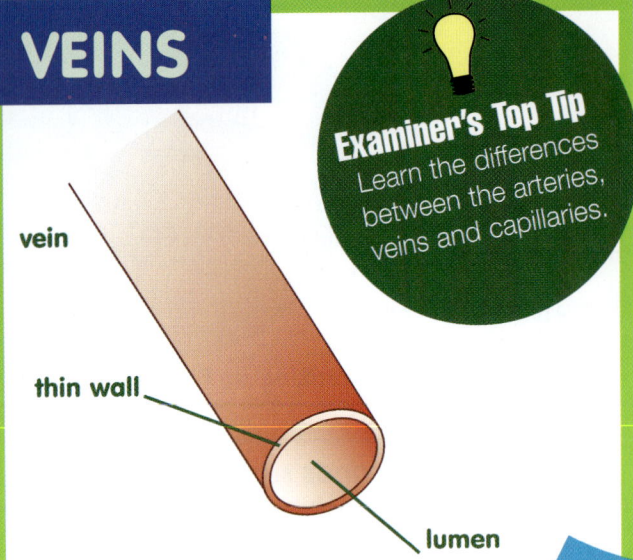

- Veins carry <u>deoxygenated</u> blood.
- The <u>pulmonary</u> <u>vein</u> is the only vein to <u>carry</u> <u>oxygenated</u> <u>blood</u>. This is because it has just been to the lungs. Find it on the diagram of the heart.
- Veins carry the blood <u>back</u> <u>to</u> <u>the</u> <u>heart</u> from the body at low pressure.
- They have <u>valves</u> to prevent the blood flowing backwards.

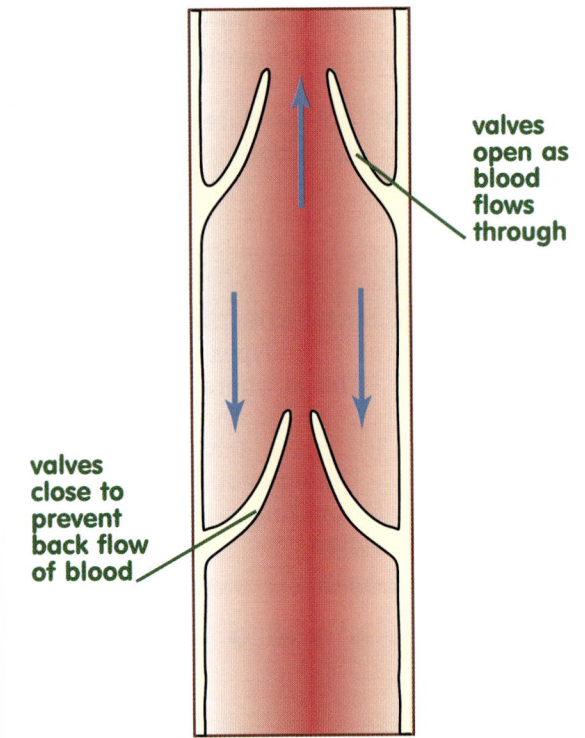

THE HEART

- The heart is a double pump.
- It has four chambers, the top two are the left and right atria and the bottom two are the left and right ventricles.
- The right side pumps blood to the lungs to be <u>oxygenated</u>.
- The left side pumps blood around the body and it becomes <u>deoxygenated</u> as it drops off oxygen to the cells.

VEINS = IN

CAPILLARIES

- Capillaries are only <u>one cell thick</u> and have very thin walls to allow oxygen and nutrients to diffuse through them.
- They are the site of exchange between the blood and the cells of the body.

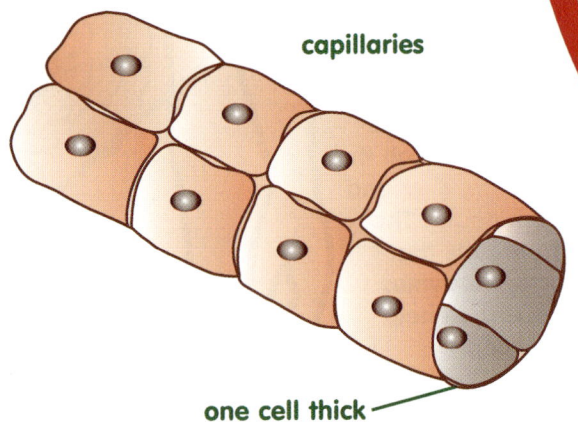

Examiner's Top Tip
Learn all the labels around the heart as you may be asked to fill in the missing labels on a diagram.

CORONARY HEART DISEASE

- The coronary arteries supply the heart with oxygen and nutrients.
- Excess cholesterol, alcohol, stress and smoking all contribute to blocking these arteries.
- Excess cholesterol can 'fur' up the arteries and block blood flow. This can result in a heart attack.

ARTERIES

- Arteries carry <u>oxygenated</u> blood.
- The <u>pulmonary artery</u> is the only artery to carry <u>deoxygenated blood</u>. This is because it is going to the lungs to pick up oxygen. Find it on the diagram.
- Arteries carry blood <u>away</u> from the heart towards the body at <u>high pressure</u>.
- They have very <u>thick</u>, <u>elastic walls</u> to withstand the high pressure.
- The high pressure in the arteries causes a <u>pulse</u> that can be felt, especially in the wrist and neck.
- Arteries narrow down into capillaries.

ARTERIES = AWAY

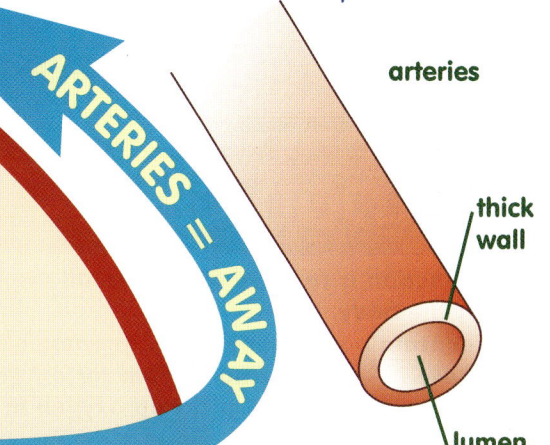

GETTING TO THE HEART OF THE MATTER

- The heart has its own blood supply called coronary arteries.

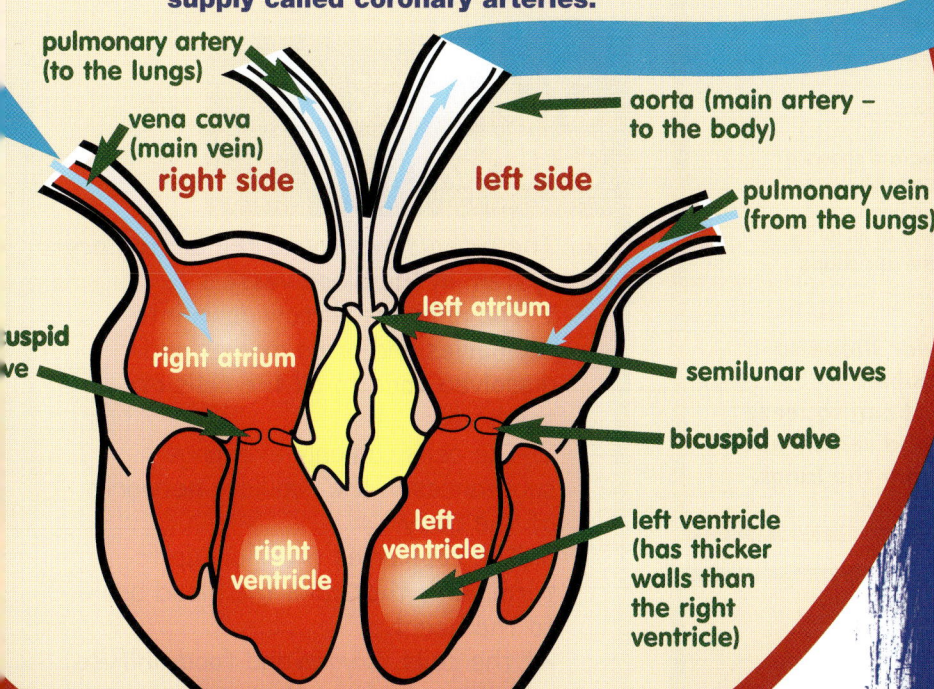

FOUR KEY POINTS TO REMEMBER...

1. <u>Arteries</u> carry blood <u>away</u> from the heart.
2. <u>Veins</u> carry blood back <u>into</u> the heart.
3. The <u>left side</u> of the heart receives <u>oxygenated</u> blood.
4. The <u>right side</u> of the heart receives <u>deoxygenated</u> blood.

QUICK TEST

1. Which blood vessels carry blood away from the heart?
2. Which blood vessels carry blood back to the heart?
3. Name two blood vessels that enter the heart.
4. Name two blood vessels that leave the heart.
5. What are valves for?
6. Which important blood vessels carry oxygenated blood?

1. Arteries. 2. Veins. 3. Pulmonary vein and vena cava. 4. Pulmonary artery and aorta. 5. To prevent back flow of blood in the heart and the veins. 6. Aorta and pulmonary vein.

WHITE BLOOD CELLS

- Their main function is defence against disease.
- They are larger than red blood cells and do have a nucleus.

nucleus

Examiner's Top Tip
Learn the functions of the four parts of the blood.

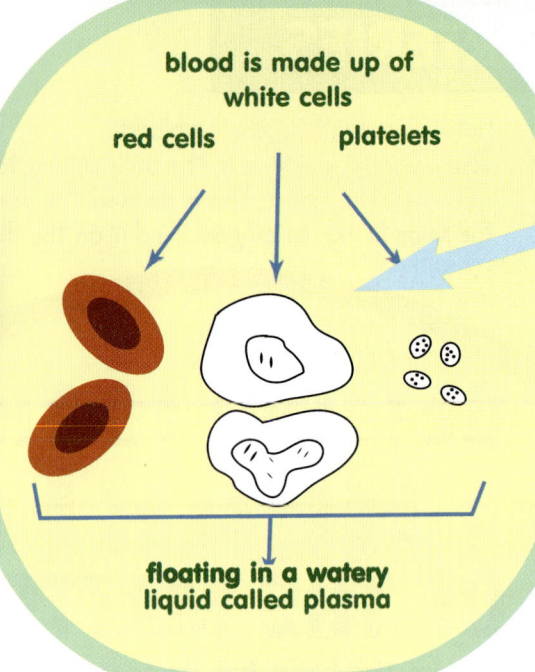

blood is made up of
white cells
red cells   platelets

floating in a watery liquid called plasma

RED BLOOD CELLS

- Their function is to carry oxygen to all the cells of the body.
- They contain a substance called haemoglobin.
- They have no nucleus (more room for oxygen).
- When the red blood cell picks up oxygen in the lungs, haemoglobin becomes oxyhaemoglobin.

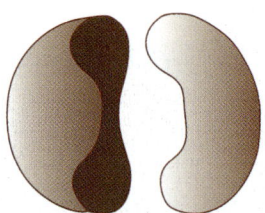

this diagram shows a red blood cell that has been sectioned to show its characteristic shape

- The red blood cell is a particular shape to absorb as much oxygen as possible.
- It is very small and flexible so it can squeeze through the small capillary blood vessels and supply the cells with oxygen from the lungs.

PLATELETS

- Platelets are fragments of cytoplasm.
- Their function is to clot the blood so you do not bleed to death if you cut yourself.

PLASMA

- Plasma is a yellow fluid.
- It consists mainly of water, but has many substances dissolved in it. These include soluble food, salts, carbon dioxide, urea, hormones, antibodies and plasma proteins.
- Its function is to transport these substances around the body.

EXCHANGE OF SUBSTANCES

- The blood flows round the circulatory system in the blood vessels.
  1. The arteries narrow down into capillaries and bring oxygen and dissolved food to all the cells of the body.
  2. The cells can only exchange substances in the capillary networks of the body.
  3. The capillaries then join up to form veins that take the blood back to the heart.
  At the cells, oxygen and food diffuse into the cells from the capillaries, and waste and carbon dioxide diffuse out of the cells into the capillaries.

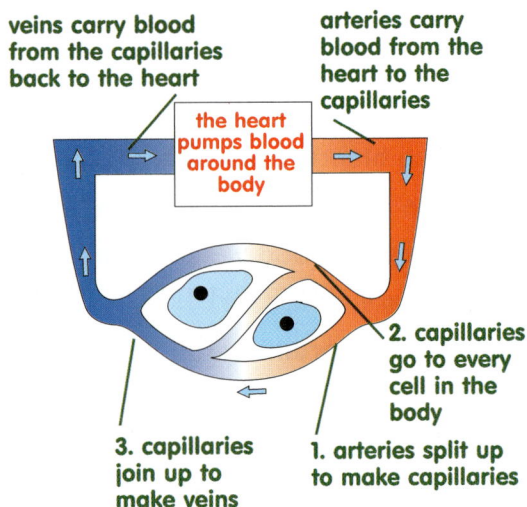

veins carry blood from the capillaries back to the heart

arteries carry blood from the heart to the capillaries

the heart pumps blood around the body

1. arteries split up to make capillaries
2. capillaries go to every cell in the body
3. capillaries join up to make veins

BLOOD AND CIRCULATORY SYSTEM

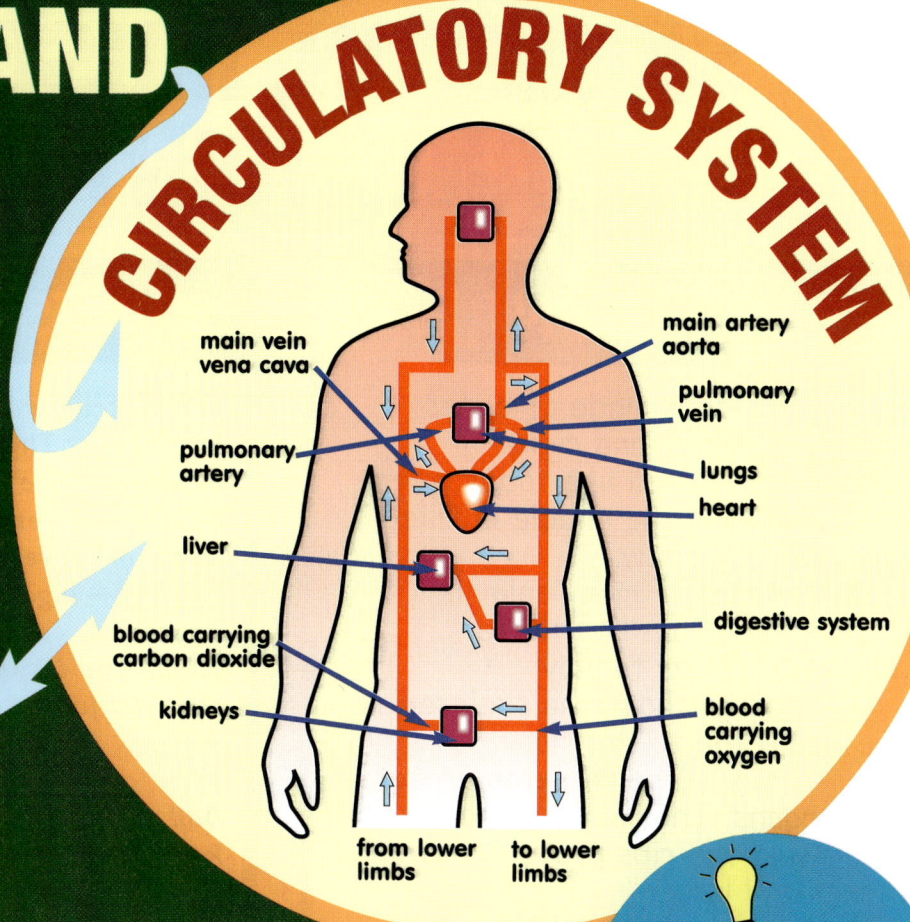

The River of Life consists of <u>red blood cells</u>, <u>white blood cells</u> and <u>platelets</u> suspended in a fluid called <u>plasma</u>.

- The <u>circulatory system</u> transports substances around the body to where they are needed and removes waste products.
- The heart is a <u>pump</u> that pushes the blood around the circulatory system.

Examiner's Top Tip
Oxygenated means the blood has oxygen, deoxygenated means the blood has given up its oxygen to the cells.

CIRCULATION

- The blood follows a specific route through the heart and around the body.
- This is to ensure all parts of the body get the substances they need and have waste substances removed.
- We have a <u>double circulation system</u>. The blood passes through the heart twice on one circuit of the body.
- The heart has two sides that act as two separate pumps.
- The <u>left side</u> of the heart has much <u>thicker</u>, <u>walled ventricles</u> as this side has to pump blood at high pressure all around the body.
- Follow the passage of blood as it leaves the heart on the left side.
  1. The main artery of the heart, the aorta, takes oxygenated blood to the capillaries in the body.
  2. The blood delivers oxygen and food to the body cells and collects waste and carbon dioxide.
  3. The deoxygenated blood travels back to the right side of the heart in the main vein, the vena cava.
  4. The blood then leaves the heart in the pulmonary artery to collect oxygen from the lungs.
  5. The pulmonary vein brings oxygenated blood back to the heart and the cycle begins again.

QUICK TEST

1. What four main things does blood contain?
2. Which type of cell has no nucleus?
3. Why is it called a double circulation system?
4. What substance is formed when haemoglobin in the red blood cells picks up oxygen in the lungs?

1. Plasma, red blood cells, white blood cells and platelets.
2. Red blood cells.
3. Because blood passes through the heart twice.
4. Oxyhaemoglobin.

SKELETON, MUSCLES AND JOINTS

THE SKELETON

- The skeleton is made of bones that are strong and rigid.
- Bones are shaped like tubes; the hollow part in the middle is filled with bone marrow.
- The skeleton of many animals including humans has three important roles to play:
1. <u>Support</u> – without the skeleton we would fall to the floor.
2. <u>Protection</u> – the skeleton protects our organs. The skull protects the brain and the ribs protect the heart and lungs.
3. <u>Movement</u> – many parts of the skeleton are jointed so that movement can take place. Movements are made by muscles. Muscles are attached to the skeleton by <u>tendons</u>.

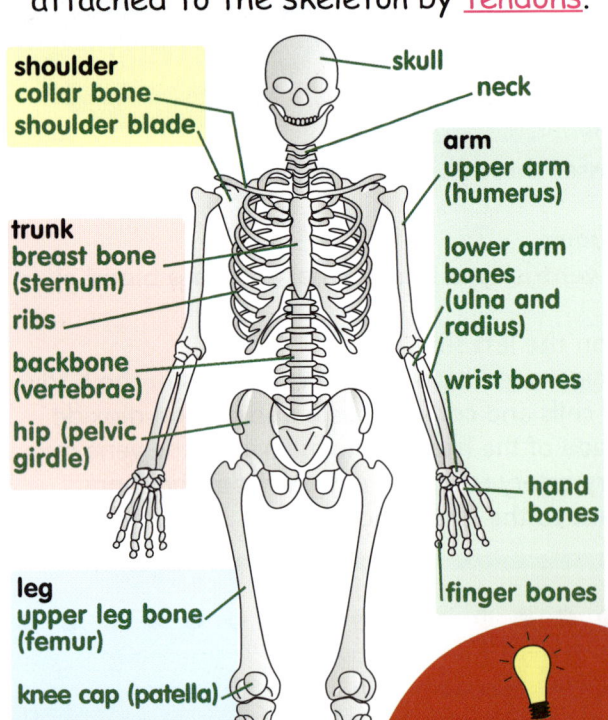

Examiner's Top Tip
Don't rush through the labelled diagrams: make sure you understand them and are able to label them yourself if they are in the exam.

JOINTS

Examiner's Top Tip
Remember tendons join muscles to bone and ligaments join bone to bone.

Joints occur when two bones meet. They allow movement. The bones are held together by strong fibres called <u>ligaments</u>.
There are several different types of joint:
1. <u>Hinge</u> – e.g. knee joint, elbow joint, wrist joint.
2. <u>Ball</u> and <u>socket</u> – e.g. hip joint, shoulder joint.
3. <u>Partly</u> <u>moveable</u> – e.g. the spine.
4. <u>Fixed</u> – e.g. the skull.
Ball and socket and hinge joints are also known as <u>synovial</u> <u>joints</u>.
The ends of the bone in these joints have a layer of <u>smooth</u> <u>cartilage</u>.
<u>Cartilage</u> acts as a <u>shock</u> <u>absorber</u> that prevents the wearing away of the surfaces. The cartilage is covered by <u>synovial</u> <u>fluid</u>. Synovial fluid helps <u>reduce</u> <u>friction</u> at the joint.

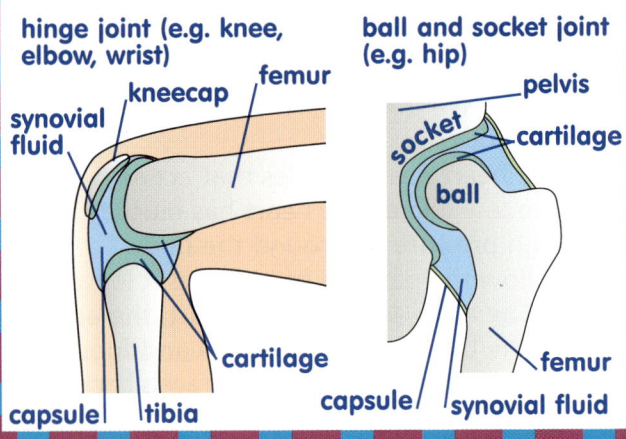

REFLEX ACTIONS

- Often the messages from the sense organs are sent very quickly to the brain or spinal cord and back again.
- For example, if you touch something hot you automatically, without thinking, move your hand away.
- This is called a <u>reflex</u> <u>action</u> and often protects you from harm.

MUSCLES

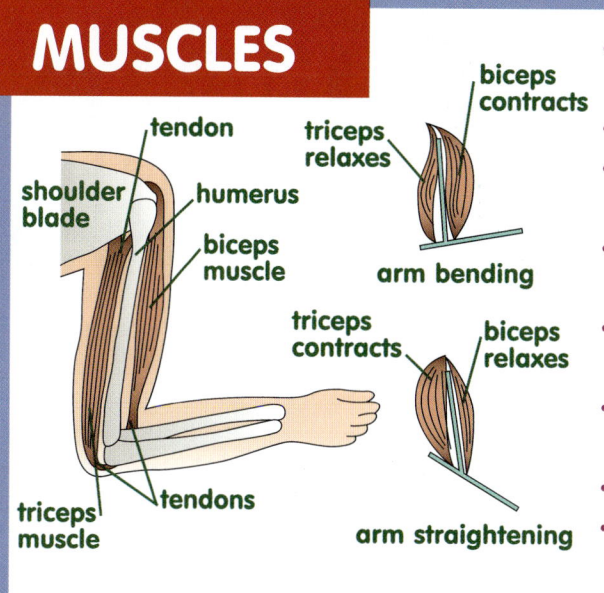

- The muscles provide the force needed to move the bones at joints.
- Muscles can only pull; they cannot push.
- When a muscle pulls it gets shorter and fatter: it contracts.
- When a muscle is not contracting it relaxes and returns to its normal size.
- Muscles all over the body work in pairs; while one contracts the other relaxes.
- These are called antagonistic pairs because they work in opposite directions to produce movement.
- Muscles are attached to bones by tendons.
- An example of an antagonistic muscle pair is the triceps and biceps of the arms.

CONTROL OF MOVEMENT

In order for muscles to move parts of your body they have to be told what to do. Your body is controlled by the central nervous system (the brain and spinal cord). The central nervous system is linked to the rest of the body by nerves. Signals travel along these nerves to the central nervous system and back to the muscle to tell it what to do.
We have sense organs that detect changes to our environment and send messages to the brain.

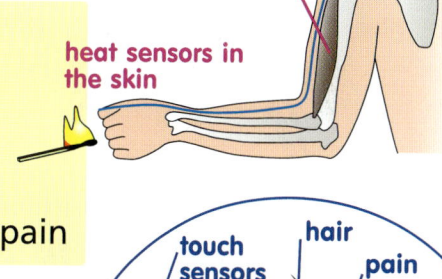

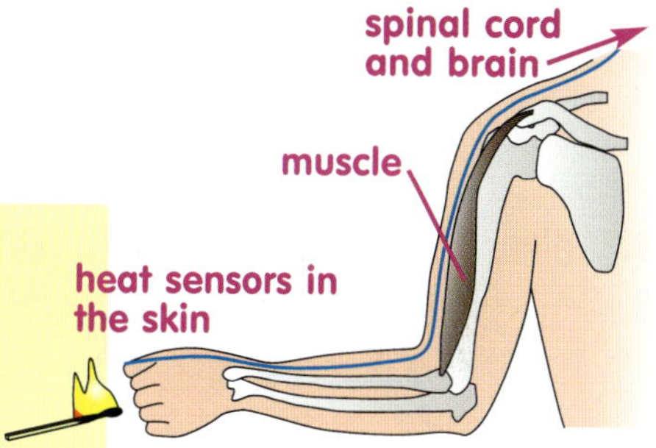

Our sense organs are:	They respond to:
• eyes	• light
• nose	• chemicals in the air
• ears	• sound
• tongue	• chemicals in food
• skin	• touch, pressure, heat and pain

- Our skin covers the whole of our body, so it is in contact with the outside environment. It has many sensors.
- The skin also has a fat layer for insulation; in hairy animals the hair also traps air for extra insulation.

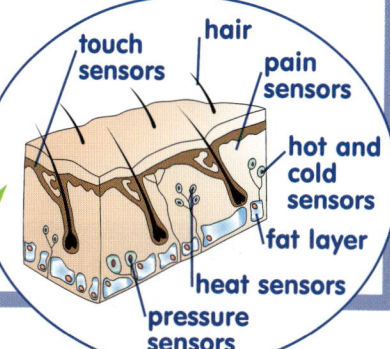

QUICK TEST

1. What is your skeleton for?
2. Where do joints occur?
3. What is synovial fluid for?
4. What are antagonistic muscles?
5. What is the function of tendons?
6. What is the function of ligaments?

1. Support, protection and movement. 2. When bones meet. 3. To reduce friction. 4. Muscles that work opposite each other to produce movement. 5. They join muscle to bone. 6. They join bone to bone.

THE LUNGS AND BREATHING

blood capillaries
alveoli
air space
The intercostal muscles between the ribs assist with breathing movements.
trachea
The heart lies between the lungs.
The trachea branches into two bronchi, each called a bronchus. They divide up, one to each lung.
The ribs protect the lungs.
The bronchi split up into many smaller branches called bronchioles.
The diaphragm is a sheet of muscle that helps breathing.
The branches end at tiny air sacs called alveoli. The alveoli are where gas exchange takes place.

- The lungs are two big air sacs in your upper body.
- Their job is to supply oxygen to your cells when you breathe in and get rid of the waste product carbon dioxide when you breathe out.
- This is called gas exchange.

Examiner's Top Tip
Learn the labelled diagram of the lungs.

BREATHING IN

- Ribs move up and out pulled by the intercostal muscles.
- The diaphragm is pulled down.
- The volume increases and pressure decreases, causing air to rush into the lungs.

ribs
intercostal muscles
lung
lung
diaphragm

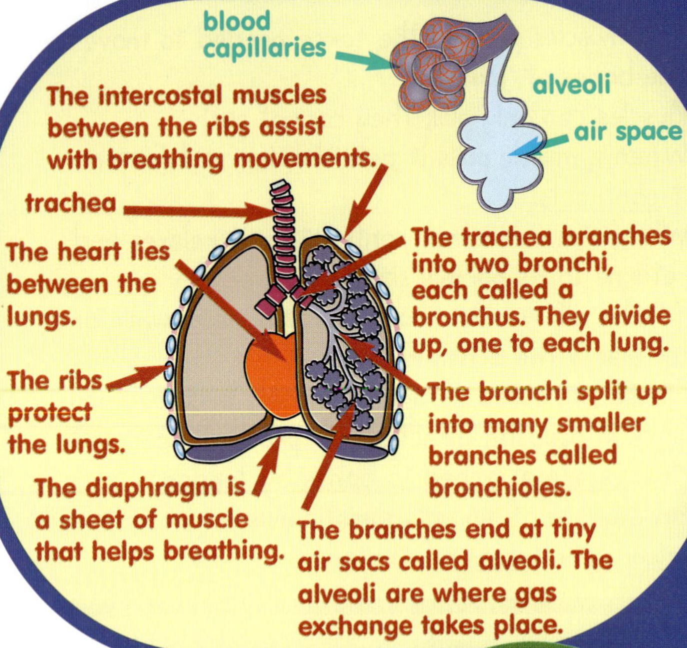

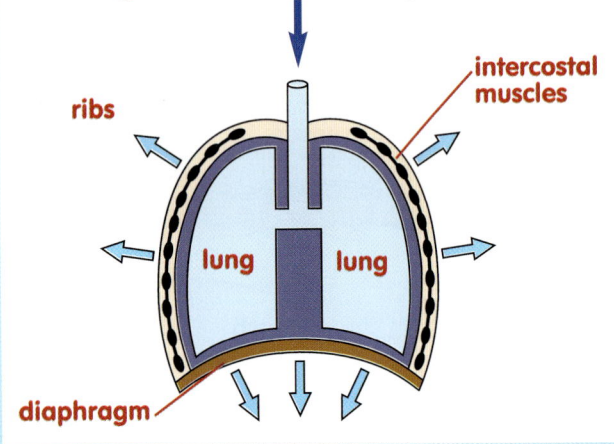

BREATHING OUT

- The intercostal muscles relax and the ribs move down and in.
- The diaphragm also relaxes and moves up.
- The volume decreases and pressure increases, forcing air out of the lungs.

ribs
intercostal muscles
lung
lung
diaphragm

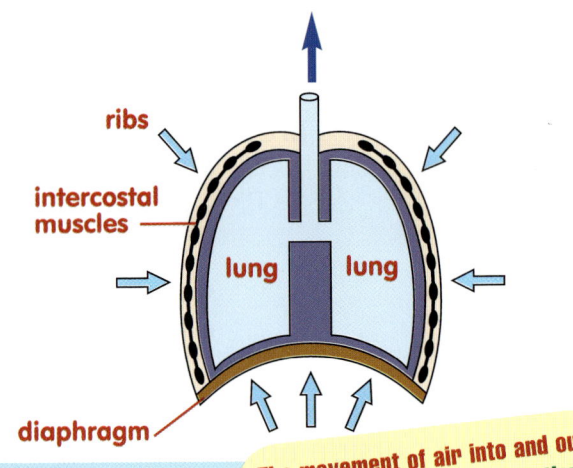

The movement of air into and out of the lungs is called ventilation.

ALVEOLI AND GAS EXCHANGE

- The alveoli are well designed for their job of gas exchange.
- There are millions of alveoli, so they present a large surface area; they are in very close contact with lots of blood capillaries.
- Their surface lining is moist, so that gases can dissolve before they diffuse across the thin membrane.
- At the lungs, oxygen diffuses into the blood and carbon dioxide diffuses into the alveoli.
- At the cells, oxygen diffuses into them and carbon dioxide diffuses out into the blood.

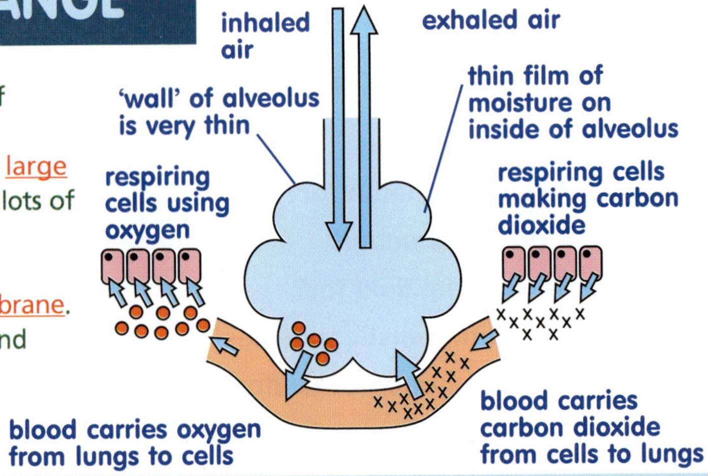

inhaled air
exhaled air
'wall' of alveolus is very thin
thin film of moisture on inside of alveolus
respiring cells using oxygen
respiring cells making carbon dioxide
blood carries oxygen from lungs to cells
blood carries carbon dioxide from cells to lungs

COMPOSITION OF GASES

INHALED AIR	EXHALED AIR
Oxygen – 21%	Oxygen – 16%
Carbon dioxide – 0.04%	Carbon dioxide – 4%
Nitrogen – 79%	Nitrogen – 79%
Water vapour – a little	Water vapour – a lot

NOTE
- Notice that we breathe out both oxygen and carbon dioxide as well as breathing them in.
- It is important to note that we breathe in more oxygen and breathe out more carbon dioxide.
- There are other differences: the air we breathe out contains more water vapour and it is warmer and cleaner compared to the air we breathe in.

AEROBIC RESPIRATION

- Breathing is necessary for respiration.
- Respiration is not breathing in and out.
- Aerobic respiration is a chemical reaction that breaks down glucose from food to release energy using oxygen.
- Every living cell in every living organism uses respiration to make energy, all of the time.
- Carbon dioxide and water are waste products removed from the body in the lungs, skin and kidneys.
- Respiration takes place inside the cytoplasm of cells on the mitochondria.

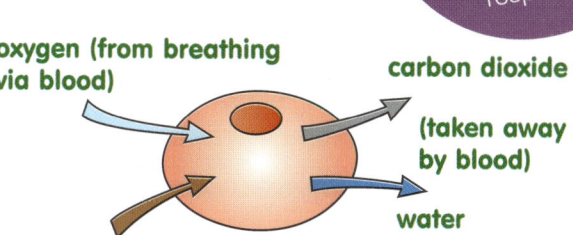

Examiner's Top Tip
Learn the word equation for respiration.

- The chemical equation for respiration is:
$C_6H_{12}O_6 + 6O_2 \rightarrow 6CO_2 + 6H_2O +$ energy

And the word equation is:

Glucose + Oxygen → Carbon Dioxide + Water + energy

SMOKING AND LUNG DISEASE

- Tar contained in tobacco smoke can cause cancer of the lung cells. It can also irritate air passages and make them narrower, causing a 'smoker's cough'.
- Bronchitis is aggravated by smoking. Smoke irritates the air passages making them inflamed. The cilia stop beating, so mucus collects in the lungs along with dirt and bacteria.
- In emphysema, the chemicals in tobacco smoke weaken the alveoli walls. The lung tissue can become damaged and make breathing difficult.

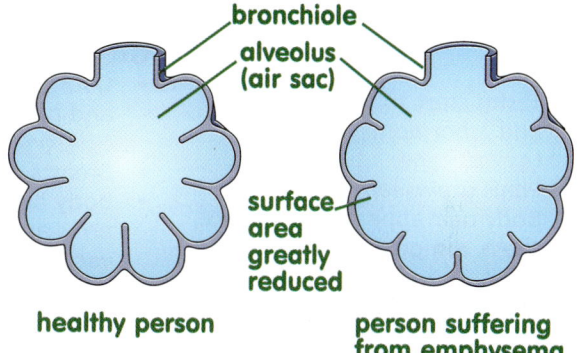

USES OF THE ENERGY PRODUCED

The energy produced during respiration is used for:
1. Making your muscles work.
2. Uptake of minerals in plants.
3. Chemical reactions.
4. Growth and repair of cells.
5. Maintaining body temperature in warm-blooded animals.

QUICK TEST

1. Where does gas exchange take place?
2. Why are the alveoli so good at gas exchange?
3. Give a definition of respiration.
4. Where does respiration take place?
5. What are the waste products of respiration?

1. In the alveoli of the lungs.
2. They have a large surface area, moist, thin walls and are close to blood capillaries.
3. Breaking down glucose with oxygen.
4. In the cell cytoplasm.
5. Water and carbon dioxide.

THE LUNGS AND BREATHING

ADOLESCENCE AND THE MENSTRUAL CYCLE

- Adolescence is a time in people's lives when the body changes from a child to an adult. Emotions also change.
- Puberty is the first stage of adolescence, most changes occur at this time.
- Puberty usually begins at the age of 10–14 in girls and a little later in boys.
- Not everybody starts puberty at the same time.

PUBERTY

Physical changes that take place during puberty include:

BOYS
- Testes start to produce sperm and a hormone called testosterone.
- Penis grows larger.
- Body hair appears on the face, chest, armpits and around the penis.
- Voice gets deeper.
- Skin produces more oil that blocks pores and causes spots.

GIRLS
- Ovaries start to release eggs and produce a hormone called oestrogen.
- Breasts grow larger.
- Body hair grows under the arms and around the vagina.
- Skin produces more oil that blocks pores and causes spots.
- Menstruation begins.

EMOTIONAL CHANGES
- Boys and girls also go through emotional changes caused by changing levels of hormones.
- Behaviour changes occur such as irritability and mood swings and an interest in the opposite sex develops.

THE HUMAN REPRODUCTIVE SYSTEM

- During puberty, males produce sperm and females start to release eggs.
- For sexual intercourse the penis becomes erect and sperms are then ejaculated into the vagina.
- The sperms swim up towards the Fallopian tube to meet an egg.
- An egg is released once a month by alternate ovaries and moves down the Fallopian tube.
- In the Fallopian tube the egg may meet a sperm and be fertilised.
- If the egg is not fertilised then it will pass out of the vagina during menstruation.

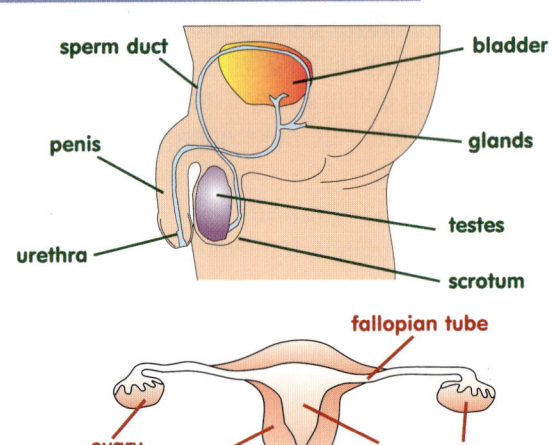

THE MENSTRUAL CYCLE

- A sequence of events occurs each month in females called the menstrual cycle.
- The menstrual cycle lasts approximately 28 days.
- The menstrual cycle involves preparing the uterus to receive a fertilised egg.
- If fertilisation doesn't occur then the egg and the lining of the uterus break down and leave the body through the vagina.
- This is sometimes called having a period and lasts between four and seven days.

REPRODUCTION

- Human reproduction involves the joining together of a male sperm and a female egg in a process called <u>fertilisation</u>.
- The fertilised egg implants itself into the uterus lining and begins its development into a baby.
- A human pregnancy lasts approximately nine months or 40 weeks.

FERTILISATION

- Fertilisation is the <u>fusing together</u> of the <u>sperm nucleus</u> and the <u>egg nucleus</u>.

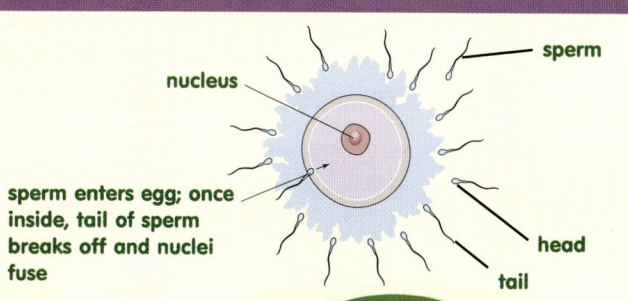

sperm enters egg; once inside, tail of sperm breaks off and nuclei fuse

AFTER FERTILISATION

- The fertilised egg divides into a ball of cells as it passes down the Fallopian tube.
- The ball of cells becomes an <u>embryo</u> and embeds itself into the uterus lining. This is called <u>implantation</u>.
- The embryo develops into a baby.

Examiner's Top Tip
The way a baby is protected and provided with food and oxygen until birth is a common exam question.

DEVELOPMENT AND PROTECTION

- During the development of the embryo it is provided with food and oxygen by the <u>umbilical cord</u>.
- Waste materials from the embryo pass back along the umbilical cord.
- The blood of the embryo and the mother do not mix but pass close together to allow the exchange of food, oxygen and waste.
- The <u>placenta</u> is an organ that grows early in the pregnancy. It acts as a barrier to help prevent harmful substances reaching the embryo.
- The embryo is attached to the placenta by the umbilical cord.
- The baby is protected inside the uterus by a sac filled with a watery liquid, called the <u>amniotic fluid</u>.
- The fluid acts as a shock absorber against minor bumps.

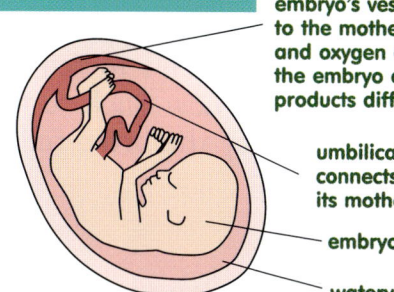

placenta: here the embryo's vessels are close to the mother's and food and oxygen diffuse into the embryo and waste products diffuse out

umbilical cord: this connects the baby to its mother

embryo

watery liquid

TWINS

- <u>Identical</u> twins are formed if the fertilised egg divides into two, and each part develops into a baby.
- <u>Non-identical</u> twins are formed when two eggs are released from the ovary and both are fertilised.

QUICK TEST

1. Where are the sperms made?
2. Where are the eggs made?
3. What is ovulation?
4. Where does fertilisation take place?
5. How is the baby supplied with oxygen and food while in the uterus?

1. In the testes.
2. In the ovaries.
3. The release of an egg in the middle of the cycle (day 14).
4. In the Fallopian tube.
5. By the umbilical cord.

DRUGS, SOLVENTS, ALCOHOL AND TOBACCO

- Smoking and solvents damage health without a doubt.
- Alcohol and drugs can also be dangerous.
- To keep healthy you need to eat a balanced diet, take regular exercise and avoid health risks.

DRUGS – WHY ARE THEY DANGEROUS?

- Drugs are powerful chemicals; they alter the way the body works, often without you realising it.
- There are useful drugs such as penicillin and antibiotics, but even these can be dangerous if misused.
- Some drugs affect the brain and nervous system, which in turn affects activities such as driving, as well as altering behaviour and increasing the risk of infection.
- Drugs affect people in many different ways; you can never be sure what will happen to you.
- An overdose can easily happen by accident as it is difficult to tell how strong a drug is or how much to take.
- Drugs which affect the brain fall into four main groups:

SEDATIVES
- These drugs slow down the brain and make you feel sleepy. Tranquillisers and sleeping pills are examples.
- They are often given to people suffering from anxiety and stress.
- Barbiturates, which are powerful sedatives, are used as anaesthetics in hospitals.
- These drugs seriously alter reaction times and give you poor judgement of speed and distances.

PAINKILLERS
- These drugs suppress the pain sensors in the brain.
- Aspirin, heroin and morphine are examples.
- Morphine is given to people in cases of extreme pain.
- Heroin can be injected, which can increase the risk of contracting HIV; it is also highly addictive. People who become addicted to heroin often resort to crime to pay for the drug and suffer personality problems.

HALLUCINOGENS
- These drugs make you see or hear things that don't exist. These imaginings are called hallucinations.
- Examples are ecstasy, LSD and cannabis.
- Hallucinations can lead to fatal accidents.
- Ecstasy can give the user feelings of extreme energy. This extra energy can lead to a danger of overheating and dehydration.

STIMULANTS
- These drugs speed up the brain and nervous system and make you more alert and awake.
- Examples include amphetamines, cocaine and the less harmful caffeine in tea and coffee.
- Overuse results in high energy levels, changes in personality and hallucinations.
- Dependence on these drugs is high and withdrawal causes serious depression.

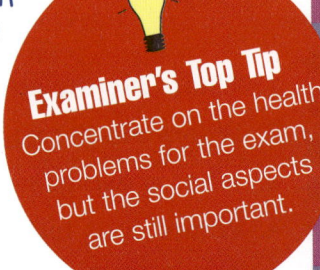

Examiner's Top Tip
Concentrate on the health problems for the exam, but the social aspects are still important.

ALCOHOL

- Alcohol is a legal drug and socially acceptable but it can still cause a lot of harm.
- Alcohol is a <u>depressant</u> and reduces the activity of the brain and nervous system.
- It is absorbed through the gut and taken to the brain in the blood.
- Alcohol damages brain cells causing irreversible brain damage.
- Alcohol can destroy parts of the liver and cause a disease called <u>cirrhosis</u>.
- Large amounts of alcohol cause people to lose control and slur their words. In this state accidents are more likely to happen.
- Alcohol can become very addictive without the person thinking they have a problem.

SOLVENTS

- Solvents include everyday products like glue and aerosols.
- Solvent fumes are inhaled and are absorbed by the lungs. They soon reach the brain and <u>slow</u> <u>down</u> <u>breathing</u> <u>and</u> <u>heart</u> <u>rates</u>.
- Solvents also damage the <u>kidneys</u> <u>and</u> <u>liver</u>.
- Repeated inhalation can cause loss of control and unconsciousness.
- Many first-time inhalers die from heart failure or suffocation if using aerosols.
- Many of the symptoms are likened to being drunk, vomiting may occur and the person may not be in control.

SMOKING

- Tobacco definitely causes health problems.
- It contains many harmful chemicals: <u>nicotine</u> is an addictive substance and a mild stimulant; <u>tar</u> is known to contain carcinogens that contribute to cancer; and <u>carbon</u> <u>monoxide</u> prevents the red blood cells from carrying oxygen.
- Some diseases aggravated by smoking include <u>emphysema</u>, <u>bronchitis</u>, <u>heart</u> <u>and</u> <u>blood</u> <u>vessel</u> <u>problems</u> <u>and</u> <u>lung</u> <u>cancer</u>.
- As well as health problems there is also the high cost of smoking and the negative social problems.

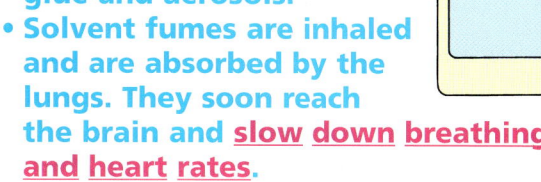

QUICK TEST

1. Which parts of the body are affected by alcohol?
2. What are stimulants?
3. Name three chemicals contained in tobacco.
4. What diseases does smoking aggravate?
5. What is the name of the disease of the liver caused by drinking excess alcohol?

1. Brain, liver and nervous system.
2. Drugs that speed up the nervous system.
3. Tar, nicotine and carbon monoxide.
4. Emphysema, bronchitis, lung cancer and heart disease.
5. Cirrhosis.

BACTERIA

- Bacteria are living organisms.
- There are three main shapes of bacteria:

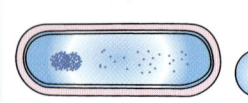 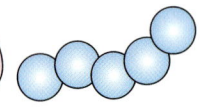 

rods (bacilli)   spheres (cocci)   spirals (spirilla)

bacterial cells have <u>no nucleus</u> but do have genes in the cytoplasm

(diagram labels: cell wall, cell membrane, cytoplasm)

- Bacteria reproduce rapidly.
- Bacteria can produce poisons, called <u>toxins</u>. For example, food poisoning is caused by bacteria releasing toxins.
- Other diseases caused by bacteria include tetanus, whooping cough and tuberculosis.
- Most bacteria are killed by antibiotics.

FUNGI

- Fungi cause diseases such as athlete's foot and ringworm.
- Fungi reproduce by <u>making spores</u> that can be carried from person to person.
- Most fungi are useful as decomposers. Yeast is a fungus that is used when making bread, beer and wine.

VIRUSES

Viruses consist of a <u>protein coat</u> surrounding a few <u>genes</u>.

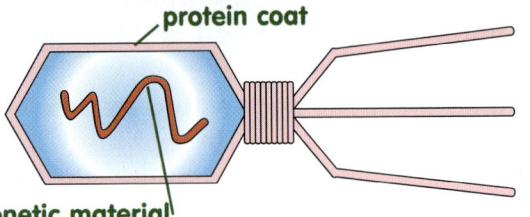

protein coat

genetic material (not in a nucleus)

- Viruses are much smaller than bacteria.
- Viruses don't feed, move, respire or grow; they just reproduce.
- Viruses can only reproduce inside the cells of a living organism.
- They <u>reproduce inside the cells</u> and release thousands of new viruses to infect new cells.
- They <u>kill the cell</u> in the process.

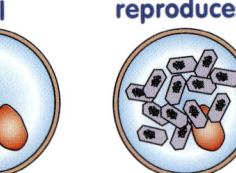 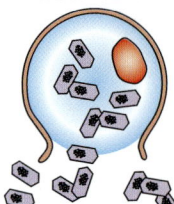

virus enters cell   virus reproduces   cell bursts – viruses invade new cells

virus   cell

- Examples of diseases caused by viruses are HIV, flu, chicken pox and measles.

DEFENCE AGAINST DISEASE

- Infectious diseases are spread in various ways; through the air, via food and water, or contact with infected people.
- Microbes – bacteria, viruses and fungi – have to enter our body before they can do any harm.
- The body has many ways of preventing microbes from entering.
- These include the skin, which provides a barrier, and the respiratory system, which makes mucus that traps dust and microbes. The eyes produce an enzyme that acts as an antiseptic and kills some microbes, and stomach acid also kills some microbes if they are swallowed.
- If the microbes do pass these barriers then your immune system springs into action.

FIGHTING DISEASE

- Microbes are **bacteria**, **viruses** and **fungi**.
- Not all microbes cause disease; some are useful.

THE IMMUNE SYSTEM RESPONSE

If the microbes get into the body then your white blood cells travelling around in your blood spring into action.

- White blood cells can make chemicals called antitoxins that destroy the toxins produced by bacteria.
- White blood cells engulf the odd bacteria or viruses before they have a chance to do any harm.
- However, if the microbes are there in large numbers then another type of white blood cell produces antibodies to fight them.

Microbes have foreign antigens on their surface.
Antibodies attach to the microbes' antigens and clump the microbes together, so they can be engulfed and destroyed.

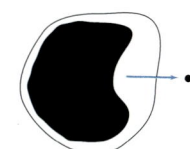

this type of white blood cell sends out antibodies which kill microbes

this type of white blood cell kills microbes by engulfing them

NATURAL IMMUNITY

- Making antibodies takes time, which is why you feel ill at first and then get better as the disease is destroyed by the white blood cells and antibodies.
- Once a particular antibody is made it stays in your body. If the same disease enters your body later the antibodies are much quicker at destroying it and you feel no symptoms. You are now immune to that disease.

ARTIFICIAL IMMUNITY

- Artificial immunity involves the use of vaccines.
- A vaccine contains dead or harmless microbes.
- These microbes still have antigens on them and your white blood cells respond to them as if they were alive by multiplying and producing antibodies.
- A vaccine is an advanced warning so that if the person is infected by the microbe the white blood cells can respond immediately and kill them.

Examiner's Top Tip
Make sure you know the difference between natural immunity and artificial immunity.

QUICK TEST

1. Name the three main types of microbes.
2. What chemicals do white blood cells produce?
3. What are vaccines?
4. Name two diseases caused by viruses.
5. Name two diseases caused by bacteria.

1. Bacteria, viruses and fungi.
2. Antitoxins and antibodies.
3. Dead or weak forms of a disease that give you artificial immunity.
4. HIV, colds, flu, chicken pox, measles (any two).
5. Food poisoning, tuberculosis, whooping cough (any two).

PHOTOSYNTHESIS

- All living things need food: animals have to find their food and plants make their own.
- Photosynthesis is a **chemical process** that plants use to make their food (glucose) using energy from the Sun. It occurs in the leaves.
- Leaves then use this food to generate other useful substances and obtain energy through respiration.
- Photosynthesis occurs in the light and respiration occurs all of the time.

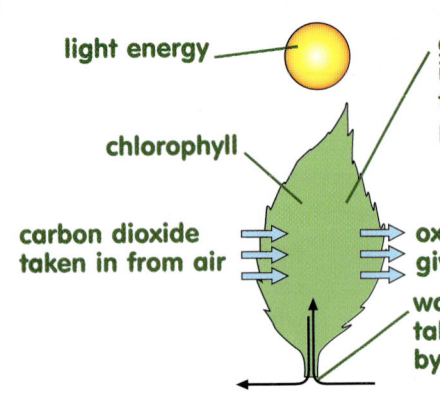

Examiner's Top Tip
It is very important to learn the word equation for photosynthesis.

The word equation for photosynthesis:

$$\text{carbon dioxide} + \text{water} \xrightarrow[\text{chlorophyll}]{\text{light}} \text{glucose} + \text{oxygen}$$

The balanced symbol equation is:

$$6CO_2 + 6H_2O \rightarrow C_6H_{12}O_6 + 6O_2$$

THE LEAF – THE ORGAN OF PHOTOSYNTHESIS

1. **Carbon dioxide** enters the leaf through tiny holes on the underside of the leaf. The holes are called **stomata**.
2. **Oxygen** produced by photosynthesis leaves through the stomata by **diffusion**.
3. **Chloroplasts** are most abundant near the upper surface of the leaf in **palisade cells**. Chloroplasts contain **chlorophyll**, a green pigment that **absorbs sunlight** energy.
4. Inside the leaf are **veins**; these are continuous with the stem and root of the plant.

- The veins contain **xylem** and **phloem**.
- **Xylem** transports **water** from the root to the leaves.
- **Phloem** transports the **glucose** up and down the plant to where it is needed, particularly the growing regions (the bud) and the storage areas (the roots).

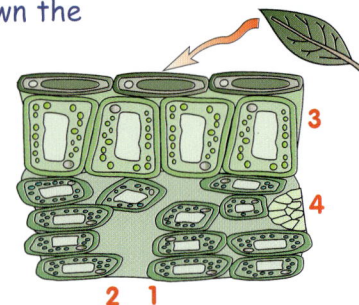

FACTORS AFFECTING THE RATE OF PHOTOSYNTHESIS

There are three things that affect the rate of photosynthesis. They are:

LIGHT
- If there is more light then the rate of photosynthesis will increase.

CARBON DIOXIDE
- If the carbon dioxide concentration is increased then photosynthesis will increase.

TEMPERATURE
- The best temperature for photosynthesis is about 30°C.
- Once the temperature rises above 45°C, photosynthesis slows down.

These three factors can be controlled in a greenhouse. This means the plants have enough light and carbon dioxide, and just the right temperature to grow well.

PHOTOSYNTHESIS EXPERIMENTS

- A plant stores the glucose as <u>starch</u> once it has been made.
- We can test whether the leaf has photosynthesised or not by testing the leaf for starch.
1. Dip a leaf in boiling water for about a minute to soften it.
2. Put the leaf in a test tube of ethanol and stand in hot water for 10 minutes. (This removes the colour.)
3. Remove and wash the leaf.
4. Lay the leaf flat in a petri dish and add <u>iodine</u> solution.
5. If starch is present the leaf should go blue/black.
- You can repeat the experiment on a plant that has been kept in the dark for 24 hours or a leaf that has been kept in a flask without carbon dioxide.
- You should find that this time the iodine stays brown, proving that light and carbon dioxide are needed for photosynthesis.

HEALTHY GROWTH

- *Minerals dissolved in water are absorbed from the soil dissolved in water by the root*
- *The root is specially designed to absorb water and dissolved minerals from the soil.*
- *These are three essential minerals needed for healthy growth:*

1. <u>Nitrates</u> are needed to make proteins.
2. <u>Phosphates</u> play an important role in photosynthesis and in helping the plant use some of its glucose for respiration.
3. <u>Potassium</u> is involved in making the enzymes used in respiration and photosynthesis work.

THE IMPORTANCE OF WATER

- Plants need water to grow. You have already learned that a plant root absorbs water from the soil and transports it up the stem to the leaf. The water passes from cell to cell.
- If the plant does not get enough water, then water in the vacuoles of plant cells moves out faster than it can be replaced and the plant wilts.
- If there is enough water then the vacuoles are firm and the plant can stand upright.
- The plant cell wall prevents the plant cell from bursting.

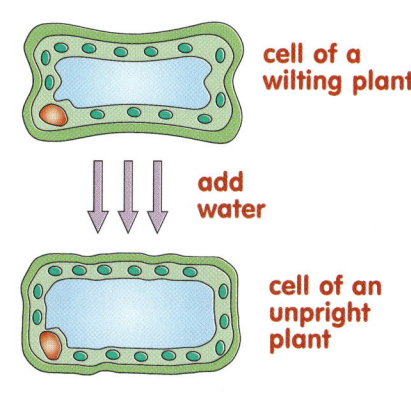

cell of a wilting plant

add water

cell of an unpright plant

QUICK TEST

1. What five things does a plant need for photosynthesis?
2. What does a plant produce in photosynthesis?
3. Where does photosynthesis take place?
4. What do the plants do with the glucose they make?
5. What are the three main minerals a plant needs?

Answers (upside down):
1. Carbon dioxide, water, chlorophyll, light and suitable temperature.
2. Oxygen and glucose.
3. The leaf.
4. They release energy in respiration, generate other useful substances and store it as starch.
5. Nitrates, phosphates and potassium.

PLANT REPRODUCTION

- Plants have male and female sex cells just like animals.
- They reproduce to form seeds inside fruits.
- Reproduction consists of pollination, fertilisation, seed dispersal, and germination.

THE FLOWER

- Many flowers contain male and female reproductive organs.
- The male sex cell is called a pollen grain.
- The female sex cell is called an ovule.

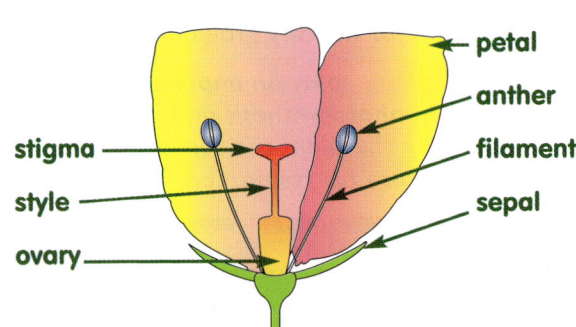

Carpel: these are the female parts of the flower and consist of the stigma, which receives the pollen grains, style and ovary. The ovary contains the ovules.

Petal: these are often brightly coloured to attract insects for pollination.

Stamen: these are the male parts of the flower (staMEN) and consist of an anther, which produces the pollen grains, and the filament.

Sepals: these protect the bud. They are green and are just below the flower petals.

POLLINATION

- This is the beginning of making a seed.
- The pollen grain from the anther must be transferred to the stigma; either of the same plant (self-pollination) or the stigma of another plant (cross-pollination).
- This can be achieved by wind or by insects.

INSECT POLLINATION
Insects such as bees carry pollen on their bodies from the anther to the sticky stigmas. Flowers that use insect pollination to reproduce usually:
- have brightly coloured petals
- have scented flowers
- contain sugary nectar.

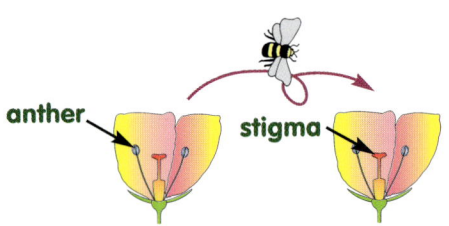

WIND POLLINATION
Flowers that use wind pollination to reproduce usually have:
- less brightly coloured petals
- no scent
- no nectar
- filaments that hang the anthers outside the flower to catch the wind.

They produce more pollen than insect pollinated plants.

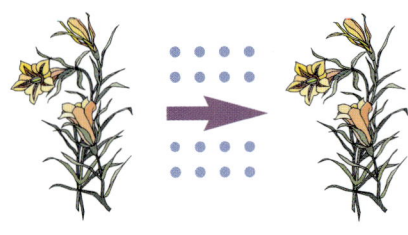

Examiner's Top Tip
Learn the differences between plants that use the wind to achieve pollination and the plants that use insects.

FERTILISATION

- Fertilisation occurs when the male pollen grain joins with a female ovule.
- The pollen nucleus fuses with the ovule nucleus. The ovule nucleus can then grow into a seed.

STEPS
- The pollen grain lands on the stigma with help from insects or the wind.
- A pollen tube grows out of the pollen down the style towards the ovary.
- The pollen nucleus moves down the tube to join with the ovule nucleus.
- Fertilisation has occurred; the ovary turns into a fruit and inside it the ovule grows into a seed.

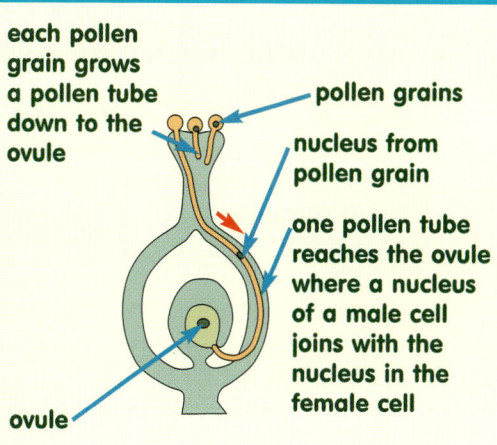

each pollen grain grows a pollen tube down to the ovule — pollen grains, nucleus from pollen grain, one pollen tube reaches the ovule where a nucleus of a male cell joins with the nucleus in the female cell, ovule

SEEDS AND SEED DISPERSAL

- Plants try to scatter their seed over as wide a range as possible so the seeds have the opportunity to grow into plants with little competition for resources.
- The scattering of seeds is called dispersal. There are three different methods used by plants.

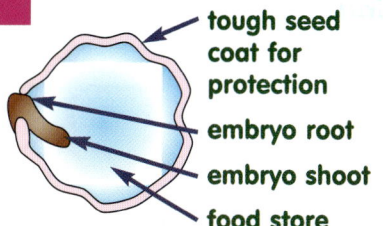

tough seed coat for protection, embryo root, embryo shoot, food store

WIND DISPERSAL
- The fruits of these plants are light and so are easily picked up by the wind.

 thistle  dandelion

ANIMAL DISPERSAL
- Animals eat the fruit, e.g. a tomato.
- The animals move to another place before producing droppings that contain the seeds.

tomato

POPPING OUT
- These pods dry out and pop open to flick out the seeds.

 sweet pea

GERMINATION
- Once settled, the seeds begin to grow into a new plant – but only if conditions are right.
- The conditions necessary for seeds to germinate are moisture, warmth and enough oxygen in the air.
- The root is sensitive to gravity and the shoot is sensitive to light so they naturally grow in the right directions.

QUICK TEST

1. What is the female part of the flower called?
2. What is the male part of the flower called?
3. What is the difference between cross-pollination and self-pollination?
4. Name the two ways that pollen can be transferred to a stigma.
5. Name three ways that seeds are dispersed.
6. What is fertilisation in plants?
7. What do the ovaries and the ovules become after fertilisation?
8. What are the best conditions for germination?

1. Carpel. 2. Stamen. 3. Cross-pollination is between two different plants; self-pollination is when the plant pollinates itself. 4. By insects or the wind. 5. By animals, popping out of pods and the wind. 6. The joining of a male pollen nucleus with a female ovule nucleus. 7. Ovaries become fruit, ovules become seeds. 8. Moisture, warmth and oxygen.

THE CARBON CYCLE

- Carbon dioxide and nitrogen are **atmospheric gases**.
- The amounts in the atmosphere should stay the same, as they are constantly recycled in the environment.

PHOTOSYNTHESIS

Plants absorb carbon dioxide from the air. They use the carbon to make carbohydrates, proteins and fats using the **Sun** as an energy source.

FEEDING

Animals eat plants and so the carbon gets into their bodies.

RESPIRATION

- Plants, animals and decomposers carry out respiration and release carbon dioxide into the air.

BURNING AND COMBUSTION

The burning of fossil fuels (coal, oil and gas) releases carbon dioxide into the atmosphere.

DEATH AND DECAY

Plants and animals die and produce waste. The carbon is released into the soil.

DECOMPOSERS

Bacteria and fungi present in the soil break down dead matter, urine and faeces, which contain carbon. Bacteria and fungi release carbon dioxide when they respire.

Examiner's Top Tip
The carbon cycle in the exam may look slightly different, so make sure you learn the processes involved.

FOSSIL FUELS

Coal is formed from plants; oil and gas are formed from animals.

DEATH BUT NO DECAY

Sometimes plants and animals die, but do not decay. Heat and pressure gradually, over millions of years, produce fossil fuels.

Examiner's Top Tip
Remember, there is only one way carbon enters the cycle (photosynthesis) and two ways it is released back into the atmosphere (respiration and combustion).

THE NITROGEN CYCLE

- Nitrogen is an important element needed for making proteins.
- Plants and animals cannot use nitrogen in the form of gas, it has to be converted to nitrates before plants can use it to make protein.
- We eat plants and get the protein into our bodies.

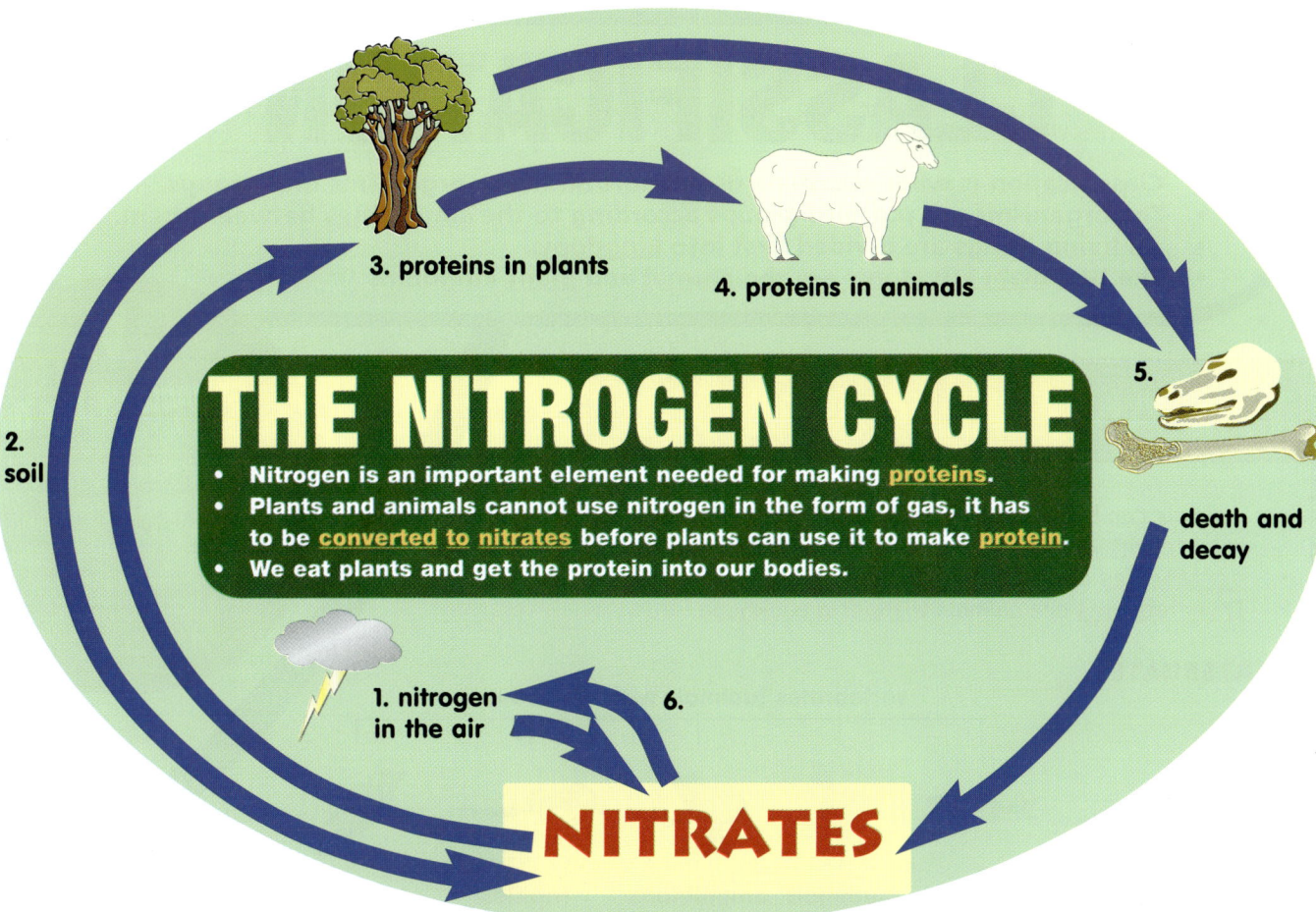

NITROGEN GAS IS CHANGED INTO NITRATES IN THE NITROGEN CYCLE

lightning

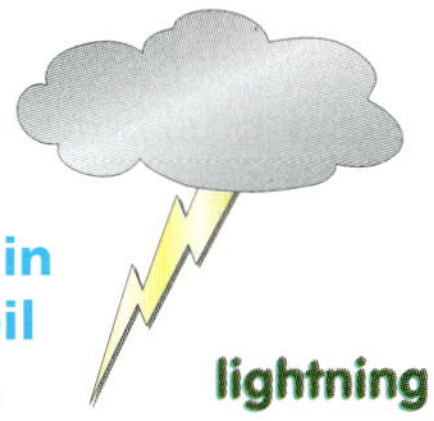

1. **Lightning** – causes nitrogen and oxygen to combine to form nitrogen oxides. These dissolve in rain and are washed into the soil to form **nitrates** in the soil.
2. **Bacteria** in the soil and in the roots of some plants convert nitrogen from the air into **nitrates**.
3. Plants take up the **nitrates** from the soil and convert them into **proteins**.
4. **Animals eat the plants**, take the protein into their bodies and use it to make their own protein.
5. Animals and plants produce waste and eventually die and decay. **Decomposers** such as **bacteria** and **fungi** convert the waste into **ammonium ions** and bacteria then turn these into **nitrates**.
6. **Denitrifying bacteria** live in waterlogged soils; they can change **nitrates** into nitrogen gas that is returned to the atmosphere. **Nitrates** can be washed out of the soil before plants take them up.

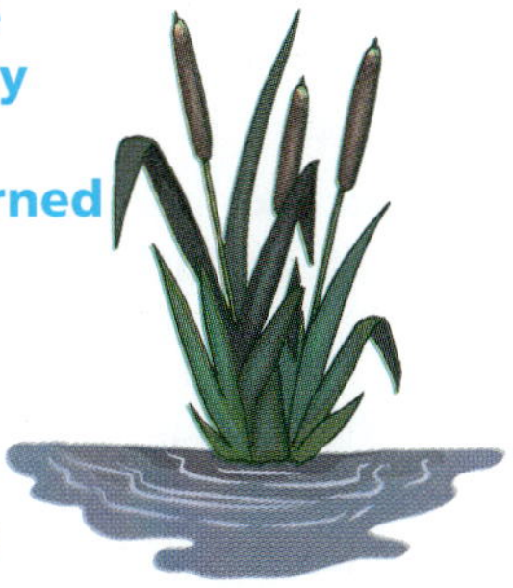

denitrifying bacteria in waterlogged soil

QUICK TEST

1. Name the process that absorbs carbon dioxide from the air.
2. What are the two ways that carbon is released back into the air?
3. What happens to the bodies of animals and plants that do not decay?
4. What do plants need nitrogen for?
5. What does nitrogen have to be converted to before it is used?

1. Photosynthesis.
2. Respiration and burning/combustion.
3. Turned into fossil fuels.
4. For making proteins.
5. Nitrates.

CLASSIFICATION

- Classification is what scientists use to sort all living organisms into groups.
- The organisms are put into groups according to the similarities between them.
- All living things are divided first into kingdoms.
- The two main kingdoms are the animal and plant kingdoms.

THE ANIMAL KINGDOM

- Animals can be divided up into two groups, the vertebrates and the invertebrates.
- Vertebrates are animals with a backbone.
- Invertebrates are animals without a backbone.

VERTEBRATES

vertebrates (animals with backbones)

fish   mammals   amphibians   reptiles   birds

Vertebrates are divided into five groups and each group has features that are specific only to it:
- Fish These live in water, have fins and scales, breathe through gills.
- Mammals These have hair on their bodies, are warm-blooded, give birth to live young and feed their young on milk from the mother.
- Amphibians These have smooth moist skin, live on water and land, but breed in water.
- Reptiles These have dry, scaly skin and most live on land.
- Birds These have feathers and wings, most can fly and they lay eggs.

INVERTEBRATES

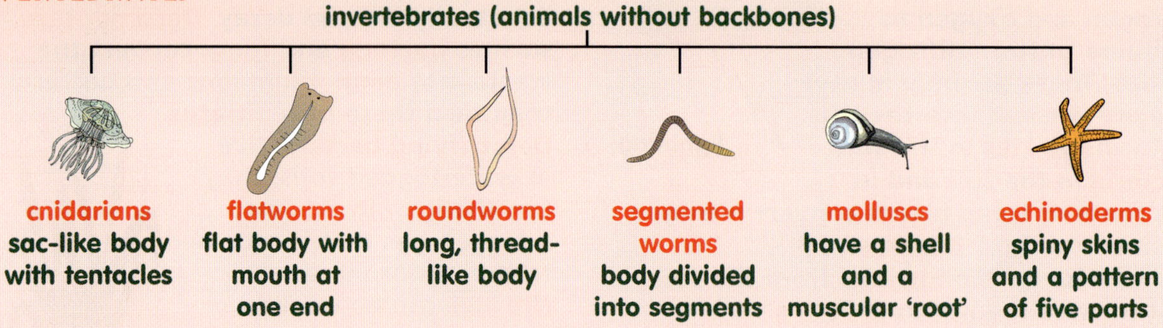

invertebrates (animals without backbones)

cnidarians	flatworms	roundworms	segmented worms	molluscs	echinoderms
sac-like body with tentacles	flat body with mouth at one end	long, thread-like body	body divided into segments	have a shell and a muscular 'root'	spiny skins and a pattern of five parts

- The invertebrates are divided into groups and each group has features specific only to it.
- Another invertebrate group is the arthropods; members have jointed legs and hard outer skeletons.
- They can be subdivided into four other groups.

arthropods

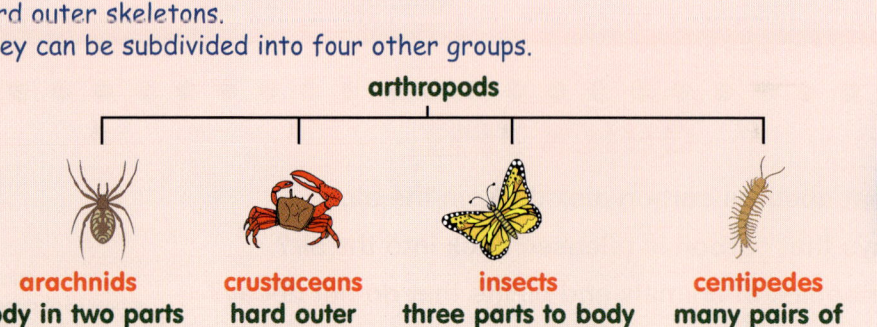

arachnids	crustaceans	insects	centipedes
body in two parts four pairs of legs	hard outer skeleton	three parts to body three pairs of legs two pairs of wings	many pairs of legs

Examiner's Top Tip
You may have found the organisms easy to identify just by looking at them, but they might not be so easy in the exam, so make sure you learn how to use both types of key.

Examiner's Top Tip
You may be asked to make up your own key to identify a group of animals or plants. Use questions that separate the organisms into two groups each time.

THE PLANT KINGDOM

Plants can be classified into the following groups:

plants

mosses and liverworts	ferns	conifers	flowering plants
no proper roots or stems	strong stems, roots	needle-like leaves	have flowers which
thin leaves that lose water	and leaves	seeds made inside cones	make seeds
make spores	make spores		

USING KEYS

- To help people <u>identify</u> living things we can use <u>keys</u>.
- Keys are a series of questions that have <u>two possible answers</u>.
- Eventually the questions divide the group until there is only one option.
- The option left will be the identification of the plant or animal.
- There are two main types of key.

TYPE 1
- Choose one organism, for example (**A**), to try to identify and go to the start.
- Answer the first question: Has it got legs?
- The answer is no, so follow the 'no' arrow.
- Answer the next question: Has it got a shell?
- The answer is yes, so follow the 'yes' arrow. You can't go any further, so the answer is a snail.
- Go back to the start and choose another animal to identify.

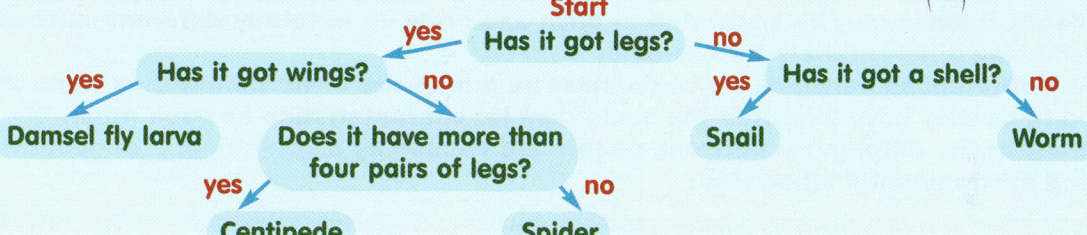

TYPE 2
- We can use a different type of key to identify the animals above.
- Again choose an organism, for example (**E**).
- Answer the first question for that organism and follow the instructions that follow:
    1. Does it have legs?   ...No, it's a worm   ...Yes, go to 2
    2. Does it have a shell?   ... No, go to 3   ...Yes, it's a snail
    3. Does it have more than four pairs of legs?   ...No, go to 4   ...Yes, it's a centipede
    4. Does it have wings?   ...No, it's a spider   ...Yes, it's a damsel fly.
- Did you find out that organism (**E**) was a worm?

QUICK TEST

1. What is classification?
2. What are invertebrates?
3. What are vertebrates?
4. Can you name the vertebrate groups?
5. Using the keys section, go back and identify the rest of the animals.

1. Sorting living organisms into groups according to their similarities.
2. Animals without a backbone.
3. Animals with a backbone.
4. Birds, mammals, fish, amphibians and reptiles.
5. A = snail, B = centipede, C = damsel-fly larva, D = spider, E = worm.

VaRIATiON
AND SELECTIVE BREEDING

- All living things vary in the way they look or behave.
- Living things that belong to the same species are all <u>slightly</u> <u>different</u>.
- Living things that belong to different species are <u>so</u> <u>different</u> that they cannot reproduce together.
- Inheritance, the environment or a <u>combination</u> <u>of</u> <u>both</u> may cause these differences.

GENETIC VARIATION

- Why do we look like we do? The answer is because we have inherited our characteristics from our parents.
- Brothers and sisters are not exactly the same as each other because they inherit different characteristics from their parents. It is completely random.
- Only identical twins have the same characteristics as each other.

ENVIRONMENTAL VARIATION

- <u>The environment consists of your surroundings and all the things that may affect you</u>.
- Identical twins may be separated at birth and grow up in totally different surroundings, following different diets for example.
- Any differences between the twins must be due to the environment they were brought up in as they have inherited the same genetic characteristics as each other.
- Many of the differences between people are caused by a <u>combination</u> of genetic and environmental influences.

VARIATION IN PLANTS

- Plants inherit characteristics in the same way as animals do.
- However, plants tend to be affected more than animals by small changes in the environment.
- Sunlight, temperature, moisture level and soil type are factors that will determine how well a plant grows.
- A plant grown in sunlight will grow much faster and may double in size compared to a plant grown in the shade, whereas an animal would not be affected.

VARIATION IN ANIMALS

- We vary partly because of the random way our characteristics are <u>inherited</u>.
- The environment can affect most of our characteristics. It is usually a combination of genetics and environment that determines how we look and behave.
- Just how significant the environment is in determining our features is difficult to assess; for example, is being good at sport inherited or is it due to upbringing?
- There are some characteristics that are not affected by the environment at all:
  1. Eye colour   2. Natural hair colour   3. Blood group   4. Certain inherited diseases

CONTINUOUS AND DISCONTINUOUS VARIATION

- Differences between animals and plants show two types of variation.
- If you measured the heights of people in your class you would find that they varied gradually from short to tall.
- Height or weight follows continuous variation.

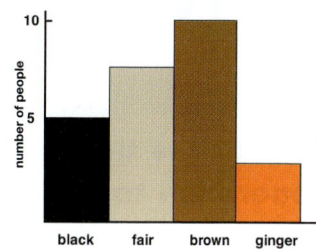

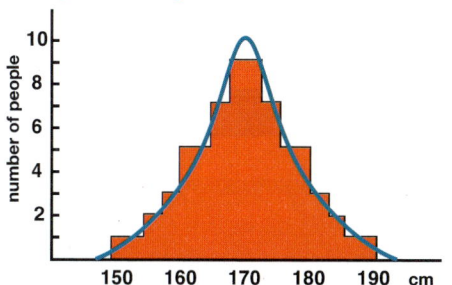

- If you looked at the hair colour of people in your class, you would find there are only a few options, not a continuous range.
- Another example is whether people can roll their tongues. You either can or you cannot; there is no in between.
- Eye colour, hair colour, blood group and rolling tongues are examples of discontinuous variation.

SELECTIVE BREEDING

Selective breeding is where features that are wanted are bred in and features that are not wanted are bred out. This is done by:
- Selecting the individuals with the best characteristics and breeding from them.
- Some of the offspring will have inherited some of the best features; the best offspring are selected and are bred together.
- This is repeated over generations until the new varieties have all the desired characteristics.
- Humans carry out selective breeding to benefit themselves in some way.

Examples include:
- Developing plants that are resistant to disease or frost, or fruit that tastes good.
- Breeding dogs for their intelligence or for showing.
- Breeding cows to produce more milk or better tasting beef.
- Breeding racehorses that can run fast.

Examiner's Top Tip
Learn examples of continuous and discontinuous variation.

small and tasty

large but tasteless

large and tasty

SELECTIVE BREEDING IN PLANTS

- Selective breeding in animals does not always produce the desired characteristics.
- This is because it relies on sexual reproduction and sexual reproduction always produces variation.
- With plants this variation can be overcome by using asexual reproduction to produce clones. Only one parent is needed.
- Clones are exact copies of the parent, so if the parent plant has large and tasty fruit so will the plants bred from it.

QUICK TEST

1. Is blood group inherited or caused by the environment?
2. Is having a scar environmental or inherited?
3. Give two examples of continuous variation.
4. Give two examples of discontinuous variation.
5. What is selective breeding?

1. Inherited.
2. Environmental.
3. Height and weight.
4. Eye colour, blood group, hair colour, tongue rolling (any two).
5. Breeding animals and plants together to produce the best offspring.

INHERITANCE AND GENETICS

- Genetics is the study of how information is passed on from generation to generation.
- Our genes inherited from our parents determine what we basically look like.

1. INHERITANCE

- Inside nearly all cells is a nucleus.
- The nucleus contains instructions that control all our characteristics.
- The instructions are carried on chromosomes.
- Inside human cells there are 46 chromosomes or 23 pairs.
- Sperm and egg cells have 23 single chromosomes.
- When they join together in fertilisation the fertilised egg has 46 chromosomes.
- Other animals have a different number of chromosomes.
- Genes are made up of a chemical called DNA and are found on the chromosomes.
- Genes occur in pairs and control all our characteristics.
- We inherit one gene from our mother and one gene from our father, making up a pair of genes for each characteristic.

Examiner's Top Tip
Remember we have a pair of genes for each characteristic. We inherit one gene from our mother and one gene from our father.

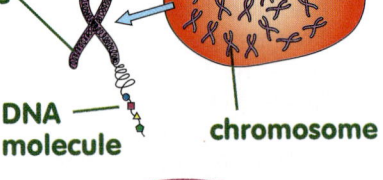

2. INHERITING DISEASES

- Sickle cell anaemia is an inherited disease of the blood.
- The red blood cells are a different shape from normal.
- This affects how much oxygen they can carry and means that they can get stuck in the capillaries.
- A person with sickle cell anaemia suffers from very painful muscles, as they do not get enough oxygen.
- There is no cure. Sickle cell disease also means that you are immune (cannot catch) malaria.

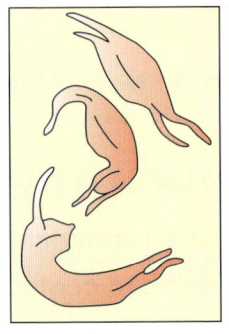
sickle cell blood cells

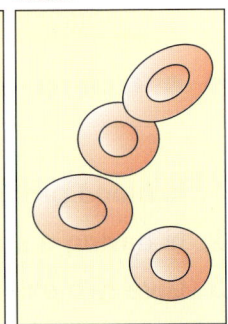
normal red blood cells

3. GENETICS

- We inherit our genes from our parents and they determine what we will look like and whether we have inherited any diseases.
- Lets look at an example; we can use any letters to represent the genes.
- Let the letter B stand for brown and the lower case letter b stand for blue.
- If the father has brown eyes then he could have 2 genes for this feature. (One from his mother and one from his father.)
- The father has two BB genes.
- If the mother has blue eyes then she will have 2 bb genes.
- We only inherit one gene from each parent so the genes of the child would be Bb. But what colour eyes would the child have?
- Only one gene can control eye colour and we call this the <u>dominant</u> gene. The dominant gene is always represented by a capital letter.
- The other weaker gene is called <u>recessive</u> and is represented by a lower case letter.
- So in this example the child would have brown eyes.
- The father could have the genes Bb and still have brown eyes. What colour eyes would the child have then?
- We can show the possibilities in a <u>punnet square diagram</u>.

father's sperm

	B	b
b	Bb	bb
b	Bb	bb

mother's eggs

- The child would have a 50% chance of having brown eyes and a 50% chance of having blue eyes.
- You can see that it is all a matter of chance which genes are inherited.

Examiner's Top Tip
If you have to choose letters to represent dominant and recessive characteristics, make sure you choose letters that are noticeably different i.e. R and r, Q and q.

4. MUTATIONS

- When a cell is dividing to grow into new organisms, or a cell is being replaced during repair, the cell information is copied exactly in each new cell but occasionally things can go wrong with the copying process.
- Remember the information in a cell is carried on chromosomes. Genes on the chromosomes control each particular characteristic.
- A **mutation** occurs when a change takes place in the chromosomes. This means that when the cell divides and copies itself the change is carried on.
- The change may happen for no reason or there might be a definite cause.
- The chances of mutation can be increased by:
  1. radiation such as x-rays and ultraviolet light
  2. certain chemicals.

5. INHERITING MUTATIONS

- Mutations that occur to body cells are not inherited; they are only harmful to the person whose body cells are altered.
- Mutations that occur when making sperm and egg cells are inherited; the child will usually develop abnormally or die at an early age.

QUICK TEST

1. Where is all the information that controls our characteristics?
2. How many chromosomes do humans have in their body cells?
3. How many chromosomes does a sperm cell have?
4. If a mouse has 40 chromosomes in each of its body cells, how many chromosomes does it have in its sperm cell?
5. What genes would a person have if they had black hair (b = black, B = brown)?

1. The nucleus. 2. 46. 3. 23. 4. 20. 5. bb.

FOOD CHAINS

- The arrows in a food chain show the transfer of energy from organism to organism.
- Food chains always begin with the Sun, then a green plant.

Examiner's Top Tip
Learn all the definitions involved in food chains and webs.

Producers – green plants use the Sun's energy to produce food energy.

Consumers – animals that get their energy from eating other living things.

Primary consumers – animals that eat the producers.

Secondary consumers – animals that eat the primary consumers.

Tertiary consumers – animals that eat the secondary consumers.

Herbivores – animals that only eat plants.

Carnivores – animals that only eat animals.

Top carnivores – animals that are not eaten by anything else except decomposers after they die.

LOSS OF ENERGY IN FOOD CHAINS

- Food chains rarely have more than four or five links in them; this is because energy is lost along the way.
- The energy is used up for staying alive, moving, growing and keeping warm, and some of the energy is lost as waste in urine and faeces.
- Not all of the animal material is eaten so not all of the energy is passed on.
- This loss of energy in a food chain means that the mass of organisms gets less at each level.

FOOD WEBS

- A food web gives us a more complete picture of what eats what.
- Most animals in a community eat more than one thing. If one kind of food runs out, they will be able to survive by eating something else.
- Food webs are made up of many food chains linked together.
- Food chains can be drawn for any environment.

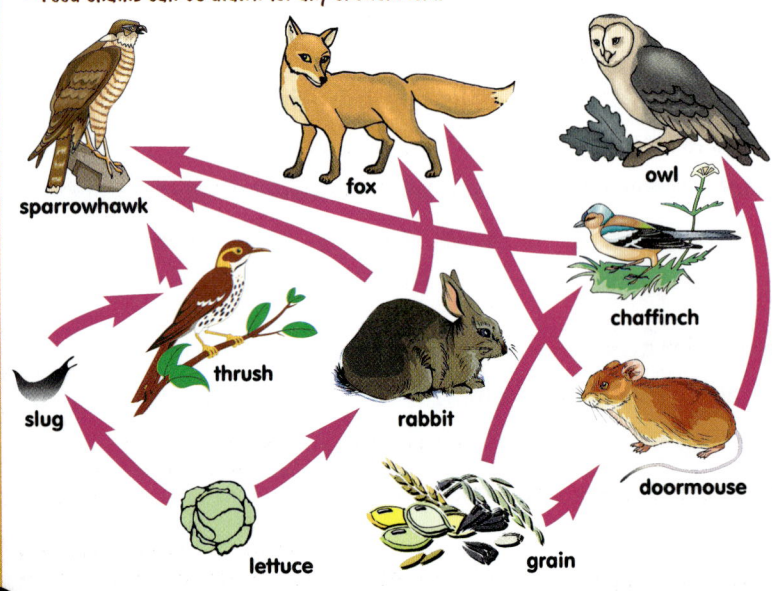

POISONS IN FOOD CHAINS

- Poisons can get into food chains with devastating consequences, especially for the top carnivore.
- An example of this is a pesticide called DDT that got into food chains. Fortunately, this is no longer used.
- As DDT passes up the food chain it becomes more concentrated.

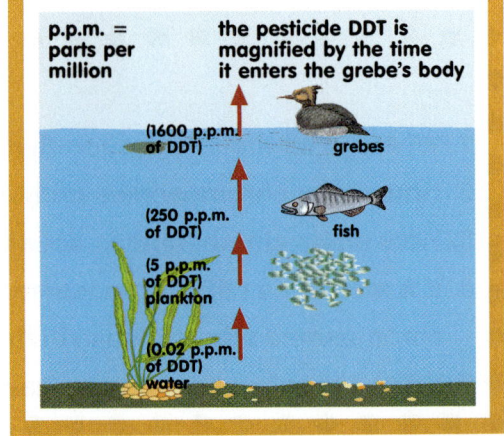

p.p.m. = parts per million

the pesticide DDT is magnified by the time it enters the grebe's body

(1600 p.p.m. of DDT) grebes

(250 p.p.m. of DDT) fish

(5 p.p.m. of DDT) plankton

(0.02 p.p.m. of DDT) water

PYRAMIDS OF NUMBERS

- If we look at the information a food chain tells us, it is simply what eats what.
- A pyramid of numbers tells us how many organisms are involved at each stage in the food chain.
- Sometimes a pyramid of numbers doesn't look like a pyramid at all as it doesn't take into account the size of the organisms.
- A rosebush is one organism but it has many leaves to support many aphids.

fox
rabbit
grass

blackbird
ladybirds
aphids
rosebush

PYRAMIDS OF BIOMASS

- A biomass pyramid takes into account the mass of an organism at each level.
- A single rosebush weighs more than the aphids and lots of aphids weigh more than the few ladybirds that feed on them.

blackbird
ladybirds
aphids
rosebush

FOOD CHAINS AND WEBS

- Food chains and webs begin with energy from the Sun.
- A food chain shows us what eats what in a community.
- A food web is made up of interconnected food chains.

grass → rabbit → fox

TYPICAL EXAM QUESTIONS

Exam questions often focus on what would happen to a food web if an animal was removed by disease or other factors.
- In the food web (left) what would happen if the rabbits were removed?
- Look at what would get eaten owing to less competition.
- What would increase in number due to not being eaten?
- Which species would go hungry due to its food source being removed?
- What effect would removing an organism have on the other animals and plants in the food web?
- Think about the effects of pesticides on the pyramid of numbers above (pesticides would kill the aphids).

QUICK TEST

1. What is a producer?
2. What is a consumer?
3. Where does the energy come from that begins a food chain?
4. What do pyramids of numbers show?
5. What do pyramids of biomass take into account?

1. A plant that produces food from the Sun's energy.
2. An animal that eats other plants and animals.
3. The Sun.
4. The numbers of organisms involved in a food chain.
5. The mass of organisms involved in a food chain.

ADAPTATION AND COMPETITION

- A habitat is where an organism lives; it has the conditions needed for it to survive.
- A community consists of living things in the habitat.
- Each community is made up of different populations of animals and plants.
- Each population is adapted to live in that particular habitat.

SIZES OF POPULATIONS

Population numbers cannot keep growing out of control; factors that keep the population from becoming too large are called limiting factors. The factors that affect the size of a population are:
- amount of food and water available
- predators or grazing – what may eat the animal or plant
- disease
- climate, temperature, floods, droughts and storms
- competition for space, mates, light, food and water
- human activity such as pollution or destruction of habitat.

Organisms will only live and reproduce where conditions are suitable; the amount of light, the temperature and the availability of food and water will affect the organisms. These factors vary with time of day and time of year; this helps explain why organisms vary from place to place, and are restricted to certain habitats. Organisms have adapted to live in certain areas.

ADAPTATION

You never see a polar bear in the desert or a camel at the North Pole. This is because they have not adapted to live there. They have adapted to live where they do; they have special features that help them survive.

A polar bear lives in cold, arctic regions of the world; it has many features that enable it to survive:
- It has a thick coat to keep in body heat, as well as a layer of blubber for insulation.
- Its coat is white so that it can blend into its surroundings.
- Its fur is greasy so that it doesn't hold water after swimming. This prevents cooling by evaporation.
- A polar bear has big feet to spread its weight on snow and ice; it also has big, sharp claws to catch fish.
- It is a good swimmer and runner to catch prey.
- The shape of a polar bear is compact even though it is large. This keeps the surface area to a minimum to reduce loss of body heat.

A camel has features that enable it to survive in the hot deserts of the world:
- The camel has an ability to drink a lot of water and store it.
- It loses very little water as it produces little urine and it can cope with big changes in temperature, so there is no need for sweating.
- Body fat is stored in the humps, so there is no insulation layer.
- Its sandy colour provides camouflage.
- It has a large surface area to enable it to lose heat.

In a community, the animal or plant best adapted to its surroundings will survive.

COMPETITION

- As the populations grow, there may be overcrowding and limited resources to support the growing numbers.
- Populations cannot keep growing out of control.
- Animals have to compete for space, food and water in their struggle to survive.
- Only those most fitted to the opportunities and limitations of their environment will survive – survival of the fittest.
- Plants compete for space, light, water and nutrients.
- If an animal or a plant can adapt to its environment then it will survive and breed.

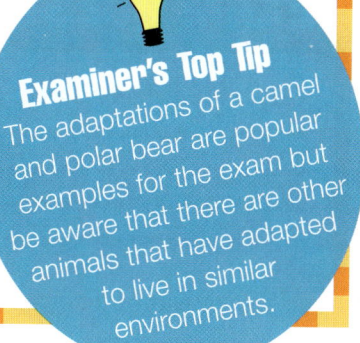

Examiner's Top Tip
The adaptations of a camel and polar bear are popular examples for the exam but be aware that there are other animals that have adapted to live in similar environments.

PREDATOR/PREY GRAPHS

- In a community, the number of animals stays fairly constant; this is partly due to the amount of food limiting the size of the populations.
- A predator is an animal which hunts and kills another animal.
- The prey is the hunted animal.
- Populations of predator and prey go in cycles.
- Follow the graph to see how the numbers of prey affect the numbers of predators and vice versa.

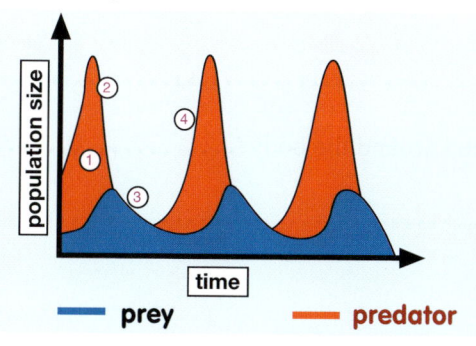

1. If the population of prey increases, there is more food for the predator, so its numbers increase.
2. This causes the number of prey to decrease as they are eaten.
3. This causes the number of predators to decrease, as there is not enough food.
4. If the predator numbers fall, the prey numbers can increase again, as they are not being eaten, and so on.

- Predators have adapted to survive by being strong, agile and fast. They have good vision and a camouflaged body. They may also hunt in packs, have a variety of prey, and often hunt the young, sick and old.
- Prey have also adapted; the best adapted escape and breed.
- Adaptations of prey include: being able to run, swim or fly fast; they often stay in large groups; they may have a horrible taste; warning colours and camouflage.

SURVIVAL

- The amount of light, temperature and availability of food and water will affect the organism and are essential for its survival.
- These factors vary in time of day and year.

DAILY ADAPTATIONS INCLUDE:
- plants closing their flowers at night for protection
- animals that are nocturnal and sleep during the day to avoid predators.

YEARLY ADAPTATIONS INCLUDE:
- animals hibernating, growing thick coats, migrating to warmer areas and storing food
- plants losing their leaves in winter and flowers dying off as there are fewer birds or insects to pollinate them.

QUICK TEST

1. What is a habitat?
2. What things do animals compete for?
3. What things do plants compete for?
4. Why do the numbers of prey and predators in a community stay fairly constant?
5. What factor determines whether animals or plants survive in their environments?

Answers:
1. Where an organism lives.
2. Food, water, and space.
3. Light, space, water and nutrients.
4. Because of the predator-prey cycle.
5. Only the best-adapted organism will survive.

EXAM QUESTIONS — Use the questions to test your progress. Check your answers on page 126.

1. Identify the labels a) b) c) and d) of this animal cell
   a) ....
   b) ....
   c) ....
   d) ....

2. Which part of the plant cell absorbs the Sun's energy for photosynthesis?
   ....

3. What type of cell is this, what substances does it contain, and what is its function?
   ....
   ....

4. Match each cell with its function:
   1. white blood cell   a) absorbs water from the soil
   2. ciliated cell   b) fights disease
   3. nerve cell   c) carries messages
   4. root hair cell   d) carries mucus

5. Name the five parts that make up the plant. ....

6. Which human organ system is responsible for transporting blood around the body? ....

7. Where are the male and female sex cells in the flower? ....

8. Finish this word equation for photosynthesis

   $$carbon\ dioxide + a)\_\_\_\_ \xrightarrow[b)\_\_\_\_]{Light} glucose + c)\_\_\_\_$$

9. Which group of vertebrates have dry, scaly skin and mostly live on land? ....

10. What happens to food in the stomach? ....

11. Where is the information stored that controls your characteristics? ....

12. What is the name of the process where digested food passes into the blood stream?
    ....

13. State three reasons why the villi on the surface of the small intestine are good for absorption.
    ....

14. What do the arrows in a food chain represent?
    ....

15. Name three diseases associated with smoking. ....

16. Complete the equation for respiration:

    $$Glucose + a)\ldots \longrightarrow Carbon\ dioxide + b)\ldots + c)\ldots$$

17. What four parts make up the human blood?..

18. What are the differences between an artery and a vein?...
....

19. Explain three ways in which white blood cells fight disease-causing microbes........................
....

20. List as many ways as you can in which the baby is protected in the womb...........................
....

21. What are antagonistic muscles? Give an example..

22. Replace the letters a–f on the diagram of the breathing system below.
    a) .... b) .... c) .... d) .... e) .... f) ....

23. What is natural immunity?..

24. Which three minerals are needed for healthy growth in a plant?...

25. What is a carpel and what does it consist of?..
....

26. What is the name of the process which farmers use to improve their crops or livestock?...........

27. List the ways in which the air we breathe out is different from the air we breathe in.
....

28. How many chromosomes does a human body cell have?..

29. What is pollination?..

30. Name the seven food groups that make up a balanced diet..
....

How did you do?

1–8	correct	....start again
9–16	correct	....getting there
17–24	correct	....good work
25–30	correct	....excellent

IGNEOUS ROCKS

- All igneous rocks are formed from molten rock which has cooled and solidified. Molten rock below the surface of the Earth is called magma. Above the Earth's surface it is called lava.
- Igneous rocks are very hard and have crystals.
- Extrusive igneous rocks have small crystals because they have formed very quickly above ground. Basalt is an example of an extrusive igneous rock.
- Intrusive igneous rocks have large crystals because they solidified slowly below the ground. Granite is an example of an intrusive igneous rock.

How do different cooling rates lead to different crystal sizes?

In liquid rock the particles move around. If the liquid rock is cooled slowly, then the particles form a few large crystals. If the liquid rock is frozen quickly many small crystals are formed.

granite has large crystals

Examiner's Top Tip
Name the three types of rock and be able to give an example of each.

SEDIMENTARY ROCKS

- Sedimentary rocks tend to be crumbly and sometimes contain fossils. Sandstone and limestone are examples of sedimentary rocks.
- Sedimentary rocks form from layers of sediment found in seas or lakes. Over millions of years these layers are buried by further sediment. The weight of these layers squeezes out the water and the particles become cemented together.
- At least 50% of a rock must be calcium carbonate for it to be called limestone. This mineral is mainly formed from the calcium-rich skeletons of sea creatures.
- The exact composition of the limestone allows scientists to work out the conditions in which limestone was formed. Some limestones contain almost pure calcium carbonate. This shows that the water in which they formed must have been very clear and clean. The nature of fossilised remains also provides evidence about the environment in which the limestone formed. Some limestones contain mud and silt. This shows that they must have been formed in muddy water, perhaps near river deltas.
- In some cases there is such a lot of mud and silt that the rock changes from a limestone to a shale or even a mudstone.
- Sedimentary rocks like sandstone can be described as porous. There are gaps between the grains of sand in the sandstone and water is able to soak into these gaps.
- Some sedimentary rocks, like rock salt are called evaporates. These were formed when water in lakes or landlocked seas evaporated, leaving behind the salts which had previously been dissolved.

sandstone

limestone

METAMORPHIC ROCKS

Metamorphic rocks are usually hard and may contain banded crystals. Metamorphic rocks are formed by high temperature and pressure on existing rocks. Metamorphic rocks are created when:
- rock is stressed as mountains are formed
- hot magma comes into contact with rock causing alteration of the existing rocks.

schist (schist and gneiss are examples of metamorphic rocks)

ROCKS

ROCKS CAN BE CLASSIFIED INTO 3 GROUPS: IGNEOUS, SEDIMENTARY AND METAMORPHIC

QUICK TEST

1. Which type of rock is formed when molten rock cools and solidifies?
2. Which type of rock is the hardest?
3. Which sort of igneous rock has small crystals and was formed quickly?
4. Which sort of igneous rock has large crystals and was formed slowly?
5. Give two examples of igneous rocks.
6. Which type of rock may contain fossils?
7. Over what sort of time period do sedimentary rocks form?
8. Give two examples of sedimentary rocks.
9. What two factors can cause existing rock to be changed into metamorphic rock?
10. Give two examples of metamorphic rocks.

1. Igneous. 2. Igneous. 3. Extrusive e.g. basalt. 4. Intrusive e.g. granite. 5. Basalt and granite. 6. Sedimentary. 7. Millions of years. 8. Sandstone, limestone. 9. Heat, pressure. 10. Schist, gneiss.

WEATHERING

Weathering is the breaking down of larger rocks into smaller pieces. There are two important ways in which rocks at the Earth's surface are weathered. These are: physical weathering and chemical weathering.

PHYSICAL WEATHERING
This happens when rocks are subjected to changes in temperature.

FREEZE THAW

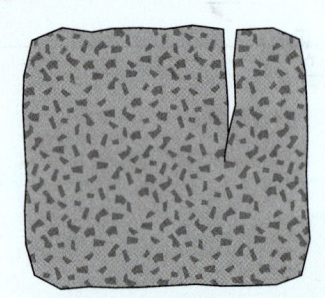

a rock with a small crack

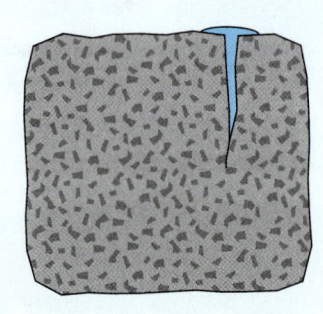

the crack fills with water

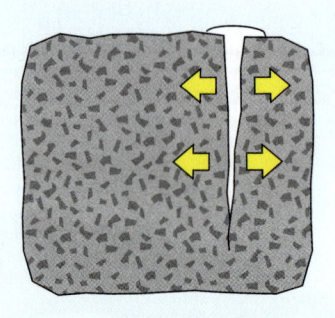

the water freezes and expands, widening the crack

- This type of weathering involves water.
- Water is unusual in that it expands when it freezes (most liquids contract on freezing).
- Water enters into a crack in the rock. When this water freezes it expands and gradually forces the crack in the rock wider apart. This type of weathering is worst in areas where the temperature often varies between just above and just below zero, as the water freezes and thaws more often, so causing more damage.

EFFECT OF THE SUN

- This type of weathering again involves changes in temperature. Rocks are very poor conductors of thermal energy. During the day the rock is gradually warmed up by the heat of the Sun, and the outer layer of the rock expands slightly. At night the temperature drops and the outside of the rock tries to contract, but cannot. Eventually the rock will be broken down.
- This type of weathering is worst in areas where there is a big variation between day and night temperatures.

CHEMICAL WEATHERING

- This type of weathering involves a chemical reaction.
- Chemical weathering damages statues, buildings and gravestones. It is worst in areas of high pollution.
- As rain falls from the sky carbon dioxide in the air dissolves in the rain to form a weak acid which attacks rocks containing calcium carbonate; these rocks include limestone, chalk and marble.
- In polluted areas other gases – including sulphur dioxide – also dissolve in the rain water, making it even more acidic.

THE ROCK CYCLE

Rocks are continually being **broken down** and then **built up** again. During the rock cycle, **one type of rock is changed into another**.

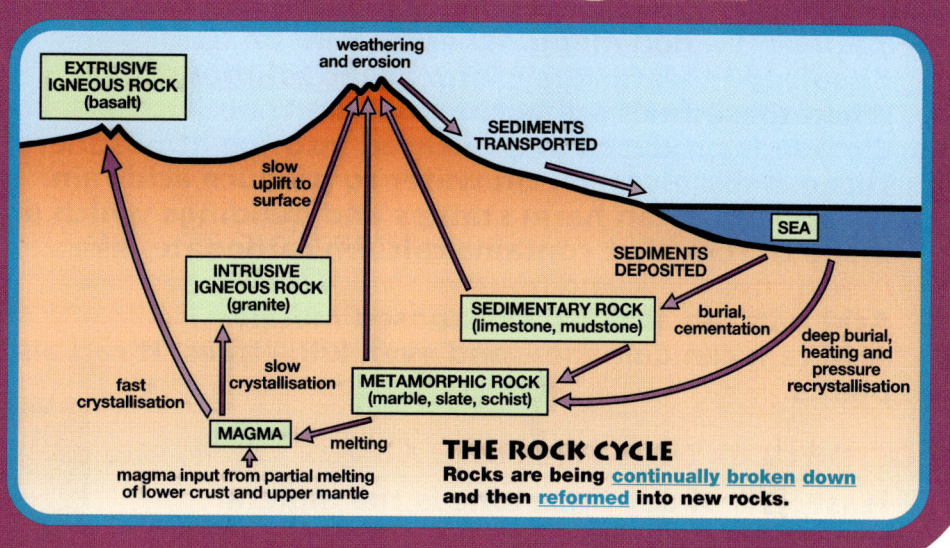

THE ROCK CYCLE
Rocks are being continually broken down and then reformed into new rocks.

STAGES OF THE ROCK CYCLE

- During weathering large rocks are broken down into smaller pieces.
- Erosion is the wearing down of rock by, for example, wind, waves and rain.
- Transportation is the movement of the eroded pieces of rock, usually by rivers and streams in this country, but also by wind and glaciers.
- Deposition occurs when sediment is laid down as the river can no longer carry it along.
- Rivers cannot carry large grains as far as smaller grains.
- As the grains are transported they rub against each other and the river bed and become increasingly more rounded, smoother and smaller.

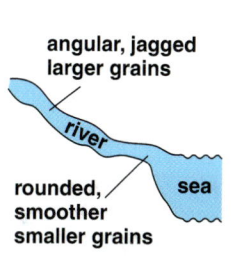

QUICK TEST

1. What is weathering?
2. What is involved in all types of physical weathering?
3. Which substance is involved in freeze-thaw weathering?
4. What happens during freeze-thaw weathering?
5. What effect does the Sun have on rocks?
6. Which gas is dissolved in all rain water and makes it weakly acidic?
7. Why is chemical weathering worst in polluted areas?
8. What is transportation?
9. What normally carries the eroded rock pieces during transportation?
10. In which process are the pieces of rock laid down as sediment?

Examiner's Top Tip
The rock cycle involves the same particles being reused over and over again. These processes happen over very long periods of time.

1. The breaking down of larger rocks to smaller pieces.
2. Changes in temperature.
3. Water.
4. Water freezes and expands in existing cracks, breaking rocks apart.
5. Rock expands during the day then tries to contract at night, and is cracked open.
6. Carbon dioxide.
7. Other gases, including sulphur dioxide, dissolve in the rain water.
8. The movement of eroded rock pieces.
9. Water/wind/glaciers.
10. Deposition.

ACID RAIN

- Fossil fuels may contain some <u>sulphur</u>.
- Sulphur is a <u>non-metal</u>. When non-metal oxides are dissolved in water they form <u>acidic solutions</u>.
- When these fuels are burnt sulphur dioxide is produced and released into the atmosphere.
- This gas dissolves in rain water to produce acid rain.
- This acid rain can harm statues and buildings which are made of rock that contains calcium carbonate, like <u>limestone</u>, <u>chalk</u> and <u>marble</u>.
- Acid rain can also attack exposed metals.
- Acid rain can damage – and even kill – trees. It can also harm animals and plants.

Formation of limestone caves

At least 50% of any limestone is the mineral calcium carbonate. <u>Limestone reacts with acids</u>. Many geologists carry small bottles of hydrochloric acid to test if a particular rock contains limestone. Limestone reacts with the acid <u>to produce carbon dioxide, water and a salt</u>. If the <u>rock fizzes</u> when a little acid is dropped on it, the rock <u>contains calcium carbonate</u>. Most other sedimentary rocks show no reaction.

When <u>carbon dioxide dissolves in rainwater it forms a weak acid</u> which <u>reacts with limestone</u>. The limestone dissolves away forming <u>fissures</u> and <u>caves</u>.

Examiner's Top Tip
Reducing the amount of fossil fuels that are burnt will decrease the amount of sulphur dioxide and carbon dioxide put into the environment.

MONITORING POLLUTION

The levels of pollutants in <u>water</u> and <u>air</u> are <u>carefully monitored</u>. If they <u>rise above acceptable limits</u> people in nearby areas are warned and <u>steps taken to reduce the pollution</u>, if at all possible. Some <u>living organisms can act as good indicators</u>. Lichen only grows well when there are low levels of air pollutants. If <u>lichen starts to die, this is a warning that the air has become polluted</u>.

CATALYTIC CONVERTERS

The exhaust fumes produced by cars contain <u>many pollutants</u>. Catalysts are chemicals that speed up chemical reactions, but are not themselves used up. <u>Catalytic converters</u> are devices fitted to the exhaust systems of cars that are made of precious metals like <u>platinum</u> or <u>rhodium</u>. The catalysts convert harmful pollutants like <u>carbon monoxide</u>, <u>unburnt hydrocarbons</u> and <u>nitrogen oxides</u> into <u>carbon dioxide</u>, <u>water vapour</u> and <u>nitrogen</u>, chemicals that occur naturally in the air.

CARBON DIOXIDE AND THE GREENHOUSE EFFECT

- The greenhouse effect is slowly heating up the Earth as a result of human activity.
- When fossil fuels are burned carbon dioxide is produced.
- Although some of this carbon dioxide is removed from the atmosphere when the gas dissolves in the oceans and is absorbed by growing plants, the overall amount of carbon dioxide in the atmosphere has gradually increased over the last 200 years.
- This carbon dioxide traps the heat that has reached the Earth from the Sun.
- Global warming may mean that ice will melt, especially at the South Pole, and cause extensive flooding.

Examiner's Top Tip
The greenhouse effect is caused by carbon dioxide.

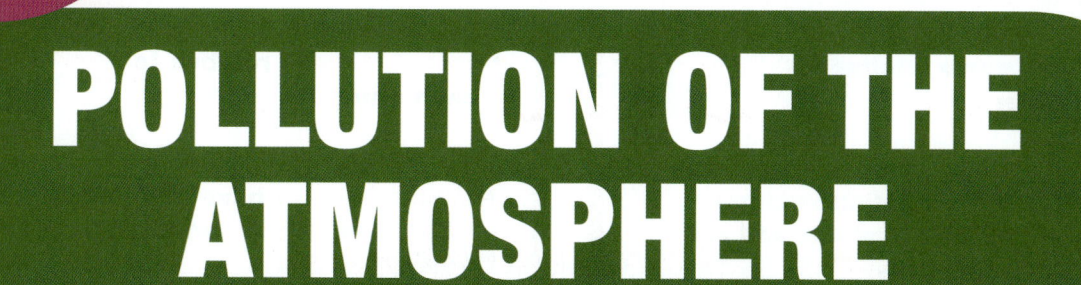

POLLUTION OF THE ATMOSPHERE

The atmosphere is being polluted in many ways.

QUICK TEST

1. What is formed when the sulphur in fossil fuels is burnt?
2. What does this form when it dissolves in rain water?
3. What environmental problems can this cause?
4. Which rock(s) does acid rain attack?
5. Which gas is responsible for global warming?
6. Why are the amounts of carbon dioxide in the environment increasing?
7. Where does some of the carbon dioxide go?
8. What does the carbon dioxide do?
9. What could be the effect of global warming on the environment?
10. Why would this be a problem?

Examiner's Top Tip
Acid rain is caused by sulphur dioxide.

1. Sulphur dioxide.
2. Acid rain.
3. It can damage statues and buildings, trees, animals and plants.
4. Limestone/chalk/marble.
5. Carbon dioxide.
6. Because fossil fuels are being burnt.
7. It dissolves in oceans.
8. Causes a gradual increase in temperature on Earth.
9. Extensive flooding.
10. We need land to live and grow food on.

SOLIDS

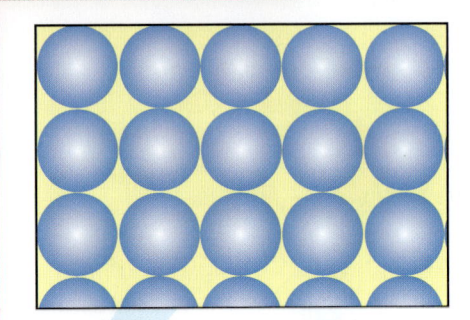

- particles are very close together
- particles are held together by strong forces of attraction
- particles vibrate but have fixed positions

KEY POINT
➡ Solids have a definite shape and volume and are hard to compress.

STATES OF MATTER

THERE ARE ③ STATES OF MATTER: SOLID, LIQUID AND GAS.

LIQUIDS

- particles are still very close together
- particles are held together by forces of attraction
- particles move relative to each other

KEY POINT
➡ Liquids have a definite volume, but not a definite shape and are hard to compress.

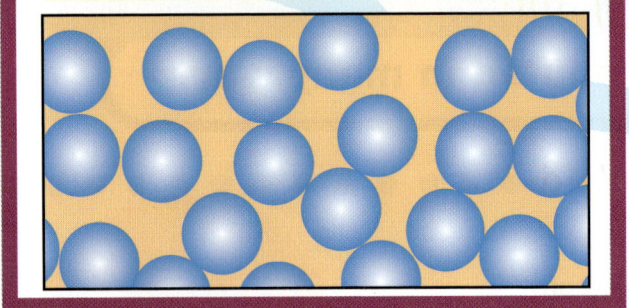

GASES

- particles are far apart from each other
- there are no forces of attraction between particles
- particles move relative to each other

KEY POINT
➡ Gases do not have a definite shape or volume and are easy to compress.

EXPANSION AND CONTRACTION

When a solid is heated it expands because the particles begin to move around more and take up more space. Railway tracks are built with small gaps to allow for the metal to expand during hot weather – otherwise they would buckle.

When a solid material is cooled it gets smaller or 'contracts'. Structures like the Eiffel Tower are slightly shorter on cold days. Liquids also expand on heating, but the results are even more dramatic. We use mercury in thermometers because as the only metal which is liquid at room temperature, it expands more on heating, so it is easier to read the exact temperature using a mercurcy thermometer.

CHANGES OF STATE

When changing from one state to another there is no change in mass.

solid (ice) → liquid (water)

MELTING AND BOILING POINTS

- Above its boiling point a substance is a gas.
- Between its melting point and its boiling point a substance is a liquid.
- Below its melting point a substance is a solid.

- At 25°C (room temperature) oxygen is a gas.
  25°C is above the boiling point of oxygen.
- At 25°C mercury is a liquid.
  25°C is above the melting point but below the boiling point of mercury.
- At 25°C iron is a solid.
  25°C is below the melting point of iron.

Substance	Melting point °C	Boiling point °C
Iron	1535	2750
Mercury	-39	357
Oxygen	-218	-183

CHANGING STATES

temperature increases →

a) The particles of the solid are heated and vibrate more.

b) The vibration of the particles overcomes the forces of attraction between the particles.

c) The particles of the liquid are heated and move more quickly.

d) The movement of the liquid particles overcomes the forces of attraction between the particles.

e) The particles in the gas move faster.

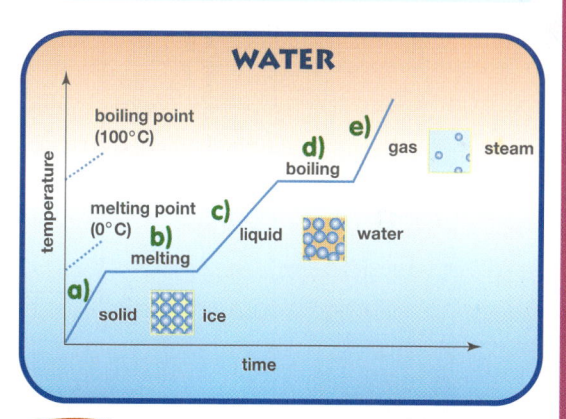

WATER

Graph showing temperature vs time for water:
- a) solid ice
- b) melting point (0°C) melting
- c) liquid water
- d) boiling point (100°C) boiling
- e) gas steam

Examiner's Top Tip
The particles themselves do not get bigger on heating, they just move around more.

Examiner's Top Tip
This is quite basic stuff so make sure you are really familiar with it. Now draw a temperature time graph to show steam condensing to form liquid water.

QUICK TEST

1. Name the three states of matter.
2. In which of the states are the particles closest together?
3. Do solids have a definite volume?
4. In which state are particles held together by forces of attraction, but the particles may move relative to each other?
5. Can liquids be compressed?
6. Are there any forces of attraction between gas particles?
7. Can gases be compressed easily?
8. In which process do liquids turn into gases?
9. In which process do solids turn into liquids?
10. Draw a temperature time graph to show solid ice melting to form liquid water.

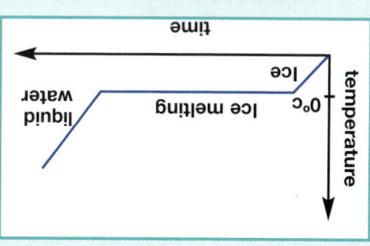

Answers:
1. Solid, liquid and gas.
2. Solid.
3. Yes.
4. Liquid.
5. No.
6. No.
7. Yes.
8. Boiling.
9. Melting.
10. See below.

STATES OF MATTER

HOW SOLUBLE?

- If a substance <u>dissolves</u> <u>well</u> in a solvent it has a <u>high</u> <u>solubility</u>. To measure <u>how</u> <u>soluble</u> a particular substance is we can find how many grams of it will dissolve in a particular solvent.

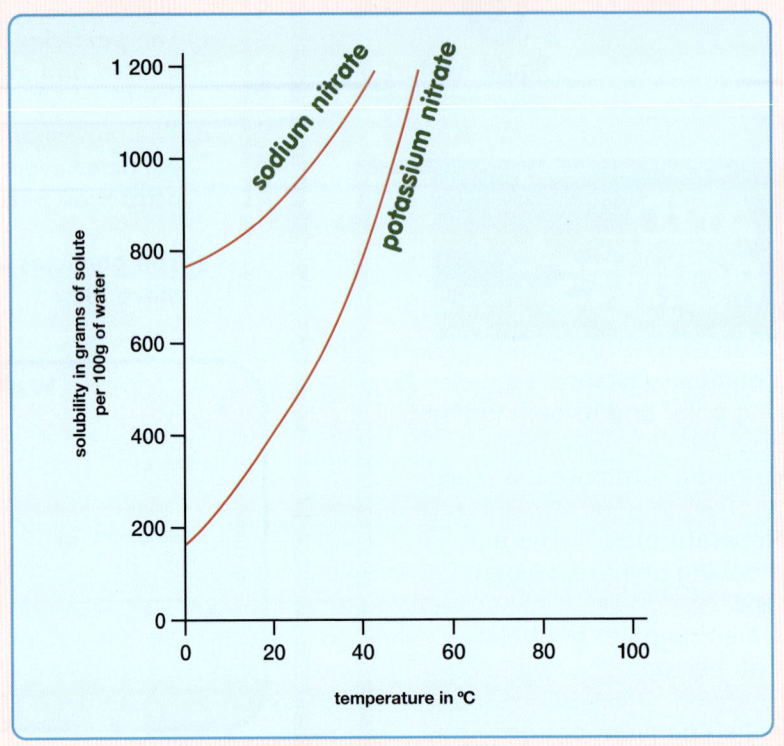

- The graph shows how the solubility of two solutes, sodium nitrate and potassium nitrate, changes as the temperature increases.
- Both of them become more soluble as the temperature rises.
- If no more solute can dissolve in a solvent it is known as a <u>saturated</u> <u>solution</u>.
- Temperature can affect solubility.
- Normally, the <u>higher</u> the temperature the <u>more</u> <u>soluble</u> the substance becomes.
- Temperature can also affect <u>how</u> <u>quickly</u> something dissolves.
- At a higher temperature the particles are moving faster, so the substance will dissolve faster.
- Sugar will dissolve faster in hot water than cold water.

a hot cup of coffee can dissolve more sugar

SOLVENTS AND SOLUTIONS

- Once a substance has dissolved, the <u>liquid</u> (often water) is called the <u>solvent</u>.
- The dissolved substance is then called the <u>solute</u>.

  solute + solvent ⇨ solution

- If a substance dissolves in the solvent it is <u>soluble</u>.
- If a substance <u>cannot</u> dissolve in the solvent it is <u>insoluble</u>.
- The insoluble substance may dissolve in a <u>different</u> solvent.

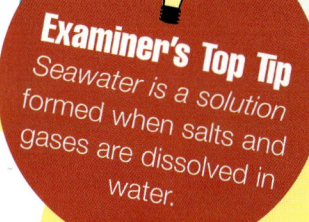

Examiner's Top Tip
Seawater is a solution formed when salts and gases are dissolved in water.

DISSOLVING

- If a solid dissolves in a liquid it forms a solution.
- However, the overall mass stays the same.

DISSOLVING SOLIDS

WHAT HAPPENS WHEN A SOLID DISSOLVES IN A SOLVENT?
<u>Salt is soluble</u>, it dissolves in water to form a solution. The <u>salt particles intermingle with the water particles</u>. In total there is the same number of particles before and after the salt dissolves, so the <u>total mass is the same</u>.

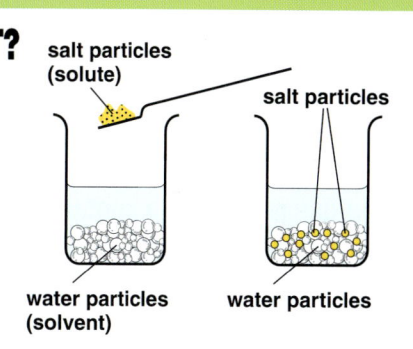

QUICK TEST

1. If 2 g of solid is dissolved in 100 g of water, what is the mass?
2. What is the solid called?
3. What is the liquid called?
4. If a substance dissolves in a solvent, what is formed?
5. What is a solid which can dissolve called?
6. How does increasing temperature affect how much dissolves?
7. What is a saturated solution?
8. Referring to the graph opposite, what is the solubility of potassium nitrate at 20°C ?
9. What is the solubility of sodium nitrate at 20°C ?
10. What happens to the solubility of potassium nitrate if it is heated?

Answers: 1. 102 g. 2. The solute. 3. The solvent. 4. A solution. 5. Soluble. 6. Normally the substance becomes more soluble. 7. No more will dissolve at that temperature. 8. 400 g per 100 g of water. 9. 900 g per 100 g of water. 10. It becomes more soluble.

DIFFUSION

The mingling of large numbers of particles is called diffusion. Gases diffuse quickly, because the particles are moving very quickly in all directions.

a smell

perfume bottle

air particles

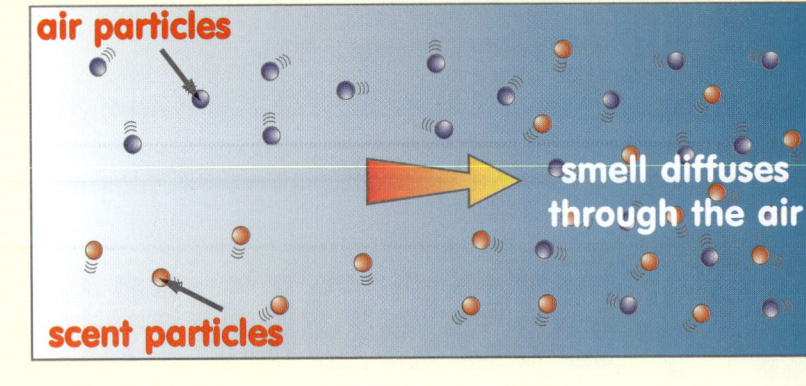

scent particles

smell diffuses through the air

You can smell a perfume because the scent particles diffuse through the air to your nose.

Liquids can mix without being stirred because liquid particles, like gas particles, can diffuse. Liquids diffuse more slowly than gases because the particles move more slowly.

GAS PRESSURE

- Gas particles are moving very quickly in all directions.
- If a gas is put into a container the gas particles crash into the walls of the container.
- The force of these collisions creates gas pressure.
- If the temperature is increased the gas particles collide harder and more often with the walls of the container, so the pressure increases.
- You can feel the effect of gas pressure when you blow up a balloon.

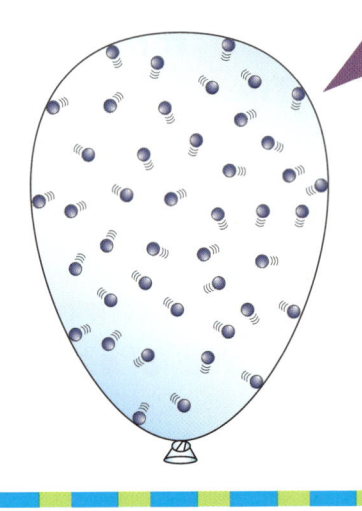

ATMOSPHERIC PRESSURE

As you read this page the gas particles in the air continually collide with you. The particles exert atmospheric pressure. We are so used to this that we don't often think about it, but it is very powerful. The effects of atmospheric pressure can be shown by the collapsing can experiment.

An 'empty' can is not really empty at all – it is full of air!

Normally the pressure on the inside and the outside of the can is equal. If some air particles from inside the can are removed, the pressure inside the can becomes less than the pressure on the outside. This causes it to collapse dramatically.

EXPANSION

- When particles are heated they move around more.
- The substance grows bigger (or expands).
- The particles themselves do not get larger, they just take up more space because they are moving more.
- Solids, liquids and gases all expand on heating.
- Solids expand the least because the particles are tightly held. Liquids expand more than solids. Gases expand the most of all the states.
- On cooling, substances become smaller (or contract).
- Expansion can exert a lot of force. Concrete roads are constructed with gaps in to allow for expansion in hot weather.

PARTICLE THEORY

Particle theory can be used to explain many everyday situations.

QUICK TEST

1. What is the mingling of particles called?
2. Why can you smell a flower across a room?
3. Why do gases diffuse quickly?
4. Can liquids diffuse?
5. What causes pressure?
6. Why does increasing temperature increase the pressure?
7. What happens to the particles as they are heated?
8. Which expands more – a solid or a liquid?
9. Do the particles themselves expand?
10. Why are concrete roads built with gaps in them?

1. Diffusion. 2. Scent molecules from the flower diffuse through the air to your nose. 3. Gas particles move quickly in all directions. 4. Yes, but more slowly than gases. 5. When gas particles crash into the walls of a container. 6. Because the gas particles crash into the walls of the container harder and more often. 7. They move around more. 8. A liquid. 9. No. 10. To allow for expansion in hot weather.

55

ELEMENTS

- Each element contains only <u>one type of atom</u>.
  There are about <u>100 different elements</u>.
- The <u>periodic table</u> is a helpful way of showing all the elements.
- Each element has a <u>symbol</u> which can be used to <u>identify</u> it.
- For example, <u>carbon</u> can be identified by the symbol <u>C</u>.

Group Period	I	II										III	IV	V	VI	VII	0/VIII
1	H 1																He 2
2	Li 3	Be 4										B 5	C 6	N 7	O 8	F 9	Ne 10
3	Na 11	Mg 12										Al 13	Si 14	P 15	S 16	Cl 17	Ar 18
4	K 19	Ca 20	Sc 21	Ti 22	V 23	Cr 24	Mn 25	Fe 26	Co 27	Ni 28	Cu 29	Zn 30	Ga 31	Ge 32	As 33	Se 34	Br 35	Kr 36
5	Rb 37	Sr 38	Y 39	Zr 40	Nb 41	Mo 42	Tc 43	Ru 44	Rh 45	Pd 46	Ag 47	Cd 48	In 49	Sn 50	Sb 51	Te 52	I 53	Xe 54
6	Cs 55	Ba 56	57–71*	Hf 72	Ta 73	W 74	Re 75	Os 76	Ir 77	Pt 78	Au 79	Hg 80	Tl 81	Pb 82	Bi 83	Po 84	At 85	Rn 86
7	Fr 87	Ra 88	89–103**	Rf 104	Db 105	Sg 106	Bh 107	Hs 108	Mt 109	Uun 110	Uuu 111	Uub 112	Uut 113	Uuq 114	Uup 115	Uuh 116	Uus 117	Uuo 118

*Lanthanides	La 57	Ce 58	Pr 59	Nd 60	Pm 61	Sm 62	Eu 63	Gd 64	Tb 65	Dy 66	Ho 67	Er 68	Tm 69	Yb 70	Lu 71
**Actinides	Ac 89	Th 90	Pa 91	U 92	Np 93	Pu 94	Am 95	Cm 96	Bk 97	Cf 98	Es 99	Fm 100	Md 101	No 102	Lr 103

Note that elements 113, 115 and 117 are not yet known, but are included in the table to show their respective positions. Elements 114, 116 and 118 have only been reported recently.

Key: Non-metal   Metalloid   Metal
Transitional   Rare-earth element (Lanthanide) and radioactive rare-earth element (Actinide)
Transactinide   'Missing' element

- In the modern periodic table the elements are arranged in order of <u>increasing atomic number</u>.
- The elements are placed in <u>rows</u> so that elements with <u>similar properties</u> are in the same <u>column</u>.
- These vertical columns are called <u>groups</u>.
- The columns are often numbered using <u>roman numerals</u>.
  For example, Group I consists of Li, Na, K, Rb, Cs, Fr.
- All the members of Group I share similar properties.
- All the elements in <u>Group I</u> have <u>one electron in their outer shell</u>.
- The horizontal rows are called <u>periods</u>.
- Most elements in the periodic table are metals. All the <u>metallic elements are solids at room temperature with the exception of mercury</u>, which is a liquid. <u>Bromine</u> is the only non-metallic element which is a <u>liquid</u> at room temperature.

ATOMS AND ELEMENTS

Examiner's Top Tip
Elements in the same group have similar properties because they have the same number of electrons in their outer shells. This is the basis for understanding all Chemistry.

- Everything is made up of <u>atoms</u>.
- Atoms are extremely <u>small</u>.
- All atoms of the same element have <u>identical</u> numbers of protons.

THE NUCLEUS

- Atoms have a <u>nucleus</u> in the centre, which is surrounded by <u>electrons</u>.
- The nucleus contains <u>neutrons</u> and <u>protons</u>.
- Neutrons have no <u>charge</u> and protons have a <u>positive</u> <u>charge</u>. This means that overall the nucleus has a <u>positive</u> <u>charge</u>.
- The electrons are very, very small, and carry a <u>negative</u> <u>charge</u> as they whiz around the nucleus.

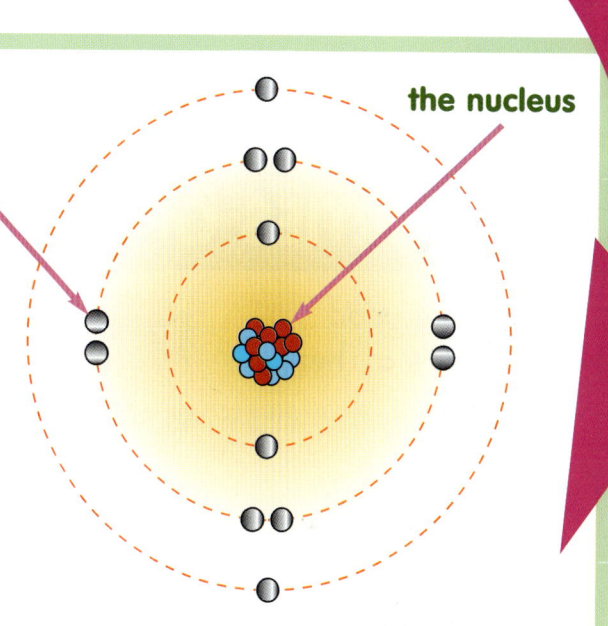

electron — *the nucleus*

QUICK TEST

1. What is special about an element?
2. How many elements have been discovered?
3. How are the elements often displayed?
4. How are atoms arranged in the periodic table?
5. What are the horizontal rows in the periodic table called?
6. What are the vertical columns in the periodic table called?
7. What is the centre part of an atom called?
8. Which particles are found in the nucleus of an atom?
9. Which particles are found in shells around the nucleus?
10. What charge do electrons have?

1. It only contains one type of atom. 2. About 100. 3. Periodic table. 4. Increasing atomic number. 5. Periods. 6. Groups. 7. Nucleus. 8. Neutrons and protons. 9. Electrons. 10. Negative.

METALS

Three-quarters of all elements are metals.

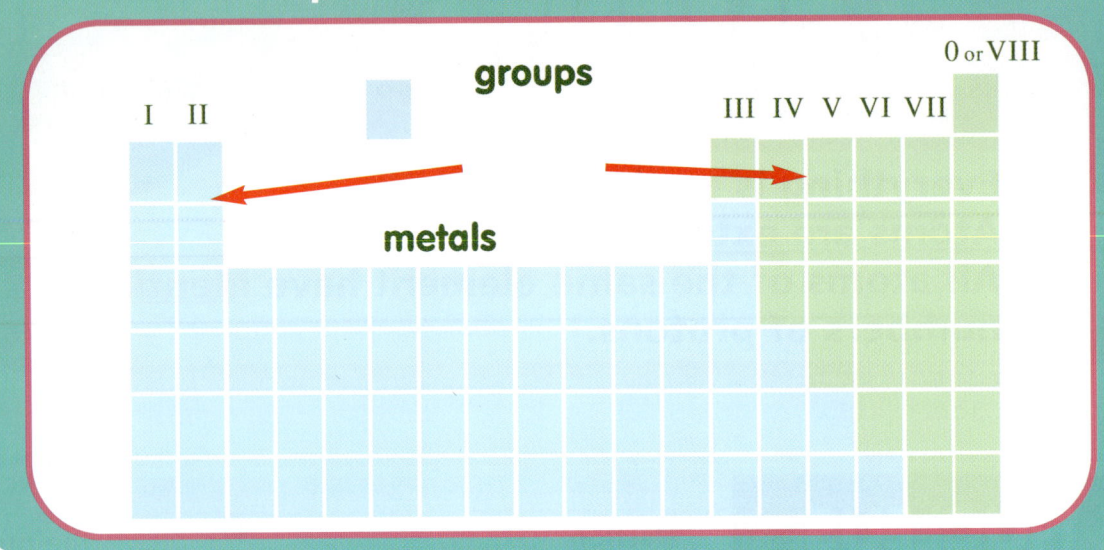

groups

metals

PROPERTIES OF METALS

Metals are good conductors of heat.

Metals have high melting and boiling points. All metals are solids at room temperature except mercury which is liquid.

Metals are shiny (when freshly cut).

Metals are sonorous (ping when hit).

Metals may be mixed together to form useful alloys.

Metals are good conductors of electricity.

Metals are strong and dense, but they are also malleable (can be hammered into shape) and ductile (can be drawn into wires).

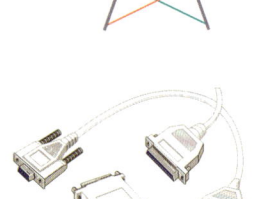

Some metals are magnetic (like iron and steel).

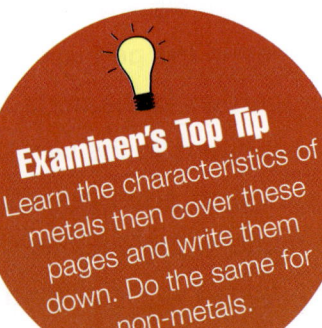

Examiner's Top Tip
Learn the characteristics of metals then cover these pages and write them down. Do the same for non-metals.

aeroplanes are made of alloys which are light and strong

NON-METALS

- Only one quarter of all elements are non-metals.

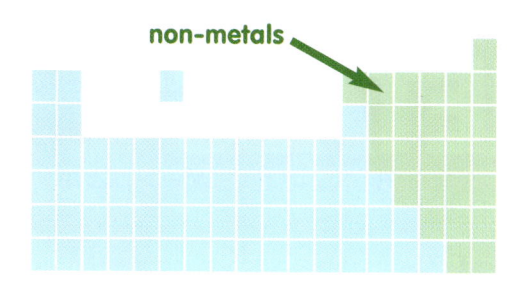

  non-metals

- Non-metals usually have low melting points and boiling points; 11 of them are gases at room temperature.
- Bromine is the only liquid non-metal at room temperature.

- Non-metals are not usually <u>shiny</u>, <u>malleable</u>, <u>strong</u>, <u>ductile</u> or <u>sonorous</u>.
- If hit they are <u>brittle</u> and tend to <u>break</u>.
- They appear <u>dull</u>.

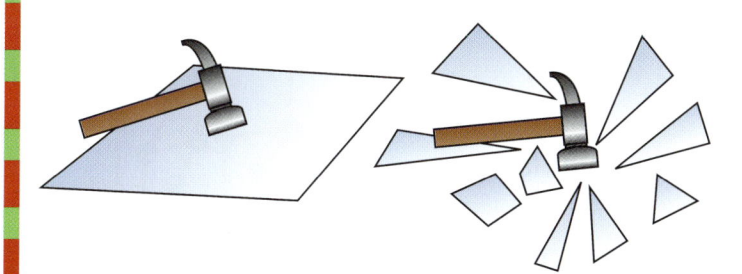

- Non-metals have <u>low</u> <u>densities</u>.

- Non-metals are poor conductors of heat.

  the wooden handle is a poor conductor of heat energy

- Non-metals usually do not conduct electricity.
- An exception is carbon which, when in the form of graphite, does conduct.

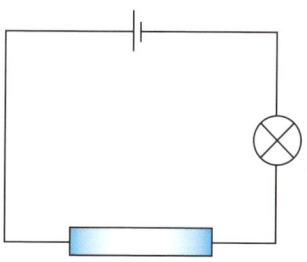

  non-metal

  electricity cannot flow and the lamp does not light

Examiner's Top Tip
Metal oxides dissolve in water to form alkaline solutions. Non-metal oxides dissolve in water to form acidic solutions.

QUICK TEST

1. Sketch the periodic table and shade the metal elements.
2. Roughly what fraction of the elements are metals?
3. Name the only metal which is not a solid at room temperature.
4. What does sonorous mean?
5. Name the properties that are common to all metals
6. Roughly what fraction of elements are non-metals?
7. Which non-metal is a liquid at room temperature?
8. Comment on the density of non-metals.
9. Do non-metals generally conduct electricity?
10. Which non-metal conducts electricity?

1. See table. 2. $\frac{3}{4}$. 3. Mercury. 4. It pings when hit. 5. Good conductors, high m.p. and b.p., strong/dense, malleable and ductile, shiny, sonorous, form alloys. 6. $\frac{1}{4}$. 7. Bromine. 8. Low density. 9. No. 10. Carbon graphite.

UNUSUAL METALS AND NON-METALS

Metals and non-metals have characteristic properties; however, there are certain elements which have unexpected properties.

NON-METALS

Carbon can exist as diamond or graphite.

DIAMOND
- Diamond is a form of the element carbon.
- In diamond all the carbon atoms are held together with very strong bonds.
- Most non-metals are soft or brittle, but diamond is very hard.
- Most non-metals are gases, one is a liquid and a few are solids with low melting points.
- Diamond has a very high melting point – over 3500°C.

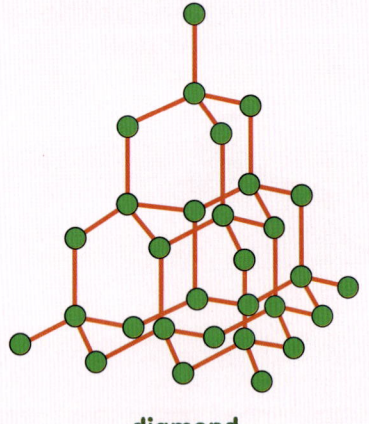

diamond

GRAPHITE
- Graphite is also a form of the element carbon.
- It is made of the same carbon atoms as diamond, but graphite has a layered structure.
- Most non-metals do not conduct electricity. Graphite is unusual because it can conduct electricity.

electricity may be conducted in this direction

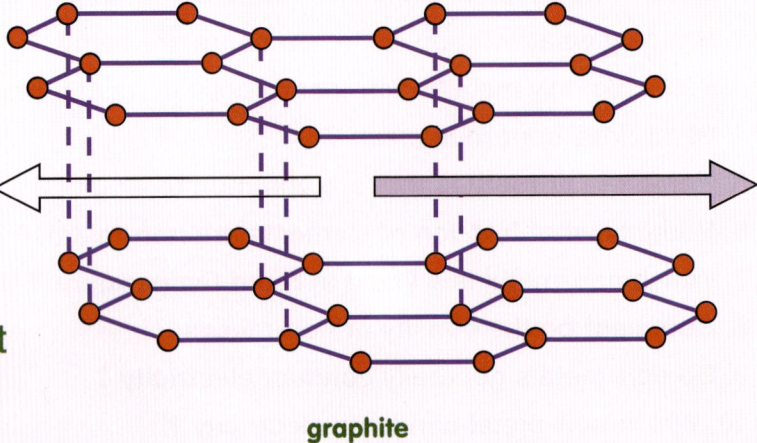

graphite

BROMINE
- Bromine is the only non-metal element which is a liquid at room temperature.

UNUSUAL METALS

MERCURY

Mercury is the only metal which is a liquid at room temperature. All other metals are solid. Liquids expand more than solids when they are heated, one reason why mercury is used in thermometers.

SODIUM

Sodium is an unusual metal.
- Most metals have a high density: sodium has a much lower density and will even float on water.
- Most metals are hard and strong: sodium is soft and can be cut with a knife.
- Most metals react slowly or not at all with water: sodium reacts very vigorously with water giving off a gas (hydrogen) and forming an alkaline solution (sodium hydroxide).

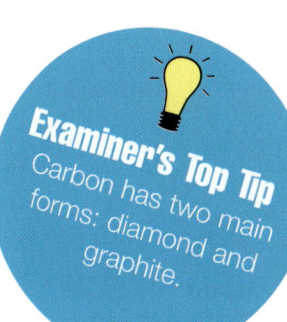

Examiner's Top Tip
Potassium and lithium behave in a similar way to sodium.

Examiner's Top Tip
Carbon has two main forms: diamond and graphite.

QUICK TEST

1. What state are most metals at room temperature?
2. Which is the only metal element which is a liquid at room temperature?
3. What happens to solids and liquids on heating?
4. What is mercury used in?
5. Why does sodium float on water?
6. Name two forms of carbon.
7. Why is graphite unusual for a non-metal?
8. Which is the only non-metal which is liquid at room temperature?

1. Solid. 2. Mercury. 3. They expand. 4. Thermometers. 5. It is less dense than water. 6. Diamond and graphite. 7. It conducts electricity. 8. Bromine.

SIMPLE CHEMICAL REACTIONS

The rusting of iron and steel is an important everyday chemical reaction. It is not a useful reaction, and we try to slow down or stop the reaction. Burning (or combustion) is another everyday reaction. When substances are burned in a controlled way it can be a very useful reaction.

RUSTING OF IRON

Iron rusts (or corrodes) faster than most metals.
Three test tubes are set up in an experiment and left for a few days.

TEST TUBE 1
Air (which contains oxygen) and water are both present.
air and water are present

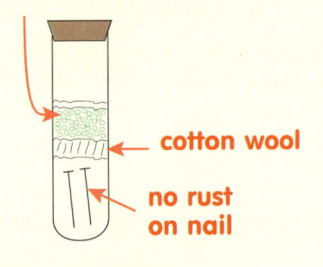

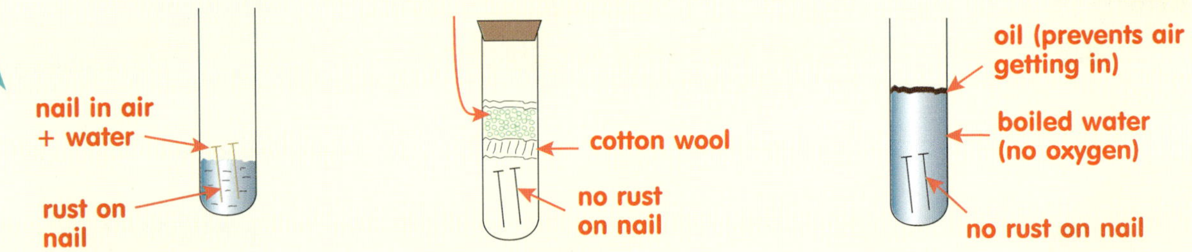

TEST TUBE 2
Air is present but there is no water. Anhydrous calcium chloride removes any water from the air.
air is present

TEST TUBE 3
The nails are resting in water. Although there is air in the test tube, any air dissolved in the water has been removed by boiling it. A layer of oil on top of the water stops any air from reaching the water.
water is present

After a few days rusting has only occurred in test tube 1.
Both oxygen and water must be present for rusting to happen.
If either the oxygen or the water is completely removed then the iron will not rust.

Examiner's Top Tip
The rusting of iron has a very slow rate of reaction.

Examiner's Top Tip
Water and oxygen must both be present for rusting to occur.

BURNING

When a substance is burned, it reacts with the oxygen in the air to form a new substance called an oxide. When magnesium is burned, in air it reacts with oxygen present to form the compound magnesium oxide.

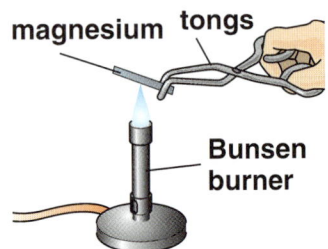

This chemical reaction can be represented by a word equation.

magnesium + oxygen → magnesium oxide

Or by a symbol equation.

$$2Mg + O_2 \rightarrow 2MgO$$

PREVENTING RUSTING

COATING THE IRON OR STEEL
- Painting the iron or coating the iron in plastic or oil can stop oxygen and water from reaching the iron, but if the coating is damaged the iron will rust.
- Steel cars are painted to stop them from rusting, but if this protective layer is damaged then the air and water can reach the steel, and it will rust.

iron is protected by paint — *if the layer is scratched water and air reaches the iron and it rusts*

no rusting occurs — *if it is scratched rusting occurs*

TIN PLATING
- If the iron is plated with tin or chromium it will not rust. Tin and chromium are both less reactive than iron. However, if the protective layer is damaged then it will begin to rust.

ALLOYING THE METAL
- If the iron is mixed with other metals such as chromium it will form the alloy stainless steel.
- This does not rust.

surgical instruments can be made from stainless steel

SACRIFICIAL PROTECTION
- If a metal which is more reactive than iron, such as zinc or magnesium, is connected to the iron, corrosion will be prevented. Because the zinc is more reactive, the zinc reacts instead of the iron.
- The iron is protected at the expense of the more reactive metal. For this reason it is called sacrificial protection.

speed boat engines are protected using zinc or magnesium

BURNING FUELS

- Fuels are substances that release energy (normally in the form of heat) when they are burned.
- The fuel methane is burned in a Bunsen burner. Methane has the formula CH_4. This shows that it contains the elements carbon and hydrogen.
- Fuels such as methane that contain carbon and hydrogen are called hydrocarbons.
- When methane is burned the carbon reacts with oxygen to form carbon dioxide, while the hydrogen reacts to form water vapour.
- The combustion of methane can be represented by a word or a symbol equation.

    methane + oxygen → carbon dioxide + water vapour
    $CH_4 + O_2 \rightarrow CO_2 + H_2O$

- If a fuel is burned in a limited supply of oxygen, incomplete combustion occurs, and carbon monoxide is also produced.

QUICK TEST

1. What does anhydrous calcium chloride do?
2. Why is the water boiled in test tube 3 of the experiment described on page 62?
3. What two things are needed for iron to rust?
4. How is stainless steel made and what are its advantages?
5. What is sacrificial protection?
6. Give an example of sacrificial protection.

1. It removes water.
2. It removes air dissolved in water.
3. Oxygen and water.
4. By alloying iron with chromium (Cr), which does not rust.
5. When magnesium (Mg) or zinc (Zn) is in contact with iron (Fe), Fe is protected as Mg/Zn reacts first.
6. It is used to protect boat engines, etc.

REACTIVITY SERIES

Most reactive —
- potassium K
- sodium Na
- calcium Ca
- magnesium Mg

Extracted from their ores by **electrolysis**

- carbon C
- zinc Zn
- iron Fe
- lead Pb

Extracted from their ores by heating with **carbon** (coke or charcoal)

- hydrogen H
- copper Cu

Least reactive —
- gold Au

Metals less reactive than hydrogen **do not** react with water or dilute acids

Examiner's Top Tip
Metals like sodium and potassium are so reactive that they must be **stored under oil**. If they are not stored in this way they react with the moisture in the air.

This order has been worked out by observing how vigorous the **reaction** is between the metal and:
- air;
- water; and
- dilute acid.

REACTIVITY SERIES

Some metals are more reactive than others. The metals can be placed in order of reactivity.

REACTING THE METALS WITH AIR

When metals are heated with air they may react with the oxygen present.

metal + oxygen ⇨ metal oxide

magnesium + oxygen ⇨ magnesium oxide

$2Mg + O_2 \rightarrow 2MgO$

Most reactive –
- potassium K
- sodium Na
- calcium Ca
- magnesium Mg

These metals react vigorously. They **burn** fiercely.

- carbon C
- zinc Zn
- iron Fe
- lead Pb
- hydrogen H
- copper Cu

These metals react **slowly** with air.

Least reactive –
- gold Au

No reaction

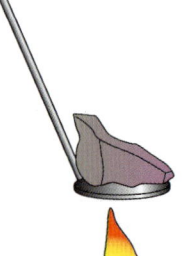

REACTING METALS WITH WATER

Some metals react with water to produce a metal hydroxide and hydrogen.

metal + water ⇒ metal hydroxide + hydrogen
sodium + water ⇒ sodium hydroxide + hydrogen

When potassium, sodium and calcium are reacted with water, bubbles can be seen. These bubbles show us that a gas is being made. The gas made in this reaction is hydrogen.

Most reactive –
- potassium K
- sodium Na — React vigorously with cold water
- calcium Ca
- magnesium Mg
- carbon C
- zinc Zn
- iron Fe — React with steam
- lead Pb
- hydrogen H
- copper Cu — No reaction
- gold Au

Least reactive –

Examiner's Top Tip
The reactivity series not only tells us how an element will react, but it also tells us how a metal should be extracted from its ore.

REACTING METALS WITH DILUTE ACIDS

Some metals (those more reactive than hydrogen) react with dilute acids to produce salts and hydrogen.

metal + acid ⇒ salt + hydrogen
calcium + hydrochloric acid ⇒ calcium chloride + hydrogen
$Ca + 2HCl \Rightarrow CaCl_2 + H_2$

Most reactive –
- potassium K, sodium Na — React violently with dilute acid
- calcium Ca, magnesium Mg — React fast with dilute acid
- carbon C
- zinc Zn
- iron Fe — Good reaction with dilute acid
- lead Pb
- hydrogen H
- copper Cu, gold Au — No reaction

Least reactive –

When magnesium reacts with acid the temperature of the acid increases. A change in temperature is evidence that a chemical reaction is taking place. The bubbles formed when magnesium reacts with dilute acid show that a gas is being made. The gas is hydrogen.

QUICK TEST

1. How should metals more reactive than carbon be extracted from their ores?
2. How should metals less reactive than carbon be extracted from their ores?
3. How was the reactivity series compiled?
4. When metals burn in oxygen what is formed?
5. What is formed when zinc is burnt in air?
6. Give a balanced equation for the reaction.
7. What is formed when potassium reacts with water?
8. Give a balanced equation for the reaction.
9. What forms when magnesium reacts with hydrochloric acid?
10. Give a balanced equation for the reaction.

1. Electrolysis.
2. Heat with carbon.
3. Observing reactions with air, water, acid.
4. Metal oxides.
5. Zinc oxide.
6. $2Zn + O_2 \Rightarrow 2ZnO$.
7. Potassium hydroxide + hydrogen.
8. $2K + 2H_2O \Rightarrow 2KOH + H_2$.
9. Magnesium chloride + hydrogen.
10. $Mg + 2HCl \Rightarrow MgCl_2 + H_2$.

METAL DISPLACEMENT REACTIONS

A more reactive metal will displace a less reactive metal from a compound.

REACTIVITY SERIES

Most reactive ↓ Least reactive

potassium K
sodium Na
calcium Ca
magnesium Mg
carbon C
zinc Zn
iron Fe
lead Pb
hydrogen H
copper Cu
gold Au

IRON AND COPPER SULPHATE

Iron is more reactive than copper.
- When an iron nail is placed in a solution of copper sulphate, the nail changes colour from silver to orange-pink.
- The nail has been coated with copper.
- The solution changes colour from blue to a very pale green.
- The solution now contains iron sulphate.

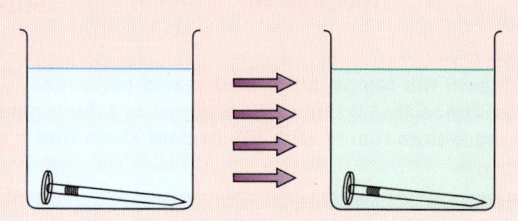

what you observe

This is an example of a displacement reaction. The more reactive metal, iron, displaces the less reactive metal, copper, from its compound, copper sulphate.

iron + copper sulphate ⇨ copper + iron sulphate
iron is more reactive

$Fe + CuSO_4 \Rightarrow Cu(s) + FeSO_4$
copper is less reactive

Iron displaces the copper from the solution.

ZINC AND IRON SULPHATE

- Using the reactivity series, zinc is more reactive than iron.
- The zinc displaces the iron from the solution.

zinc + iron sulphate ⇨ zinc sulphate + iron
$Zn + FeSO_4 \Rightarrow ZnSO_4 + Fe$

- This shows that zinc is more reactive than iron and iron is more reactive than copper.

The order of reactivity is:

most   zinc

        iron

least   copper

Examiner's Top Tip
An understanding of the reactivity series and displacement reactions can help you to predict and explain many chemical reactions.

COPPER AND MAGNESIUM SULPHATE

If the metal which is added is less reactive than the metal in the compound then no reaction will occur.

copper + magnesium sulphate ⇨ no reaction

THE THERMIT REACTION

This is a very useful <u>displacement</u> <u>reaction</u>.
It is used to produce <u>molten</u> <u>iron</u> to mend railway tracks.
- Aluminium is heated with iron oxide.
- Aluminium is more reactive than iron, so the aluminium <u>displaces</u> the iron.
- Aluminium oxide and iron are produced.

The reaction gives out a lot of heat, or is very <u>exothermic</u>; the iron produced is molten and can therefore be poured into gaps in the rails.

Aluminium + iron oxide ⇨ aluminium oxide + iron

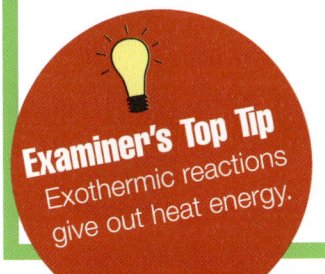

Examiner's Top Tip
Exothermic reactions give out heat energy.

METAL DISPLACEMENT REACTIONS

QUICK TEST

1. What is the rule for displacement reactions?
2. Which metal is more reactive: iron or copper?
3. What is the word equation for the reaction between iron and copper sulphate?
4. Write a balanced symbol equation for the reaction.
5. Which metal is the more reactive: iron or zinc?
6. What is the word equation for the reaction between zinc and iron sulphate?
7. Write a balanced symbol equation for the reaction.
8. Which metal is more reactive: copper or magnesium?
9. Write a word equation for the reaction between magnesium and copper sulphate.
10. What happens when copper is placed in a solution of zinc sulphate?

1. A more reactive metal will displace a less reactive metal from a compound.
2. Iron.
3. Iron + copper sulphate ⇨ iron sulphate + copper.
4. $Fe + CuSO_4 \Rightarrow FeSO_4 + Cu$.
5. Zinc.
6. Zinc + iron sulphate ⇨ zinc sulphate + iron.
7. $Zn + FeSO_4 \Rightarrow ZnSO_4 + Fe$.
8. Magnesium.
9. Magnesium + copper sulphate ⇨ magnesium sulphate + copper.
10. No reaction.

INDICATORS

- There are many different indicators.

Indicator	Acid	Neutral	Alkali
Universal Indicator	red	green	purple
Blue litmus	red	blue	blue
Red litmus	red	red	blue
Phenolphthalein	colourless	colourless	pink

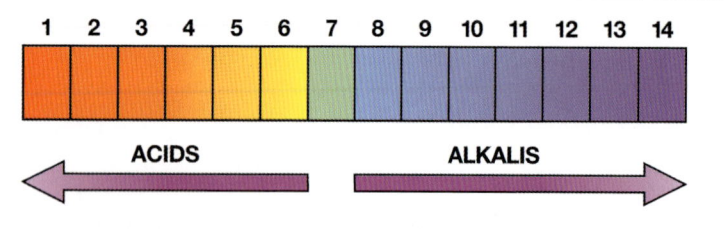

1 2 3 4 5 6 7 8 9 10 11 12 13 14

← ACIDS   ALKALIS →

Examiner's Top Tip
Many people do not realise that alkalis are often more corrosive than acids of the same strength. Always wear goggles when handling acids and alkalis.

ACIDS

- Acidic solutions have a pH less than 7.
- The strongest acids have a pH of 1.
- The weakest acids have a pH of 6.
- Many foods, such as lemons and vinegar contain acids. These foods taste sour.

COMMON LABORATORY ACIDS ARE:
- hydrochloric acid
- sulphuric acid
- nitric acid

The soluble oxides of non-metals form acidic solutions.

If water is added to an acid it becomes more dilute and less corrosive.

ALKALIS

- Alkalis are also called bases.
- Alkalis are soluble bases.
- Alkalis have a pH of more than 7.
- The strongest alkalis have a pH of 14.
- The weakest alkalis have a pH of 8.
- Alkalis often make good cleaning materials.

COMMON LABORATORY ALKALIS ARE:
- sodium hydroxide
- potassium hydroxide
- calcium hydroxide

Examiner's Top Tip
Bee stings are acidic. Wasp stings are alkaline.

TREATING SOILS

- Many plants only grow really well at a certain pH.
- Food crops in particular do not thrive if the soil is too acidic.
- Farmers add lime to the soil to neutralise the acid so the pH of the soil is right for the plant that is being grown.

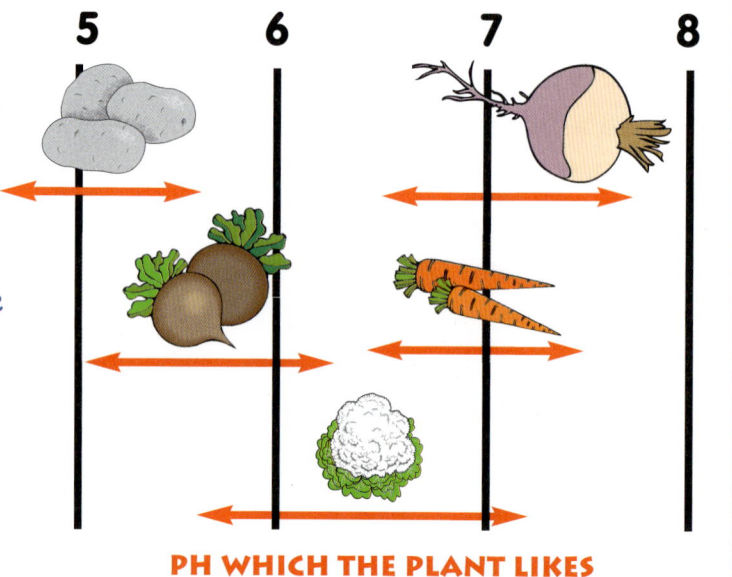

5   6   7   8

PH WHICH THE PLANT LIKES

ACIDS AND ALKALIS

Indicators are used to show whether a solution is acidic, alkaline or neutral by changing colour.

TREATING INDIGESTION

Examiner's Top Tip
Hydrogen, H^+ ions make solutions acidic.

- Your stomach contains <u>hydrochloric</u> <u>acid</u>.
- It helps you to digest your food.
- If more acid than usual is produced you get <u>indigestion</u>.
- To stop this indigestion this <u>extra</u> <u>acid</u> needs to be neutralised with an alkali.

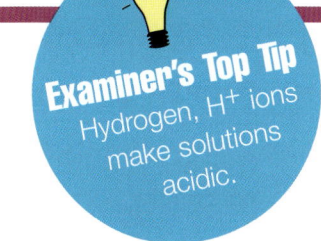

- Some indigestion tablets contain calcium carbonate.

hydrochloric acid + calcium carbonate ⇨ calcium chloride + water + carbon dioxide
extra acid in the stomach   **base in the indigestion tablet**   **salt**   **water**

NEUTRALISATION

Examiner's Top Tip
Learn what colour indicators will be in different types of solution.

The reaction between an acid and a base is called <u>neutralisation</u>.
acid + alkali ⇨ a neutral salt + water

The type of salt produced depends on the metal in the alkali used and on the acid used.

The <u>temperature</u> <u>increases</u> when an acid is added to an alkali. This shows that a <u>chemical</u> <u>reaction</u> is taking place.

QUICK TEST

1. What colour is Universal Indicator in neutral solution?
2. What colour is blue litmus in neutral solution?
3. What is the pH of a neutral solution?
4. What is the pH of the strongest alkali?
5. What is the pH of a weak acid?
6. What colour is Universal Indicator in water?
7. What colour is red litmus in water?
8. Name three common acids.

1. Green. 2. Blue. 3. 7. 4. 14. 5. 6. 6. Green. 7. Red. 8. Hydrochloric acid, sulphuric acid, nitric acid.

METAL CARBONATES

Metal carbonates can be neutralised by acids.
Most carbonates are insoluble, so they are bases, but they are not alkalis.
When carbonates are neutralised carbon dioxide is given off:

metal carbonate + acid ⇒ salt + water + carbon dioxide
copper carbonate + hydrochloric acid ⇒ copper chloride + water + carbon dioxide
zinc carbonate + sulphuric acid ⇒ zinc sulphate + water + carbon dioxide

MAKING COPPER CHLORIDE

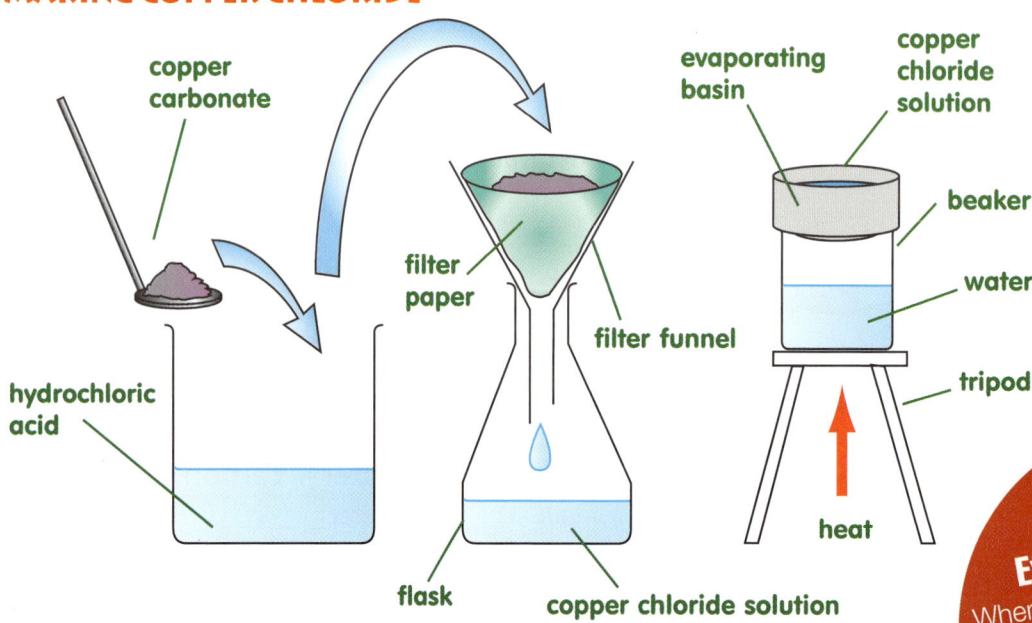

- Copper carbonate is added to the acid until it stops fizzing.
- The unreacted copper carbonate is then removed by filtering.
- The solution is poured into an evaporating dish.
- It is heated until the first crystals appear.
- The solution is then left for a few days for the copper chloride to crystallise.

Examiner's Top Tip
Sulphuric acid makes sulphate salts. Hydrochloric acid makes chloride salts. Nitric acid makes nitrate salts.

Examiner's Top Tip
When bubbles are observed during a chemical reaction it shows that a gas is being made.

Examiner's Top Tip
When acids react with metals, a salt and the gas hydrogen are produced. When acids react with metal carbonates, a salt, water and the gas carbon dioxide are produced.

METALS

Metals can be reacted with acids to form a salt and hydrogen:
- metal + acid ⇒ salt + hydrogen

zinc + hydrochloric acid ⇒ zinc chloride + hydrogen
$2Zn + 2HCl \Rightarrow 2ZnCl + H_2$

METAL OXIDES

Metal oxides are also bases; they can be reacted with acids to make salts and water:
- metal oxide + acid ⇒ salt + water

copper oxide + hydrochloric acid ⇒ copper chloride + water
$CuO + 2HCl \Rightarrow CuCl_2 + H_2O$

MAKING SALTS

METAL HYDROXIDES

We have seen that metal hydroxides can be neutralised with acids to make salt and water:

metal hydroxide + acid ⇨ salt + water

SOME USES OF SALTS

Potassium nitrate
This salt is widely used as a fertiliser.

Copper sulphate
This salt is used in electroplating, in the dying of textiles and as a wood preservative.

Silver nitrate
Silver nitrate is used in photography.

QUICK TEST

1. What is formed when hydrochloric acid reacts with potassium hydroxide?
2. What is formed when sulphuric acid reacts with sodium hydroxide?
3. Which gas is given off when carbonates react with acid?
4. What is formed when hydrochloric acid reacts with zinc carbonate?
5. What is formed when sulphuric acid reacts with magnesium carbonate?
6. How could you get a sample of a soluble salt?
7. What is formed when hydrochloric acid reacts with magnesium?
8. What is formed when sulphuric acid reacts with zinc?

1. Potassium chloride + water.
2. Sodium sulphate + water.
3. Carbon dioxide.
4. Zinc chloride + water + carbon dioxide.
5. Magnesium sulphate + water + carbon dioxide.
6. Remove unreacted solid by filtering, then evaporate off the water.
7. Magnesium chloride + hydrogen.
8. Zinc sulphate + hydrogen.

COMMON TESTS AND APPARATUS

COMMON TESTS

CARBON DIOXIDE
The gas is bubbled through limewater.
Carbon dioxide turns limewater milky.

HYDROGEN
If a lighted splint is nearby hydrogen will burn with a 'squeaky pop'.

OXYGEN
Oxygen relights a glowing splint.

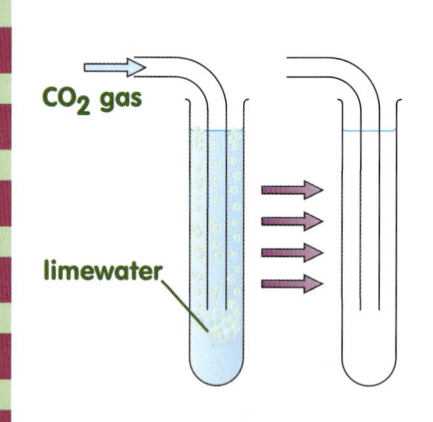

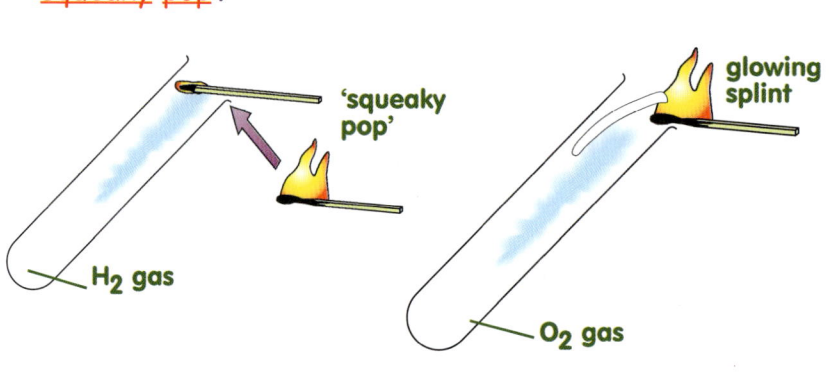

APPARATUS

Below is some of the apparatus found in the science laboratory.

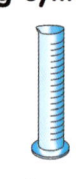

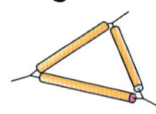

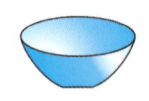

- beaker
- Bunsen burner 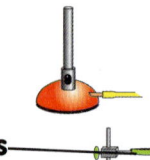
- boss clamp stand
- conical flask
- evaporating basin
- filter funnel 
- gauze 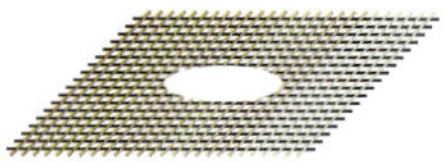
- measuring cylinder
- spatula
- test tube
- thermometer
- triangle
- tripod

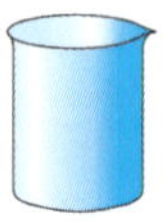

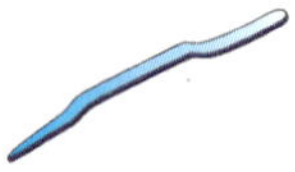

Examiner's Top Tip
Choose apparatus which is suitable for the job.

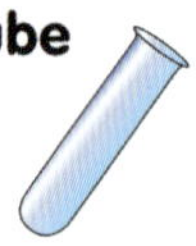

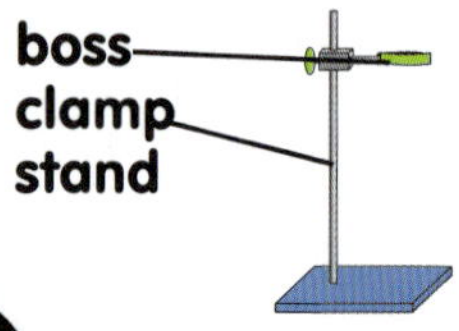

Examiner's Top Tip
Some chemicals carry more than one hazard.

SAFETY HAZARDS

OXIDISING
- Provides oxygen which allows other materials to burn more fiercely.

TOXIC
- Can cause death, if swallowed, breathed in or absorbed through the skin.

CORROSIVE
- Attacks and destroys living tissues, including eyes and skin.

HIGHLY FLAMMABLE
- Catches fire easily.

HARMFUL
- Similar to toxic but less dangerous.

IRRITANT
- Not corrosive but can cause reddening or blistering of the skin.

COMMON GASES

CARBON DIOXIDE

Carbon dioxide is a compound with the formula CO_2. It is produced when fuels containing carbon are burned in oxygen. The fuel methane contains the elements carbon and hydrogen.

The combustion of methane.
methane + oxygen → carbon dioxide + water vapour

Carbon dioxide is also produced when metal carbonates react with acids.
The reaction between hydrochloric acid and copper carbonate.
copper carbonate + hydrochloric acid → copper chloride + water + carbon dioxide

The bubbles of carbon dioxide show that a chemical reaction is taking place. As carbon dioxide escapes from the flask, the mass of the flask decreases.

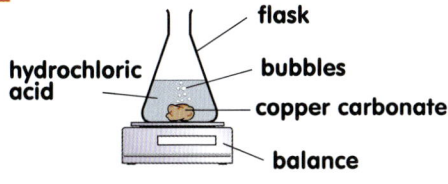

HYDROGEN

Hydrogen is produced when metals react with acids.
The reaction between magnesium and sulphuric acid.
Magnesium + sulphuric acid → magnesium sulphate + hydrogen

The bubbles of hydrogen show that a chemical reaction is taking place. The mass of the test tube decreases as the hydrogen is lost. The temperature of the acid also increases, another sign that a chemical reaction is taking place.

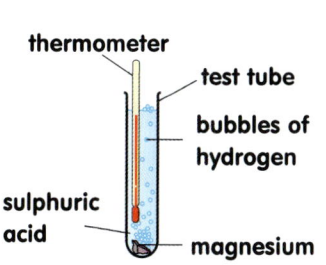

OXYGEN

Oxygen is the second most abundant gas in the air. Oxygen is required for burning and rusting. When a metal is burned it forms a metal oxide.
Combustion of magnesium.
magnesium + oxygen → magnesium oxide
Magnesium is a shiny silvery metal, while magnesium oxide is a white ash. This change in colour is evidence that a chemical reaction has taken place.

COMMON TESTS AND APPARATUS

QUICK TEST

1. Sketch the hazard symbol for oxidising.
2. Sketch the hazard symbol for highly flammable.
3. Sketch the hazard symbol for toxic.
4. Sketch the hazard symbol for corrosive.
5. What is the test for carbon dioxide?
6. What is the test for hydrogen?
7. Which piece of apparatus would you use to measure the volume of a liquid?
8. Which piece of apparatus would you use to separate a solid from a liquid?

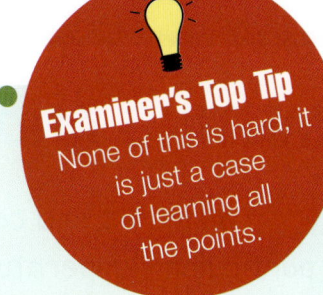

Examiner's Top Tip
None of this is hard, it is just a case of learning all the points.

1. See above.
2. See above.
3. See above.
4. See above.
5. Gas is bubbled through limewater which turns milky.
6. Lighted splint gives 'squeaky pop'.
7. A measuring cylinder.
8. Filter funnel.

MIXTURES

If there are two or more different atoms, but they are not combined, they are a mixture of different elements.

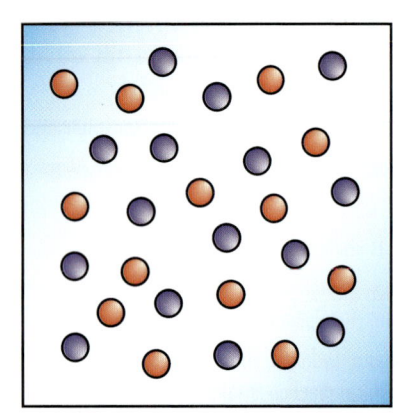

If there are two or more different compounds, but they are not combined, they are a mixture of compounds.

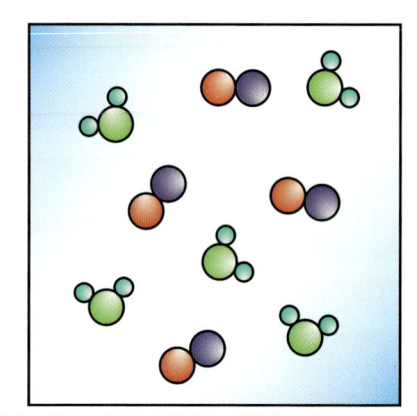

FIXED COMPOSITION

- A mixture contains two or more atoms or compounds that are not combined or joined together.
- Mixtures are easy to separate.
- Compounds are much harder to separate.
- Mixtures do not have a fixed composition.
- Compounds do have a fixed composition.

SEA WATER

Sea water is a mixture. It contains particles of water, salts and gases. These particles are mixed together, but they are not joined.

MELTING AND BOILING POINTS OF PURE SUBSTANCES

Pure elements and compounds melt at a particular temperature and boil at a particular temperature.

The graph shows how when ice is heated its temperature increases. At 0°C the solid ice melts to form liquid water. The temperature stays the same until all the ice has melted. Only once all the ice has melted does the water begin to increase in temperature. This graph shows that pure ice melts at a particular temperature, 0°C.

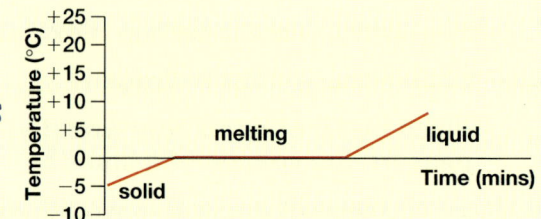

Pure elements and pure compounds melt at a particular temperature called the melting point.

AIR

- Air is a mixture of gas particles. It is composed of about 80% nitrogen molecules and about 20% oxygen molecules.
- There are also very small amounts of other gases, including carbon dioxide, water vapour and noble gases, including argon and neon.
- These gas particles are mixed together, but they are not joined.
- Air can be separated by the fractional distillation of liquid air.
- Oxygen is used in the production of steel and is needed for combustion and respiration.
- Nitrogen is used to make fertilisers and explosives.
- Argon is placed inside light bulbs because it does not react with the hot tungsten filament.
- Neon is used in neon lights and in the barcode readers found in shops.

a molecule of carbon dioxide, a compound consisting of carbon and oxygen

a molecule of oxygen, an element

a molecule of nitrogen, an element

a molecule of water, a compound consisting of oxygen and hydrogen

ROCKS

- Most rocks contain a mixture of different minerals.
- Minerals are compounds because they have a fixed composition.
- Granite is an igneous rock.
- It contains a mixture of minerals.
- It consists mainly of the minerals feldspar, quartz and mica.
- The exact proportion of these minerals is not fixed, and will vary from rock to rock.

MELTING POINTS

Mixtures do not melt at one fixed temperature. Instead, each component in the mixture melts at its own particular melting point.

Butter is a good example of a mixture. On a warm day butter will begin to melt. If you look carefully, some of it will have already melted while other parts are still solid. Mixtures melt over a range of temperatures.

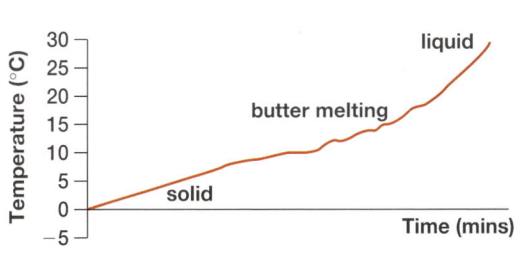

*Mixtures melt over a **range** of temperatures.*

QUICK TEST

1. Can mixtures be separated easily?
2. Why is a mixture different to a compound?
3. Can you have a mixture of compounds?
4. Do compounds have a fixed composition?
5. Do mixtures have a fixed composition?
6. Is sea water a mixture?
7. What does sea water contain?
8. What does air contain?
9. What percentage of air is nitrogen?
10. What are most rocks a mixture of?

Examiner's Top Tip
Learn the examples of mixtures discussed on this spread.

1. Yes.
2. It is not joined.
3. Yes.
4. Yes.
5. No.
6. Yes.
7. Water, salts and gases.
8. Nitrogen, oxygen, water vapour, carbon dioxide, argon and neon.
9. 80%.
10. Different minerals.

SEPARATION TECHNIQUES

- In a mixture the constituent parts are <u>not joined together</u>.
- Mixtures can be <u>separated</u> quite easily.

FILTRATION

- *Filtration is used to <u>separate</u> a mixture of a solid and a liquid.*
- *The mixture is poured through a <u>filter paper</u>. Only the liquid passes through and is called the <u>filtrate</u>. The solid is collected on the filter paper and is called the <u>residue</u>.*

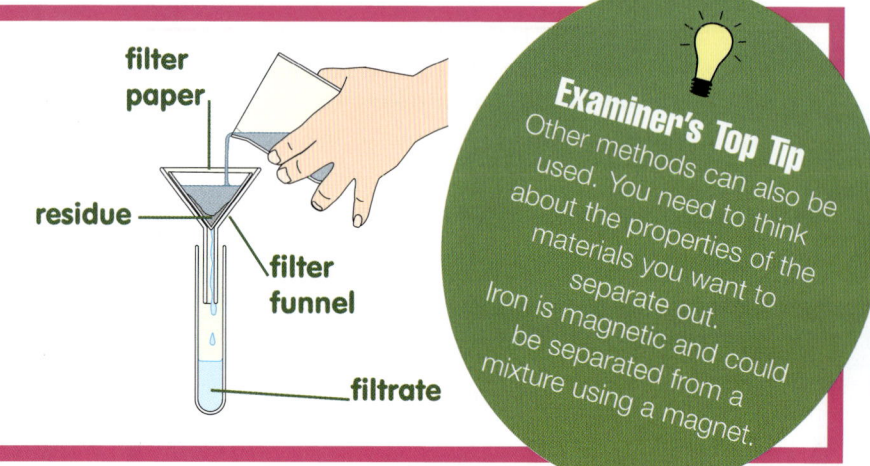

Examiner's Top Tip
Other methods can also be used. You need to think about the properties of the materials you want to separate out. Iron is magnetic and could be separated from a mixture using a magnet.

FILTRATION AND EVAPORATION

- A mixture of salt and sand can be separated using these two techniques.
  When water is added and the mixture is stirred, the soluble salt will dissolve.
  The insoluble sand does not dissolve.
  The mixture can then be filtered: the dissolved salt passes through the filter, while the sand can be collected from the filter paper.

- Solutions of a solvent and a solute can be separated by evaporation.
  The solvent, in this case water, can be evaporated, leaving the solute (salt) behind.
  The salt forms crystals; this process is called crystallisation.

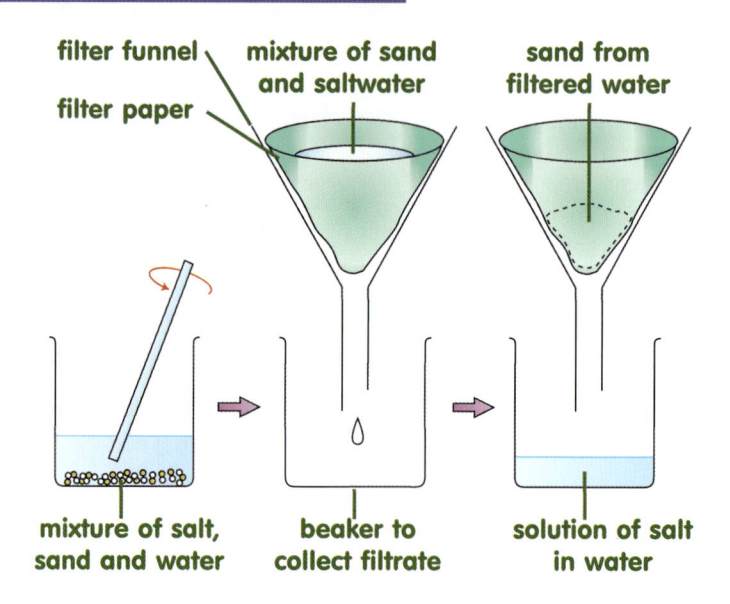

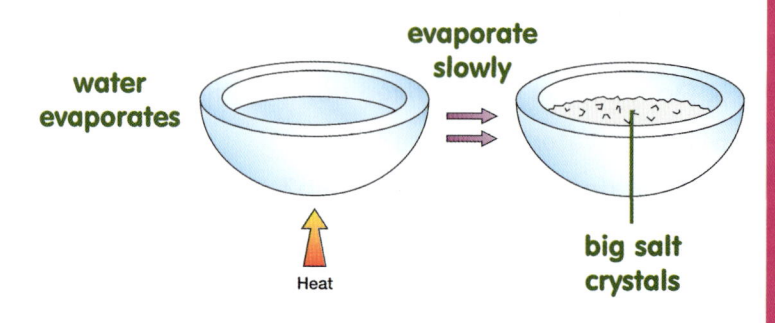

76

CHROMATOGRAPHY

- Chromatography can be used to separate mixtures of different coloured dyes. The different dyes have different solubilities.
- This method can be used to find which dyes make up black ink. A spot of ink is placed on a piece of filter paper and this is placed in a beaker containing a small amount of solvent.
  The solvent travels across the filter paper carrying the dyes with it. Each dye has a slightly different solubility, so travels a slightly different distance across the paper.
- This black dye contains red, blue and yellow dyes.

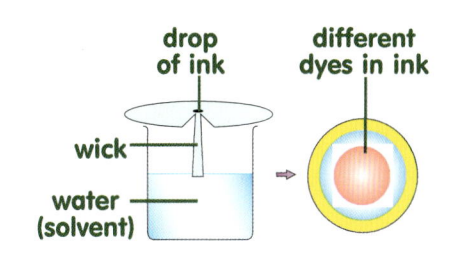

DISTILLATION

DISTILLATION

- Distillation can be used to separate a solvent from a solution.
- It can be used to separate water from a solution of salt and water. The solution is heated. The water boils and water vapour is formed. The water vapour cools and condenses to form liquid water which is collected in a beaker. This water is called 'distilled water' and is very pure.

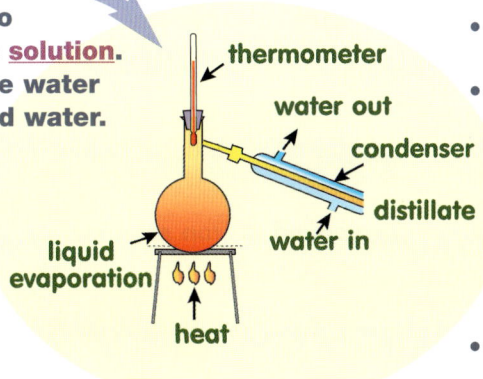

FRACTIONAL DISTILLATION

- Fractional distillation can be used to separate a mixture of two or more liquids.
- It can be used to separate alcohol and water.
- The liquids still boil at their own boiling temperatures, even though they are now in a mixture. The alcohol boils at 78°C. Some water will also evaporate, but it will condense in the fractionating column and fall back into the flask.
- Only the alcohol passes into the condenser, where it forms pure liquid alcohol which is collected in the beaker.

QUICK TEST

1. In a mixture are the constituent parts joined?
2. In a compound are the constituent parts joined?
3. How should a mixture of solid and liquid be separated?
4. How can crystals of a salt be obtained from a mixture of salt and water?
5. Which technique should be used to separate a mixture of different coloured dyes?
6. Why do different dyes travel different distances?
7. How can water be separated from a mixture of salt and water?
8. How can a mixture of alcohol and water be separated?

1. No. 2. Yes. 3. Filtration. 4. Through crystallisation which will evaporate the water. 5. Chromatography. 6. They have different solubilities. 7. By distillation. 8. Through fractional distillation

FORMING COMPOUNDS

- During a chemical reaction a <u>new</u> <u>substance</u> is made.
- These new chemicals are the <u>products</u> of the reaction. The starting chemicals are called the <u>reactants</u>.
- The products can have <u>very</u> <u>different</u> <u>properties</u> from the reactants. Heating iron with sulphur gives iron sulphide.

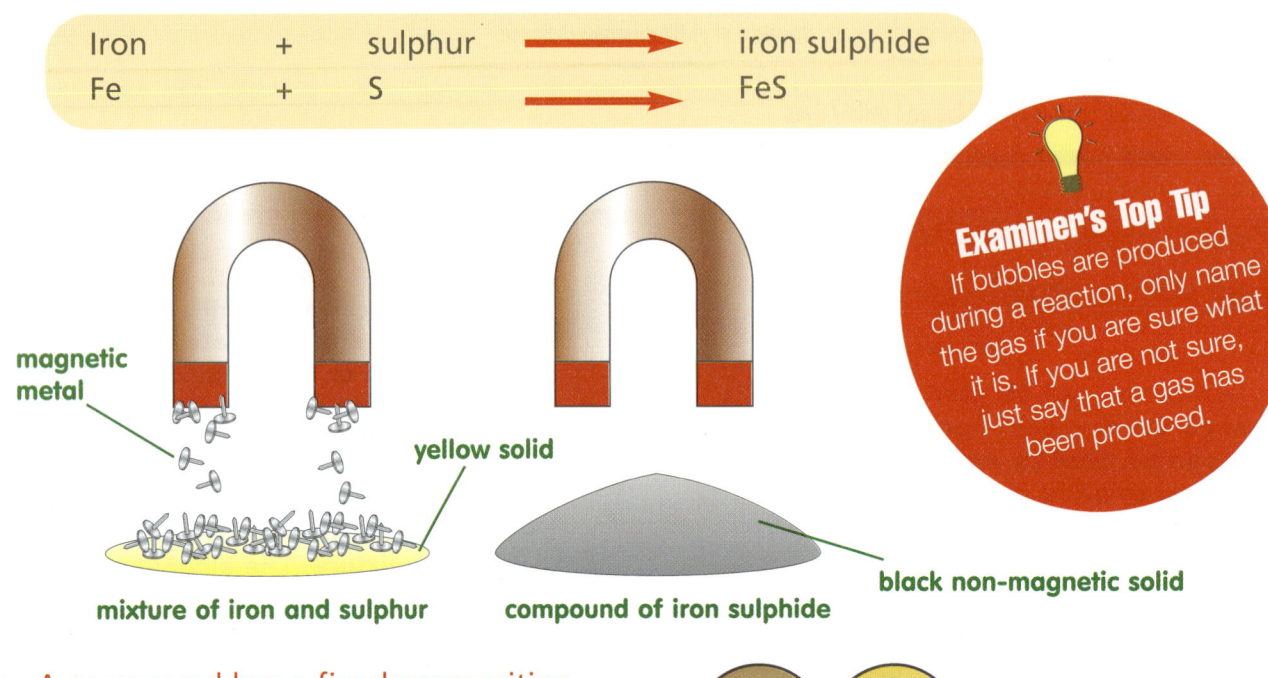

Iron	+	sulphur	→	iron sulphide
Fe	+	S	→	FeS

magnetic metal

yellow solid

mixture of iron and sulphur

compound of iron sulphide

black non-magnetic solid

Examiner's Top Tip
If bubbles are produced during a reaction, only name the gas if you are sure what it is. If you are not sure, just say that a gas has been produced.

- A compound has a fixed composition.
- Iron sulphide FeS contains one atom of iron for each atom of sulphur.

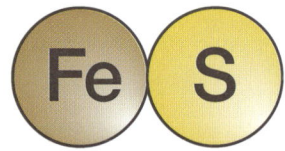

CAN COMPOUNDS REACT?

We have seen that chemical reactions can take place between elements. Chemical reactions can also take place between <u>compounds</u>. If a chemical reaction takes place <u>new</u> <u>substances</u> <u>are</u> <u>made</u>. There are three things to look out for that show that a chemical reaction is occurring.

- **Temperature change**
  Most chemical reactions <u>give</u> <u>out</u> <u>heat</u> <u>energy</u>, so we can <u>measure</u> <u>an</u> <u>increase</u> <u>in</u> <u>temperature</u>.

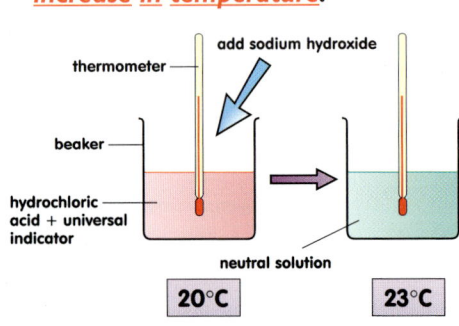

  thermometer — add sodium hydroxide
  beaker
  hydrochloric acid + universal indicator
  neutral solution
  20°C 23°C

- **Gas is produced**
  <u>Bubbles</u> <u>show</u> <u>that</u> <u>gas</u> <u>is</u> <u>being</u> <u>produced</u>. If the reaction is carried out in a beaker placed on a mass balance, then the <u>mass</u> <u>of</u> <u>the</u> <u>beaker</u> <u>goes</u> <u>down</u> as the <u>gas</u> <u>(which</u> <u>has</u> <u>mass)</u> <u>escapes</u> <u>into</u> <u>the</u> <u>air</u>.

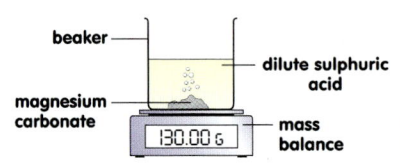

  beaker
  magnesium carbonate
  dilute sulphuric acid
  mass balance
  130.00 g   129.80 g

- **Change in colour**
  iron nail
  test tube
  copper sulphate   iron sulphate + copper

COMPOUNDS

Atoms may form molecules. A molecule has two or more atoms joined together.

- If the atoms are of the same element, they form a **molecule** of the **element**.

- If atoms of two or more elements are joined together, they form **molecules** of a **compound**.

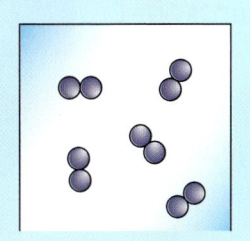

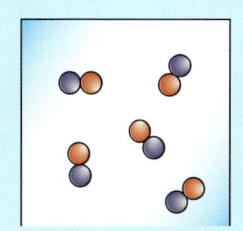

QUICK TEST

1. What does this represent?

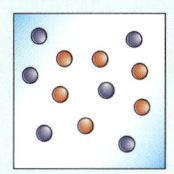

2. What does this represent?

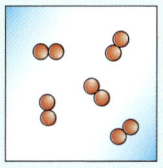

3. What does this represent?

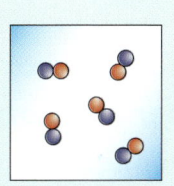

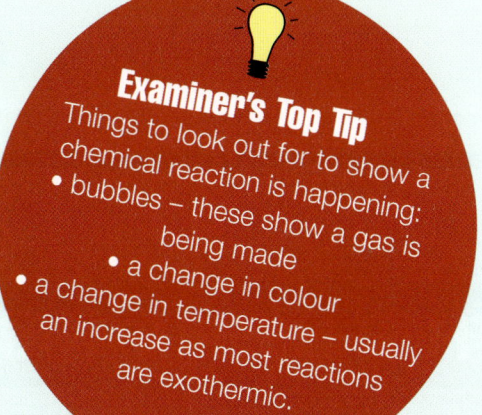

4. If you saw bubbles during a chemical reaction, what is being made?
5. What piece of apparatus would you use to find if the temperature had increased?
6. What are the chemicals at the start of a chemical reaction called?
7. What are the chemicals made by a chemical reaction called?
8. How can you tell if a chemical reaction has occurred when iron and sulphur are heated to form iron sulphide?
9. Do compounds have a fixed composition?
10. Can the elements in a compound be separated easily?

Examiner's Top Tip
Things to look out for to show a chemical reaction is happening:
- bubbles – these show a gas is being made
- a change in colour
- a change in temperature – usually an increase as most reactions are exothermic.

1. Atoms of two elements.
2. Molecules of an element.
3. Molecules of a compound.
4. Gas.
5. Thermometer.
6. Reactants.
7. Products.
8. Iron is no longer magnetic, there is change in colour, etc.
9. Yes.
10. No.

CHANGING THE NAMES

If atoms of two elements join together in a chemical reaction, it can be represented in a <u>word</u> <u>equation</u>:

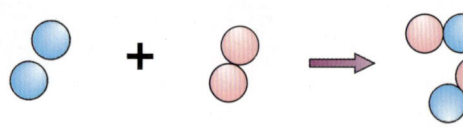

- sodium + chlorine ⇨ sodium chloride

sodium   chlorine   sodium chloride (a compound)

This can also be represented using <u>symbols</u>:

- $2Na$ + Cl_2 ⇨ $2NaCl$

The name of the compound is given by the two elements that have joined.
- The <u>chlorine</u> has changed to <u>chloride</u>.

In a similar way the names of these non-metals change when they form compounds.

- oxygen ⇨ oxide
- fluorine ⇨ fluoride
- bromine ⇨ bromide
- iodine ⇨ iodide
- sulphur ⇨ sulphide

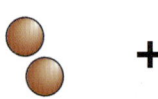

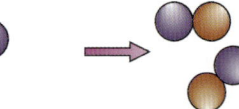

magnesium   oxygen   magnesium oxide (a compound)

$2Mg$ + O_2 ⇨ $2MgO$

Examiner's Top Tip
In all chemical reactions the overall mass does not change. Overall mass before = overall mass after the reaction.

OTHER USEFUL NAMES

- **OH is called hydroxide, so NaOH is sodium hydroxide.**
- **SO_4 is called sulphate, so $CuSO_4$ is copper sulphate.**
- **CO_3 is called carbonate, so $MgCO_3$ is magnesium carbonate.**

Examiner's Top Tip
If a name ends with 'ate' it shows that oxygen is present, for example calcium carbonate has the formula $CaCO_3$.

CARBON DIOXIDE (CO_2)

Carbon dioxide is formed from <u>one</u> <u>carbon</u> and <u>two</u> <u>oxygen</u> atoms.
- carbon + oxygen ⇨ carbon dioxide

The <u>di-</u> shows that there are <u>two</u> oxygen atoms.

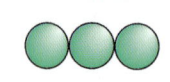

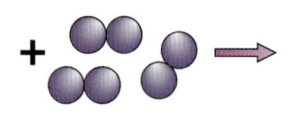

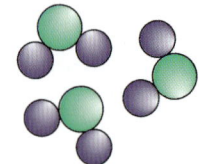

carbon   oxygen   carbon dioxide (a compound)

NAMING COMPOUNDS

When atoms of two or more elements join together they form a compound. Compounds are difficult to separate.

WATER (H_2O)

Water is formed from two hydrogen atoms and one oxygen atom.
- hydrogen + oxygen ⇨ water

hydrogen   oxygen   water (a compound)

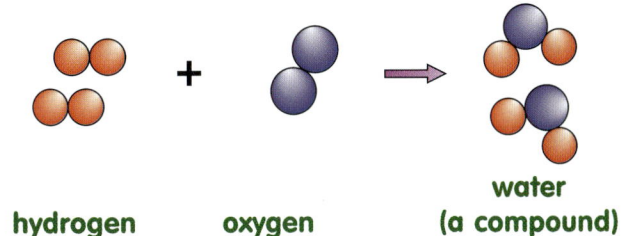

INTERPRETING FORMULAE

The chemical formula of a compound is very useful. It shows the relative number of atoms of each element that is present. Example: copper sulphate has the formula $CuSO_4$.
This shows that copper sulphate contains three different elements: copper, sulphur and oxygen.
The formula also shows the relative number of atoms of each element present:
1 copper atom, 1 sulphur atom and 4 oxygen atoms.   Cu   S O_4
                                                          1 + 1 + 4 = 6

QUICK TEST

1. Can components in a mixture be separated easily?
2. Can elements in a compound be separated easily?
3. What is a compound?
4. What is the name of the compound formed when magnesium reacts with oxygen?
5. What is the name of the compound formed when magnesium reacts with bromine?
6. In the compound magnesium chloride, $MgCl_2$, what are the relative numbers of magnesiumn and chlorine atoms?
7. In the compound carbon monoxide, CO, what are the relative numbers of carbon and oxygen atoms?
8. Write a word equation for the reaction between sodium and chlorine.
9. Write a word equation for the reaction between hydrogen and oxygen.
10. Write a word equation for the reaction between calcium and oxygen.

Examiner's Top Tip
Compounds have a fixed composition.

1. Yes.
2. No.
3. When atoms of two or more elements are joined together.
4. Magnesium oxide.
5. Magnesium bromide.
6. 1 Mg to 2 Cl.
7. 1 C to each O.
8. Sodium + chlorine ⇨ sodium chloride.
9. Hydrogen + oxygen ⇨ water.
10. Calcium + oxygen ⇨ calcium oxide.

BALANCING THE EQUATION

When hydrogen burns in oxygen, water is made.

- Hydrogen + oxygen ⇨ water
- H_2 + O_2 ⇨ H_2O

The formulae are correct, but the equation is not balanced because there are different numbers of atoms on each side of the equation. This is not correct because atoms cannot be created or destroyed in a chemical reation. The formulae for hydrogen and oxygen cannot be changed, but the numbers in front of the formulae can be changed.

HOW TO BALANCE AN EQUATION

Looking at the equation we can see that there are two oxygen atoms on the left-hand side but only one on the right-hand side.

So a 2 is placed in front of the H_2O:

- $H_2 + O_2$ ⇨ $2H_2O$

Now the oxygen atoms are balanced, but while there are two hydrogen atoms on the left-hand side there are four hydrogen atoms on the right-hand side.

So a 2 is placed in front of the H_2:

- $2H_2 + O_2$ ⇨ $2H_2O$

- **The equation is then balanced.**

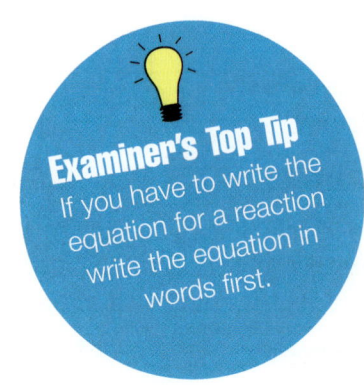

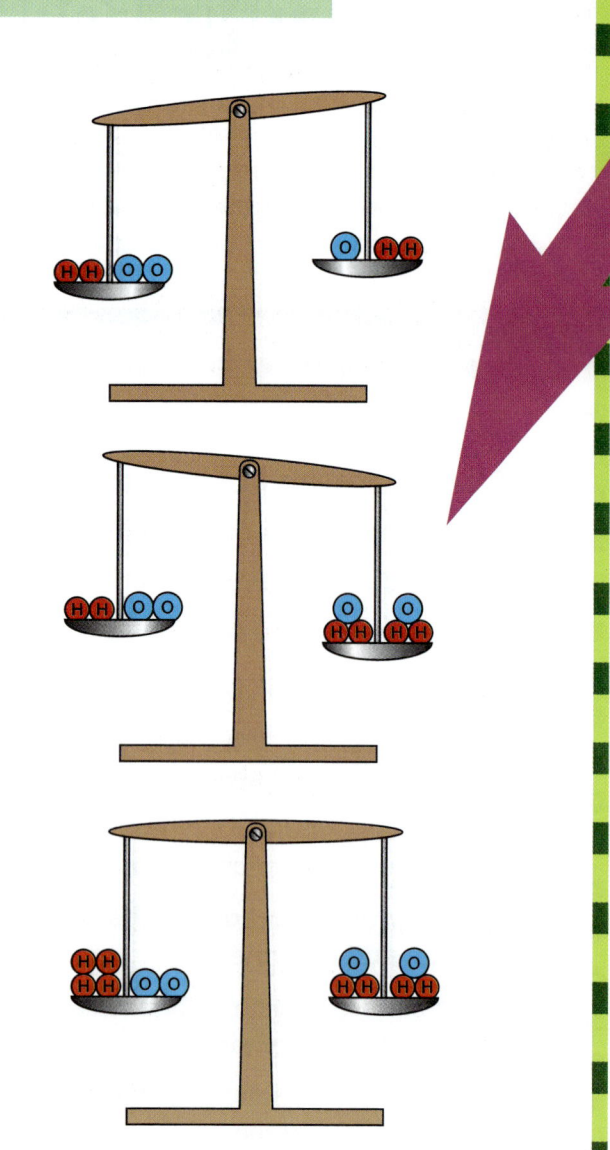

Examiner's Top Tip
If you have to write the equation for a reaction write the equation in words first.

CHEMICAL FORMULAE

- Symbol equations show the number of atoms.
- The chemical formula for water is H_2O.
- This means that every water molecule consists of two hydrogen atoms and one oxygen atom.

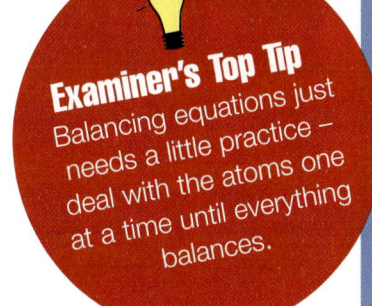

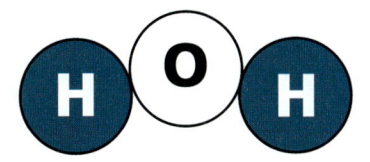

H — O — H

- The chemical formula for copper sulphate is $CuSO_4$.
- This means that every copper sulphate molecule consists of one copper atom, one sulphur atom and four oxygen atoms.
- When a chemical reaction takes place it can be represented using a <u>balanced</u> <u>equation</u>.
- There must be the same number of atoms on <u>both</u> <u>sides</u> of the equation. <u>Atoms</u> <u>cannot</u> <u>be</u> <u>created</u> <u>or</u> <u>destroyed</u>.
- This means that in chemical changes the overall mass before and after is the same.

Examiner's Top Tip
Balancing equations just needs a little practice – deal with the atoms one at a time until everything balances.

BALANCING EQUATIONS

QUICK TEST

Consider $CaCO_3$. For each atom of Ca:

1. How many carbon atoms are present?
2. How many oxygen atoms are present?

Consider H_2SO_4. For each atom of H_2:

3. How many hydrogen atoms are present?
4. How many oxygen atoms are present?
5. Why must there be the same number of atoms on both sides of the equation?
6. Balance the equation $Na + Cl_2 \Rightarrow NaCl$
7. Balance the equation $H_2 + Cl_2 \Rightarrow HCl$
8. Balance the equation $C + CO_2 \Rightarrow CO$

Examiner's Top Tip
When balancing an equation always check that the formulae you have written down are correct.

1. One.
2. Three.
3. Two.
4. Four.
5. Atoms cannot be created or destroyed.
6. $2Na + Cl_2 \Rightarrow 2NaCl$
7. $H_2 + Cl_2 \Rightarrow 2HCl$
8. $C + CO_2 \Rightarrow 2CO$

EXAM QUESTIONS – Use the questions to test your progress. Check your answers on page 127.

1. Why is copper used in electrical wiring?
   Choose one answer.
   a) copper is shiny
   b) copper does not react with water
   c) copper is a good conductor of electricity.

2. Three inks, yellow, blue and green, were compared using chromatography.
   a) Which ink is made of two substances?..
   b) Name the two colours this ink is made from..

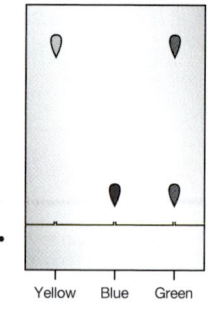

   Yellow Blue Green

3. The table below shows the melting and boiling temperatures of four elements.

Element	Melting temperature °C	Boiling temperature °C
fluorine	−220	−188
chlorine	−101	−34
bromine	−7	59
iodine	114	184

Using the table name one substance which at room temperature is:
   a) a solid..
   b) a liquid..
   c) a gas..

4. A student heated some magnesium in a crucible.
   She did not lose any of the magnesium oxide that was formed.
   The mass of the crucible was measured before and after heating.
   a) Write a word equation for the reaction..
   b) Why has the mass of the contents increased during this reaction?

   ....

   30.00 g — empty crucible
   30.24 g — crucible and magnesium
   30.40 g — crucible and magnesium oxide

5. Iron oxide reacts with carbon monoxide to form iron and carbon dioxide.
   a) Name three compounds mentioned here..
   b) Name one element mentioned here..

6. Limestone is mainly calcium carbonate. It decomposes on heating to form calcium oxide and the gas carbon dioxide.
   Write a word equation for this reaction..

7. Four metals were placed in solutions of different metal sulphate solutions. The results are shown in the table below. (If a reaction occurred a tick is shown, if no reaction took place a cross is shown.)

Metal	Magnesium sulphate	Copper sulphate solution	Iron sulphate solution	Zinc sulphate solution
magnesium	–	✓	✓	✓
copper	✗	–	✗	✗
iron	✗	✓	–	✗
zinc	✗	✓	✓	–

a) Using the table write down the order of reactivity for these four metals. Write the most reactive metal first.

....

b) Give a word equation for the reaction between magnesium and zinc sulphate.

....

8. Methane (natural gas) is burnt in Bunsen burners
   Complete a word equation for methane burning in plenty of oxygen.
   ....

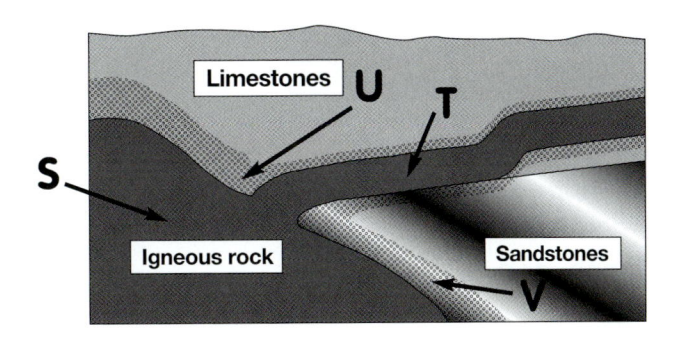

9. The diagram shows a cross section of rock. T is a small igneous intrusion.
   Why are the crystals at T smaller than those at S? ....

10. Which gas, found in the air, is required for both respiration and rusting?
    ....

11. The main compound in limestone is calcium carbonate. It has the formula $CaCO_3$.
    How many different elements are there in the compound calcium carbonate? ....

12. When sulphuric acid reacts with sodium hydroxide the salt sodium sulphate and water are produced.
    a) What is the name of this type of chemical reaction? ....
    b) The equation below shows the reaction between sulphuric acid and sodium hydroxide. Balance the equation.

    .... H_2SO_4 + ... $NaOH$ → Na_2SO_4 + ... H_2O

13. Glucose has the formula $C_6H_{12}O_6$.
    a) When glucose is burned, which gas in the air does the glucose react with? ....
    b) Give the name of the two products of the complete combustion of glucose. ....

14. a) What is the gas produced when a metal reacts with an acid? ....
    b) Give a word equation for the reaction between zinc and hydrochloric acid. ....

15. A compound has the formula KOH. When this compound is dissolved in water it forms a solution. This solution is tested with Universal Indicator paper. What colour would the Universal Indicator turn?
    ....

How did you do?

1–3	correct	start again
4–6	correct	getting there
7–11	correct	good work
12–15	correct	excellent

SPEED

The speed of an object is a measure of how fast it is moving.

CALCULATING SPEEDS

To find the speed of an object we need to know how far it has travelled and how long it took to travel this distance. Then we use the equation.

$$\text{speed} = \frac{\text{distance}}{\text{time}} \quad \text{or} \quad s = \frac{d}{t}$$

EXAMPLE
Calculate the speed of a sprinter who runs 100 m in 10 s.

$$s = \frac{d}{t} = \frac{100 \text{ m}}{10 \text{ s}} = 10 \text{ m/s}$$

This answer tells us that the sprinter, on average, ran 10 m every second.

EXAMPLE
Calculate the speed of a car which travels 300 km in 5 hours.

$$s = \frac{d}{t} = \frac{300 \text{ km}}{5 \text{ h}} = 60 \text{ km/h}$$

The car, on average, travels 60 km each hour.

Examiner's Top Tip
Whenever you do a calculation be sure to write down the units of your answer. An answer of 10 to the question opposite may not have gained you full marks. An answer of 10 m/s will get you all the marks available.

SPEED AND VELOCITY

We often use the words speed and velocity as if they have the same meaning, but there is a small but important difference.
- A speed tells us how fast an object is moving.
- A velocity tells us how fast an object is moving and in which direction.
- 20 m/s is a speed. 20 m/s northwards is a velocity.

CALCULATING DISTANCES AND TIMES

Some questions may give you the speed of an object and ask you to calculate either:
a) the distance it travels in a certain time or
b) the time it takes to travel a certain distance.

Both of these are very easy to do once you know how to use the formula triangle. We draw the triangle with the letters in the same place as they are in the formula. So $s = \dfrac{d}{t}$

is drawn in the formula triangle as:

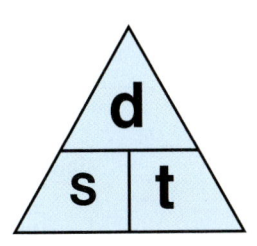

EXAMPLE
A cannonball after being fired travels at 75 m/s for 4 s. How far has the ball travelled?
d = s x t = 75 m/s x 4 s = 300 m

To find the formula to calculate time we simply cover the t in the triangle

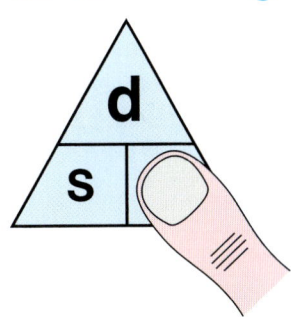

Now we can see that $t = \dfrac{d}{s}$

EXAMPLE
A cyclist travels 80 km at an average speed of 20 km/h. How long does the journey take?
$t = \dfrac{d}{s} = \dfrac{80 \text{ km}}{20 \text{ km/h}} = 4$ hours

To find the formula to calculate the distance we simply cover the d in the triangle:

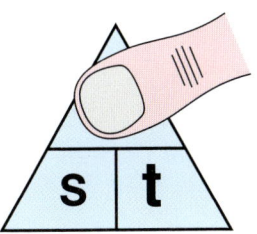

Now we can see that d = s x t

Examiner's Top Tip
Practise using your formula triangle. It is very useful for lots of formulæ you will need in your exams.

ACCELERATION

If an object is **speeding up** it is **accelerating**. If an object is **slowing down** it is **decelerating**.

QUICK TEST

1. What two measurements do you need to calculate the speed of an object?
2. Name two units you could use to measure the speed of an object.
3. Calculate the speed of a woman who runs 400 m in 80 s.
4. How long will it take a boy cycling at 20 m/s to travel 400 m?
5. How far will a bus travel in 5 hours if its speed is 60 km/h?

1. Distance travelled and time taken.
2. m/s and km/h.
3. 5 m/s.
4. 20 s.
5. 300 km.

GRAPHS OF MOTION

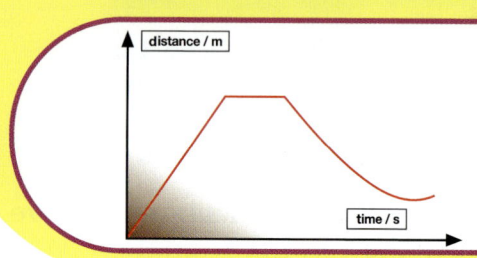

It is often useful to show the <u>journey of an object</u> in the form of a <u>graph</u>. There are two types of graph: <u>distance–time</u> graphs and <u>speed–</u> or <u>velocity–time</u> graphs.

Examiner's Top Tip
It is very easy in an exam to mix these graphs up. Before writing your answer, double-check the words next to the y-axis. Is it a distance–time graph or a velocity–time graph?

DISTANCE–TIME GRAPHS

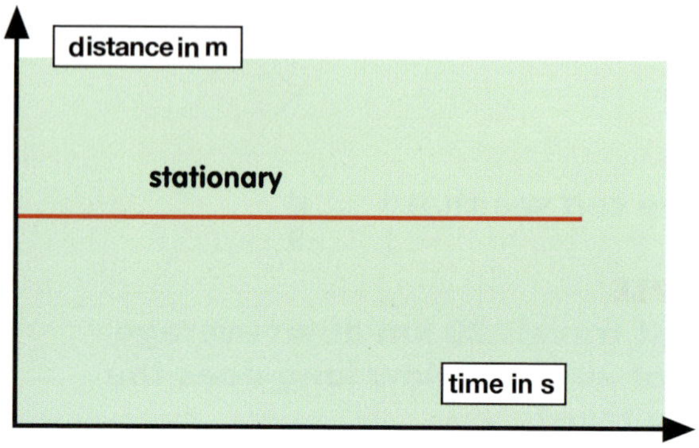

Horizontal line: object is <u>not moving</u>.

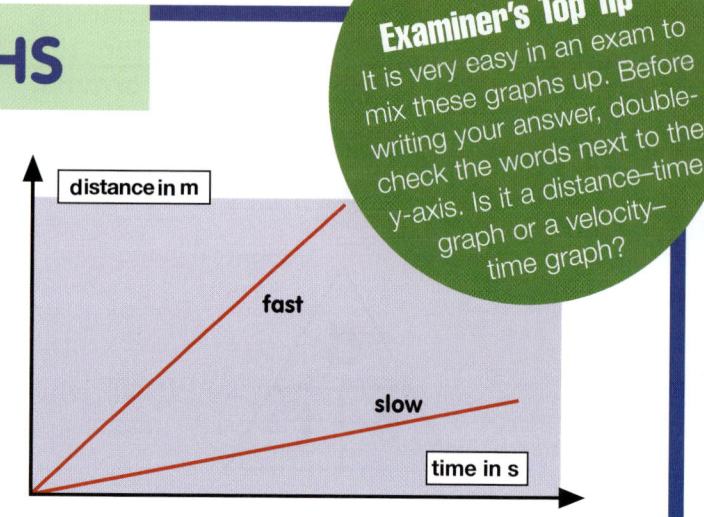

Sloping straight line: object moving at <u>constant speed</u>. Steeper straight line: object moving at a <u>greater constant speed</u>.

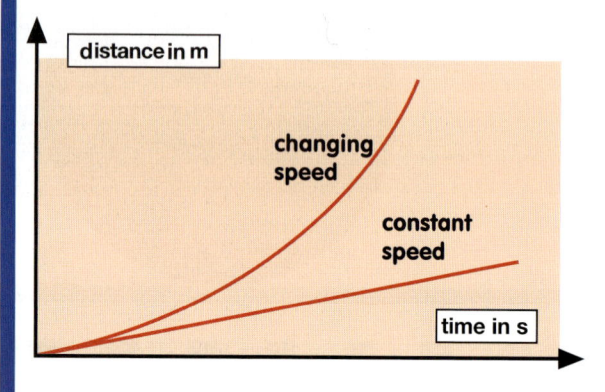

Steepness or gradient of line changes: speed of object is <u>not constant</u>.

<u>Speed</u> of an object is equal to the <u>gradient of the line</u>.
Speed of object = $\frac{y}{x}$ = $\frac{150}{5}$ = 30 m/s

This example shows how a distance-time graph can be used to describe a journey.
A man walking at a constant speed travels 200m in 100 s. He then stops for 150s. He completes the final leg of his journey travelling 100m in 50s.

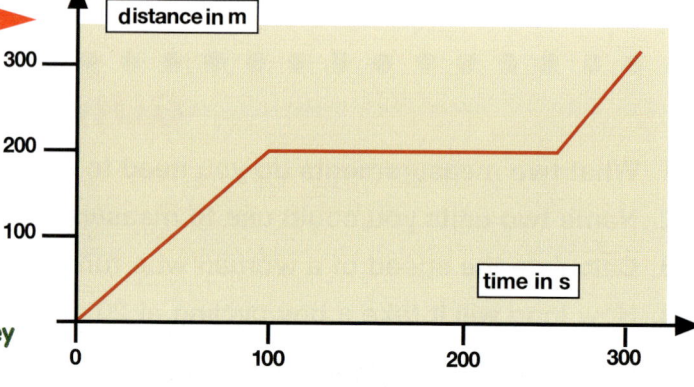

distance-time graph for this journey

88

SPEED– OR VELOCITY–TIME GRAPHS

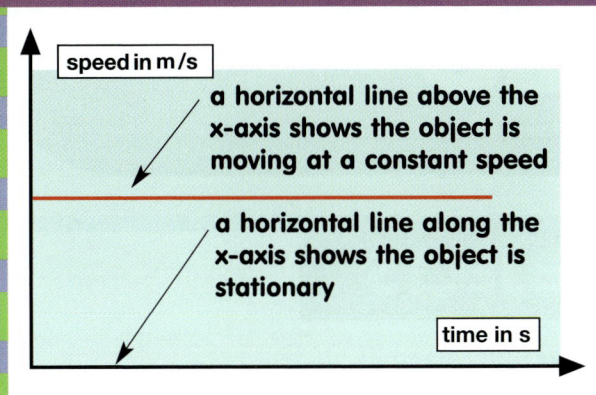

A **horizontal line** along the axis shows the object is **stationary**.
A **horizontal line** above the axis shows the object is moving at **constant speed**.

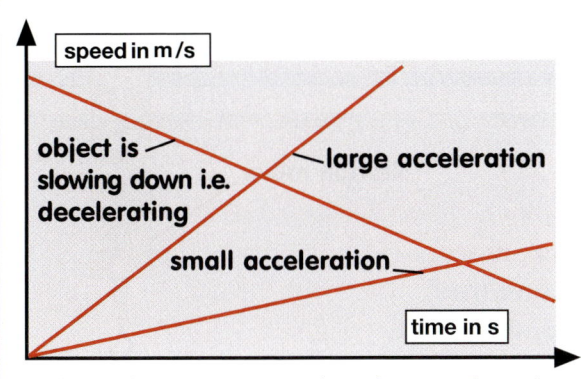

A line sloping upwards: shows the object is increasing its speed, i.e. **accelerating**.
A line sloping downwards: shows the object decreasing its speed, i.e. **decelerating**.
The **steeper the line** the **greater the acceleration or deceleration** of the object.

EXAMPLE

The example below shows how a speed-time graph can be used to describe the journey of a motorist.

A motorist starting from rest accelerates to a speed of 40 m/s in 4 s. She travels at this speed for 10 s before decelerating to a halt in 8 s.

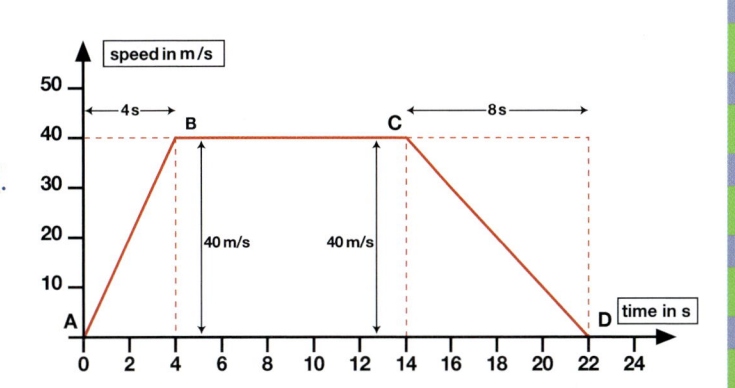

Examiner's Top Tip
If you have to draw a graph remember to:
- use a sharp pencil and don't press too hard. You may want to rub it out!
- use a ruler for straight lines and axes
- label the axes and include units.

QUICK TEST

1. On a distance–time graph what do the following show?
   a) a horizontal line
   b) a steeply sloping straight line
   c) a straight line sloping just a little.
2. On a speed–time graph what do the following show?
   a) a horizontal line
   b) a straight line sloping steeply upwards
   c) a straight line sloping gently downwards.

1. a) A stationary object. b) Large constant speed. c) Small constant speed. 2. a) Constant speed. b) Large acceleration. c) Small deceleration.

89

FORCES

EFFECTS OF FORCES ON OBJECTS

When forces are applied to an object they may:

- start the object moving if it is stationary
- stop the object if it is already moving
- speed the object up
- slow the object down
- change the direction of the object
- change the shape of the object.

MEASURING FORCES

We can measure the size of a force using a **Newton meter**. This consists of a spring and a scale; the scale measures how much the spring stretches when a force is applied to it. The larger the force the more the spring extends. We measure forces in **Newtons** (N). An average-sized apple weighs about 1 N.

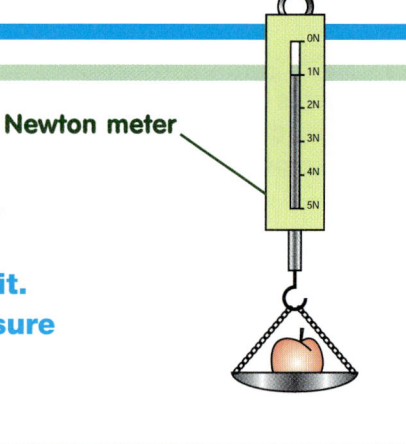

Newton meter

BALANCED FORCES

If several forces are applied to an object, they may cancel each other out. The forces are balanced.
- If the forces applied to an object are balanced they will have no effect on its motion.
- If the object is stationary it will remain stationary.
- If the object is moving it will continue to move in the same direction and at the same speed.

EXAMPLE

If the driving force of this aircraft equals the drag, it will travel at a constant speed. If the lift force equals the weight, the aircraft will stay at a constant height.

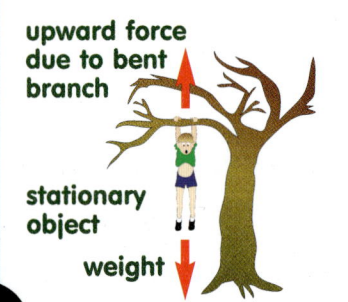

balanced forces: no motion

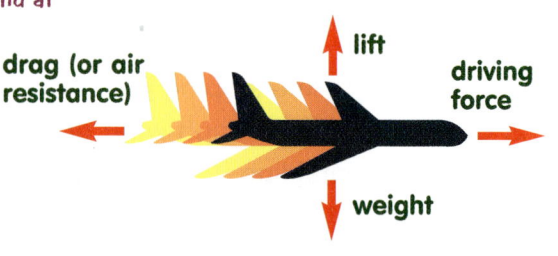

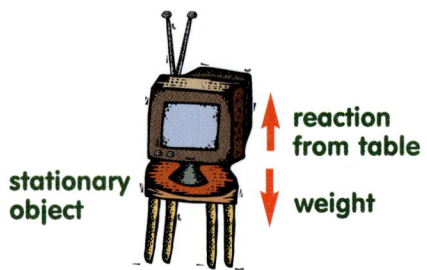

drag (or air resistance) — lift — driving force — weight

upward force due to bent branch — stationary object — weight

upthrust from water — stationary object — weight

stationary object — reaction from table — weight

UNBALANCED FORCES

If the forces applied to an object do not cancel each other out, i.e. they are <u>unbalanced</u>, they will affect its motion.

If the object is stationary it may start to move.
If it is already moving it may:
- stop moving
- speed up
- slow down
- change direction.

stationary object made to move: unbalanced forces

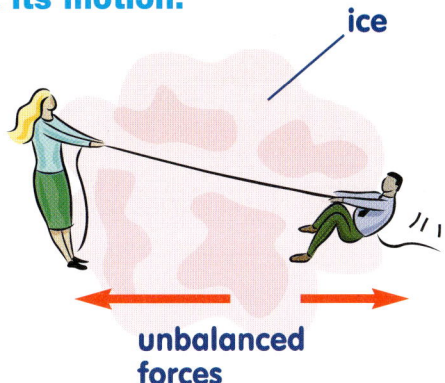

ice

unbalanced forces

FORCES AND ACCELERATION

An object whose motion (speed or velocity or direction) is changing is <u>accelerating</u>. The size of the acceleration depends on:

- The size of the force: the larger the force the greater the acceleration for the <u>same mass</u>.
- The mass of the object: the larger the mass the smaller the acceleration for the <u>same force</u>.

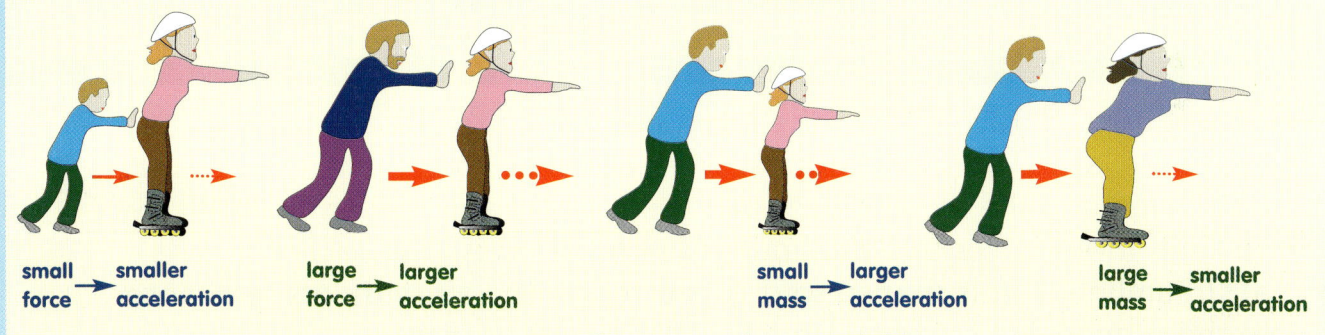

small force → smaller acceleration

large force → larger acceleration

small mass → larger acceleration

large mass → smaller acceleration

- The mass of an object is a measure of how much material it contains. It is usually measured in kg.

QUICK TEST

1. Name five things that might happen to an object's motion when a force is applied to it.
2. What do we use a Newton meter for?
3. In what units do we measure forces?
4. What effect do balanced forces have on the motion of an object?
5. What does the size of the acceleration of an object depend on?

Examiner's Top Tip
Remember: balanced forces mean no change to speed or direction, unbalanced forces cause change.

1. Speed up, slow down, stop, start and change direction.
2. To measure the size of a force.
3. Newtons (N).
4. No effect.
5. Mass of object and size of force.

FRICTION AND TERMINAL VELOCITY

FRICTION

Whenever an object moves or tries to move, friction is present.

Friction opposes motion

Friction between surfaces can make them hot and wear them away.

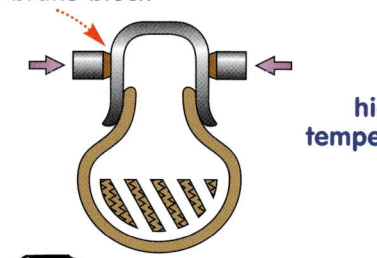

worn brake block

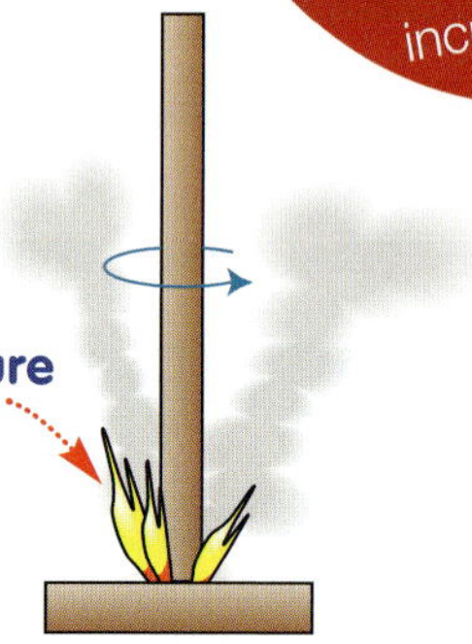

high temperature

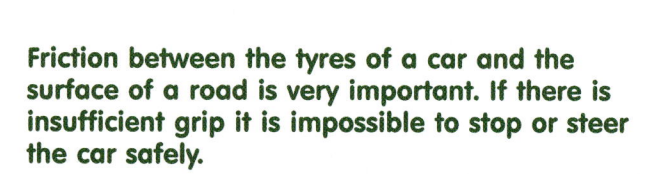

runners

Friction

Friction between the tyres of a car and the surface of a road is very important. If there is insufficient grip it is impossible to stop or steer the car safely.

Examiner's Top Tip
Remember streamlining and lubricating reduce friction. Rough surfaces and high speeds increase friction.

REDUCING FRICTION BY STREAMLINING AND LUBRICATING

- As a bobsleigh travels down the run it gains speed.
- There are large frictional forces at work between the bob sleigh and the air, and between the runners and the ice.
- To keep these forces to a minimum the bobsleigh is:
  a) streamlined – It is shaped so it cuts through the air with less resistance.
  b) the runners are coated with a lubricant, such as wax.

MOVING THROUGH AIR

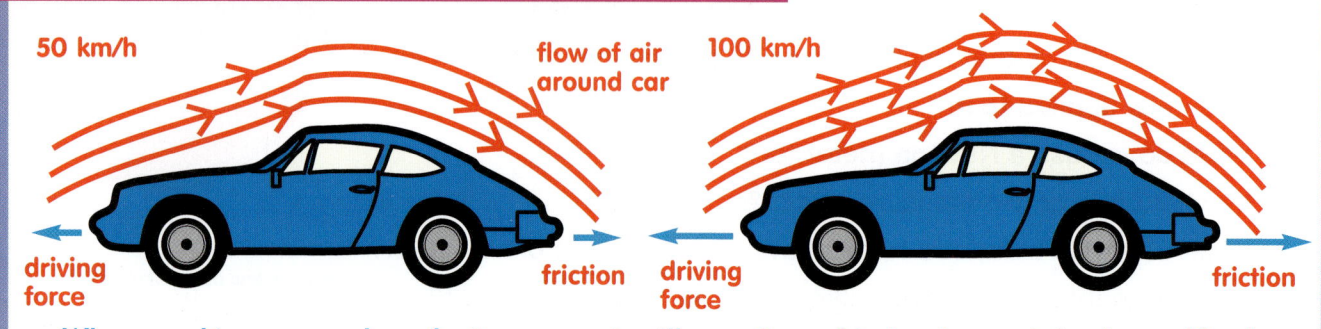

50 km/h

flow of air around car

100 km/h

driving force — friction

driving force — friction

- When an object moves through air or water it will experience frictional or resistive forces (drag) which will try to prevent its motion.
- The faster the object moves, the larger these resistive forces become.

TERMINAL VELOCITY: CARS

Action
Driver begins journey by pressing accelerator.

Accelerator is kept in same position.

Accelerator is kept in same position.

Result
The driving force from the engine makes the car accelerate.

As the speed of the car increases the air resistance increases. The car will have a smaller acceleration.

The air resistance and the driving force are equal and balanced. The car travels at a constant speed, called its terminal velocity.

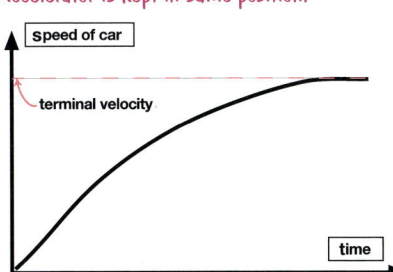

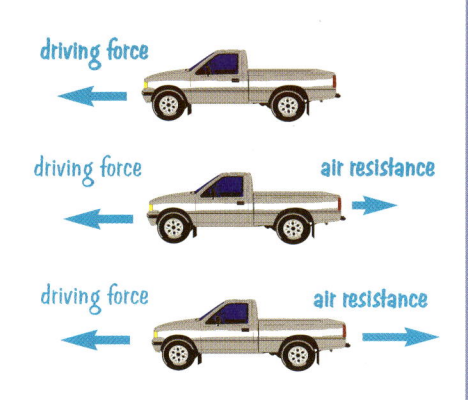

TERMINAL VELOCITY: FALLING OBJECTS

SKY DIVER

Action	Result
Sky diver jumps	Gravity makes sky diver accelerate.
Speed of sky diver increases	Air resistance increases, so acceleration of sky diver decreases.
Sky diver is still falling	Air resistance and pull of gravity are equal and balanced. He now falls at a constant speed, called his terminal velocity.

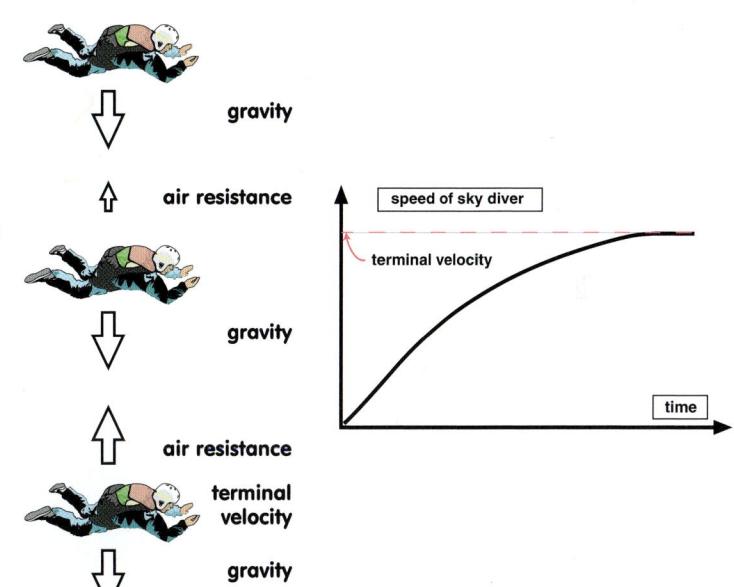

FRICTION AND TERMINAL VELOCITY

QUICK TEST

1. In which direction does friction act?
2. What is streamlining?
3. What is a lubricant?
4. Name one situation where the presence of friction is an advantage.
5. What happens to a moving object if the driving force and the resistive forces are balanced?
6. Friction can cause .... and ....

Answers: 1. Opposite direction to motion. 2. Shaping to reduce air resistance. 3. Substance used to reduce friction between surfaces. 4. Striking a match. 5. Constant velocity. 6. Wear and heat.

93

MOMENTS

- Forces sometimes make objects **turn** or **rotate**.
- The **turning effect of a force** is called a **moment**.
- You created a moment with your fingers when you opened this book.

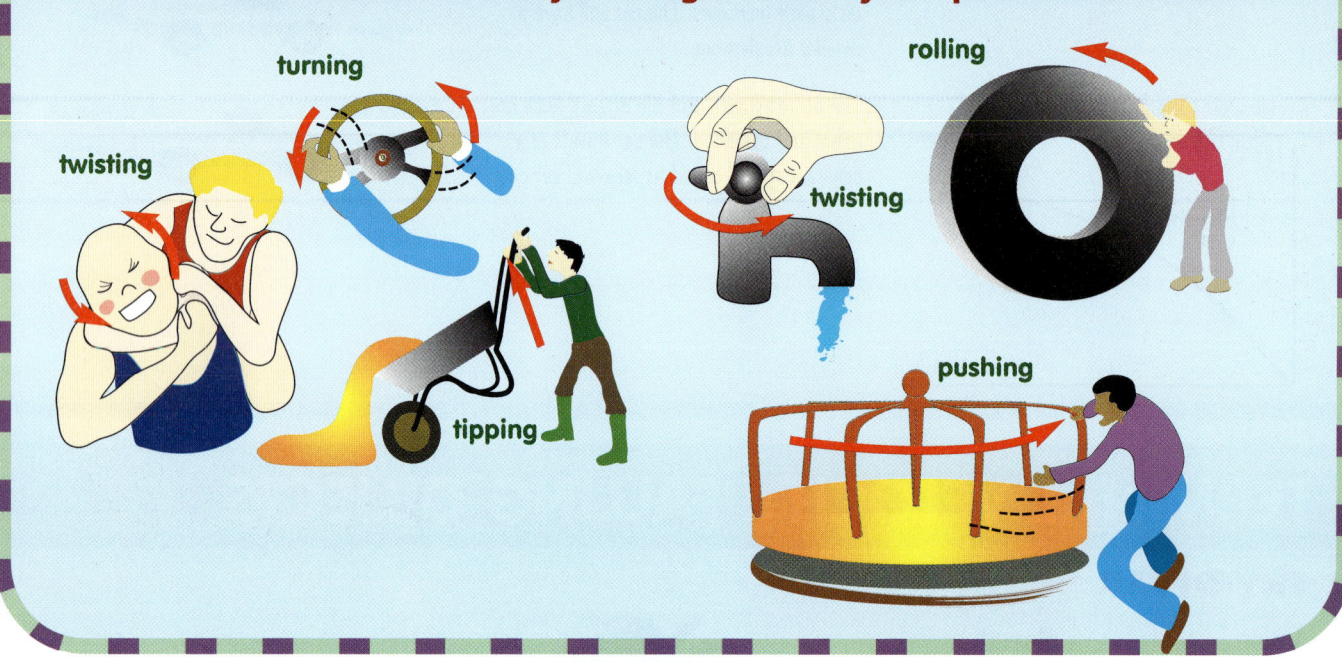

twisting, turning, tipping, twisting, rolling, pushing

THE SIZE OF A MOMENT

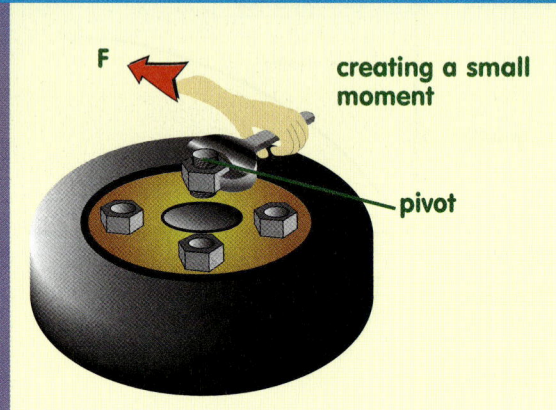

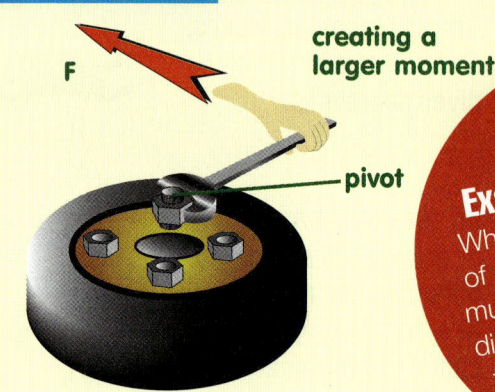

creating a small moment

creating a larger moment

Examiner's Top Tip
When calculating the size of a moment remember it must be the perpendicular distance of the force from the pivot you use in the equation.

- This moment is trying to undo a nut. The point the spanner will turn around is called **the pivot**.

- If the nut is too stiff we can increase the size of the moment by:

a) using a longer spanner or

b) applying a bigger force to the spanner.

- The size of a moment can be calculated using the equation:

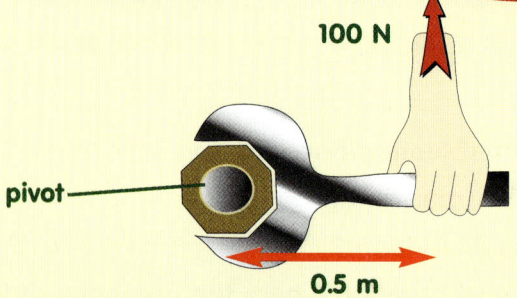

We measure moments in Nm.

100 N

pivot

0.5 m

- The moment being applied to this spanner is 100 N × 0.5 m = 50 Nm

moment of a force = force × perpendicular distance of force from pivot

BALANCING MOMENTS

- If two equal and opposite moments are applied to an object there will be no turning: the moments are balanced.
- In the diagram opposite, the anticlockwise moments created by the waiter are balanced by the clockwise moments created by the woman.
- When balanced:

clockwise moments = anticlockwise moments

(known as the Principle of Moments.)

If this see-saw balances, the clockwise moments created by the girl must be equal to the anticlockwise moments created by the boy.

300 N × 2 m = 400 N × 1.5 m

EXAMPLE

A boy weighing 600 N sits 2.5 m from the centre of a see-saw. How far from the centre of the see-saw should his friend sit so that the see-saw balances? His friend weighs 750 N.

- If the see-saw balances:

clockwise moments = anticlockwise moments

750 N × d = 600 N × 2.5 m

d = $\frac{600 \text{ N} \times 2.5 \text{ m}}{750 \text{ N}}$

d = 2.0 m

Examiner's Top Tip
Don't forget to include units with your answers to calculations.

Key Terms

Make sure you understand these terms before moving on:
- moment
- pivot
- perpendicular distance
- clockwise and anticlockwise moments

QUICK TEST

1. What is a moment?
2. A force of 200 N is applied perpendicular to and at the end of a spanner 0.4 m long. Calculate the moment created by the force.
3. Suggest two ways in which you could increase the moment applied by the spanner.
4. Under what conditions will two moments applied to the same object balance?
5. A man weighing 1200 N sits 1.5 m to the left of the centre of a see-saw. His friend weighs 1100 N and sits on the opposite side, 1.8 m from the centre. Why does the see-saw not balance?
6. Which way does the seesaw in question 5 turn?

1. Turning effect of a force defined as force × perpendicular distance.
2. 80 Nm.
3. Apply a larger force and apply same force at point further from pivot.
4. Clockwise moments = anticlockwise moments.
5. Clockwise moments do not equal anticlockwise moments.
6. Clockwise.

PRESSURE

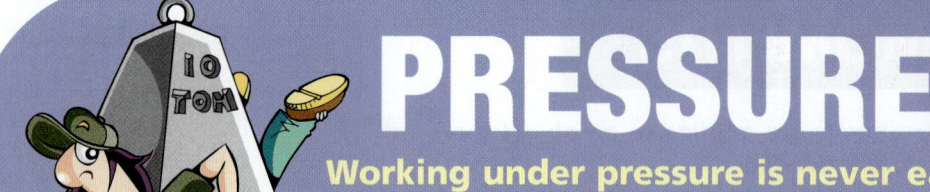

Working under pressure is never easy. But if you understand how pressure is created you will deal with it much better.

WHAT IS PRESSURE?

Pressure is a measure of how concentrated or spread out a force is.

- If a force is applied over a small area it creates a large pressure.
- If the force is applied over a large area it creates a small pressure.

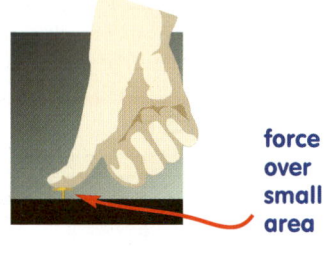

force over small area

low pressure

If a knife is sharp the pressure under its blade is high and cutting the cheese is easy. If the blade is blunt the pressure would be lower and cutting the cheese much more difficult.

If the handles of a carrier bag are thin they can create an uncomfortably high pressure on your hands.

PRESSURE IN LIQUID

- The movement of particles in a liquid creates pressure.
- This pressure increases with depth.
- This pressure is the same in all directions.

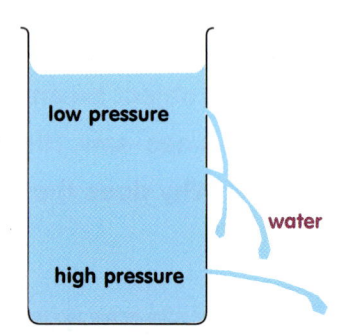

low pressure

water

high pressure

The water gushes out of the lowest hole fastest because pressure in a liquid increases with depth.

This submarine will feel the same pressure all over its surface.

CALCULATING PRESSURE

We can calculate the pressure created by a force using the equation:

pressure = $\dfrac{\text{force}}{\text{area}}$ or $P = \dfrac{F}{A}$

- We measure pressure in <u>pascals (Pa)</u>. 1 Pa = 1 N/m²

EXAMPLE
A crate weighing 1000 N is standing upright on one of its sides which measures 2 m × 2 m. Calculate the pressure created on the ground by the crate.

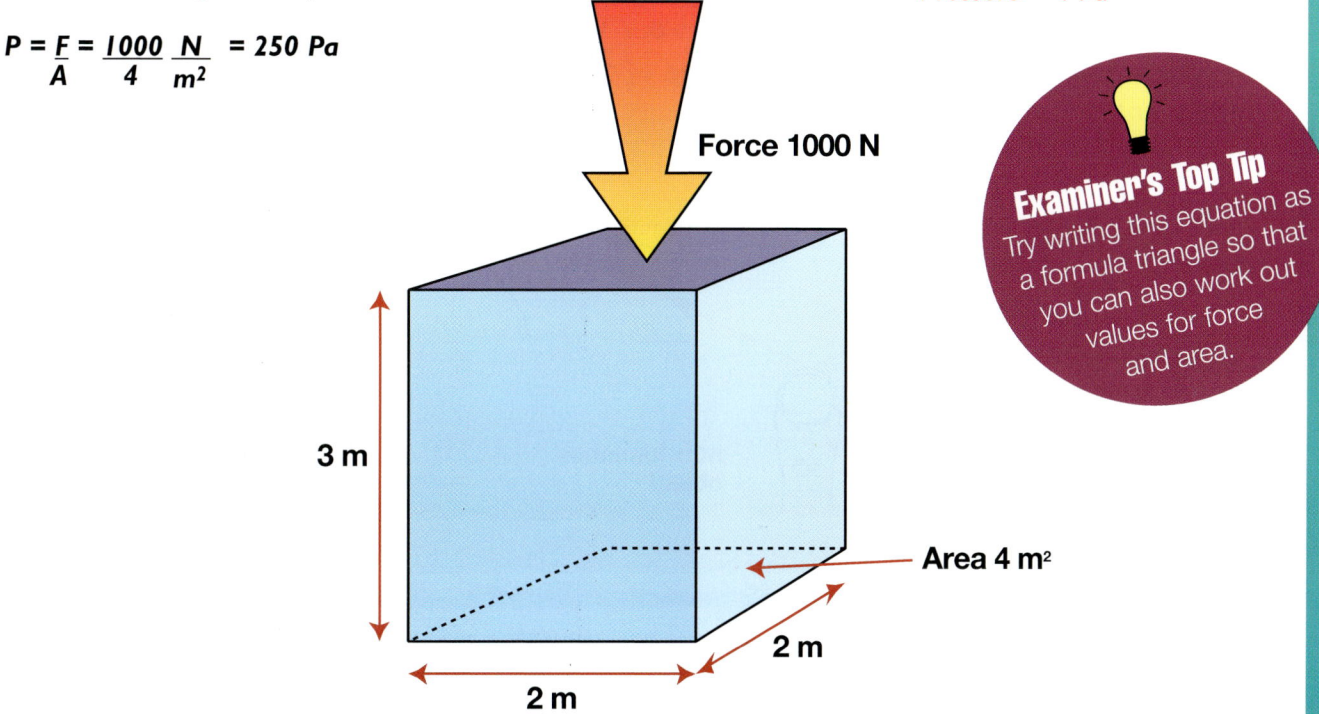

$P = \dfrac{F}{A} = \dfrac{1000 \text{ N}}{4 \text{ m}^2} = 250 \text{ Pa}$

Force 1 N
Area 1 m²
Pressure = 1 Pa

Force 1000 N
3 m
2 m
2 m
Area 4 m²

Examiner's Top Tip
Try writing this equation as a formula triangle so that you can also work out values for force and area.

QUICK TEST

1. How do we create a high pressure?
2. How can we avoid or reduce a high pressure?
3. Why are full carrier bags sometimes painful to carry?
4. In what units do we measure pressure?
5. Why does a sharp knife cut through a piece of cheese easier than a blunt knife?
6. Calculate the pressure created when a force of 50 N is over an area of 2.5 m².
7. Calculate the pressure created when a crate weighing 4000 N is standing on the side of the crate measuring 4 m × 2 m.
8. Draw a formula triangle for the equation $P = \dfrac{F}{A}$.
9. What force when applied to an area of 2 m² will create a pressure of 40 Pa?
10. Where in a lake is the water pressure greatest?

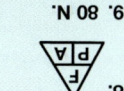

1. Large force over a small area.
2. Spread the force over a large area.
3. Weight of contents concentrated over very small area.
4. Pascal (Pa).
5. Greater pressure under blade.
6. 20 Pa.
7. 500 Pa.
8. (triangle F / P A)
9. 80 N.
10. At the bottom.

LIGHT RAYS AND REFLECTION

Light travels in **straight** **lines**.

SEEING OBJECTS

- We see <u>luminous</u> <u>objects</u> such as fires, light bulbs and stars because some of the light they <u>emit</u> enters our eyes.
- We see non-luminous objects because some of the light they <u>reflect</u> enters our eyes.

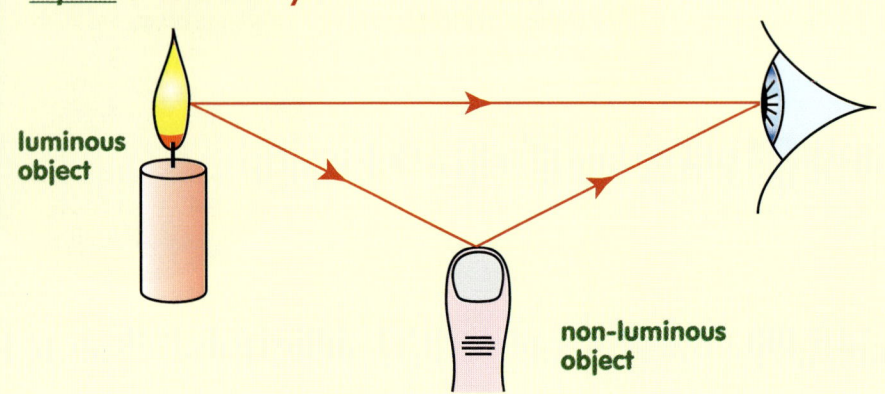

luminous object

non-luminous object

Examiner's Top Tip
Always put arrowheads on rays. If the ray changes direction, put one arrowhead on the ray before the change and one after.

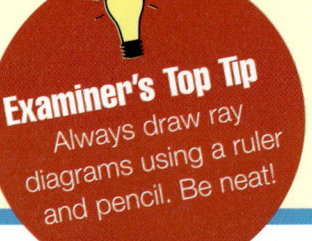

Examiner's Top Tip
Always draw ray diagrams using a ruler and pencil. Be neat!

SHADOWS

- We can see through a <u>transparent</u> object, e.g. a pane of glass, because the light <u>can pass</u> through it.
- We cannot see through an <u>opaque</u> object, e.g. a piece of wood, because the light <u>cannot pass</u> through it.
- An opaque object placed in front of a source of light will create <u>a shadow</u>.
- A <u>translucent</u> object allows light to pass through it but we cannnot see through it: e.g. tracing paper, frosted glass.
- A shadow is a dark area where there is <u>little</u> or <u>no</u> <u>light</u>.
- The shadow will have the <u>same</u> <u>shape</u> as the object creating it.
- This is because light travels in straight lines.

THE SPEED OF LIGHT

- Light travels very quickly.
- Over short distances it seems to arrive <u>almost</u> <u>instantaneously</u>.
- It takes light just eight minutes to travel from the Sun to the Earth.
- It travels at a speed of <u>300</u> <u>million</u> <u>metres</u> a second.
- Sound travels at a speed of just 340 metres a second.
- Because light travels much more quickly there is sometimes a <u>delay</u> between <u>seeing</u> <u>and</u> <u>hearing</u>.
- The fireworks in the diagram are seen to explode but then there is a delay before we hear the explosion.

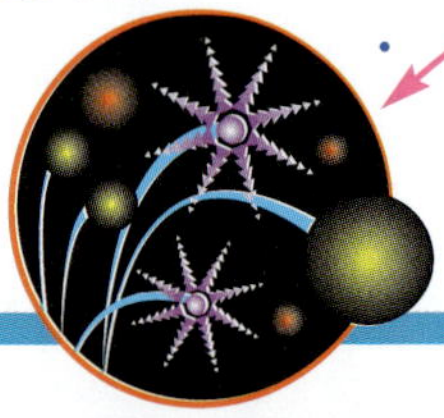

REFLECTION FROM A PLANE MIRROR

- When a ray of light strikes a plane mirror it is reflected so that the angle of incidence is equal to the angle of reflection. The angles are always measured from the normal.

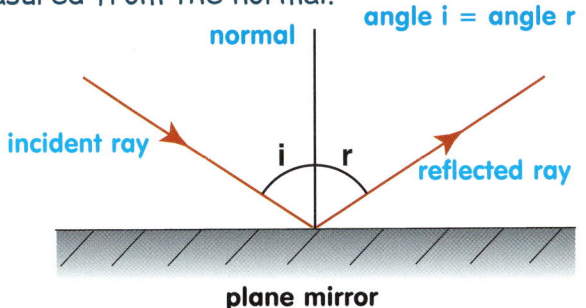

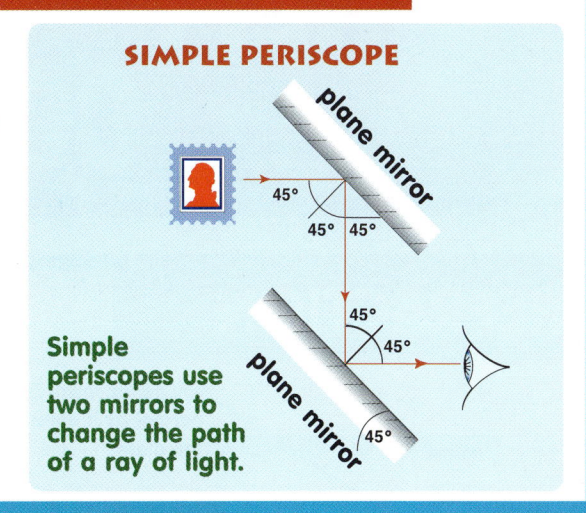

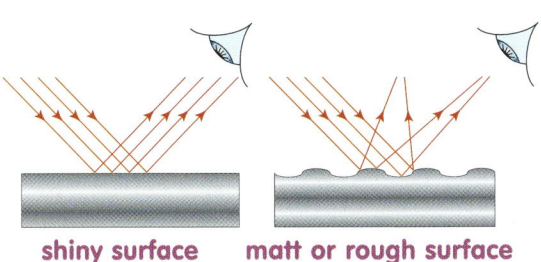

SIMPLE PERISCOPE

Simple periscopes use two mirrors to change the path of a ray of light.

PLANE AND DIFFUSION REFLECTION

shiny surface

- All the rays are reflected in the same direction. Lots of light enters our eyes so the surface looks shiny or glossy.

matt or rough surface

- Because the light is scattered, only a little of it enters our eyes so the surface appears dull or matt.

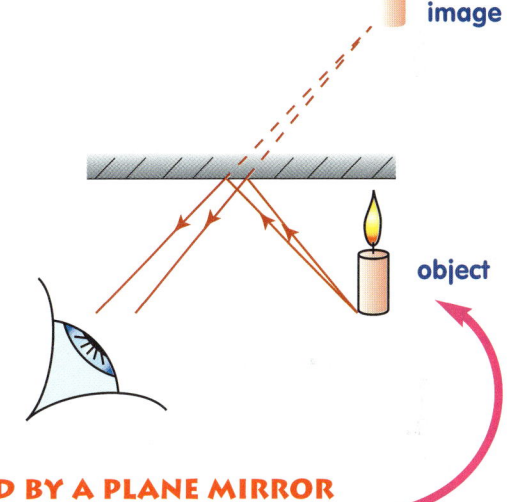

THE IMAGE CREATED BY A PLANE MIRROR
The image of an object is:
- upright
- the same size as the object
- the same distance behind the mirror as the object is in front
- laterally inverted, i.e. the left is on the right and the right is on the left
- a virtual image, i.e. it cannot be formed on a screen placed behind the mirror.

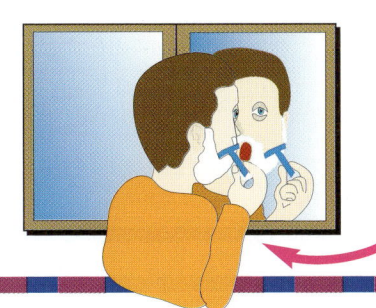

QUICK TEST

1. How do we know light travels in straight lines?
2. What is an opaque object?
3. What is a transparent object?
4. What is a luminous object?
5. How do we see a non-luminous object?
6. The angle of incidence is equal to ....
7. Describe the image that is created by a plane mirror.

1. Shadows are the same shape as the object.
2. One which light cannot pass through.
3. One which is see-through.
4. One which gives off its own light.
5. By the light it reflects.
6. The angle of reflection.
7. Upright, same size, same distance behind mirror and laterally inverted.

REFRACTION AND COLOUR

REFRACTION

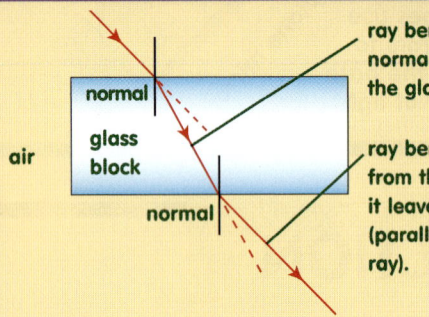

- ray bends towards normal as it enters the glass
- ray bends away from the normal as it leaves the block (parallel to original ray).

- When a ray of light enters a glass block, it slows down and bends towards the normal.
- This change of direction is called refraction.
- When the ray emerges from the block, it speeds up and bends away from the normal.
- If the ray meets the surface at 90° the ray slows down but there is no change in direction.

no refraction at either surface

Examiner's Top Tip
When revising any topic about light be sure to practise drawing ray diagrams using a ruler and pencil.

STRANGE EFFECTS OF REFRACTION

This pencil looks bent because the rays of light are refracted as they emerge from the water. This swimming pool is deeper than it appears. This is also caused by refraction.

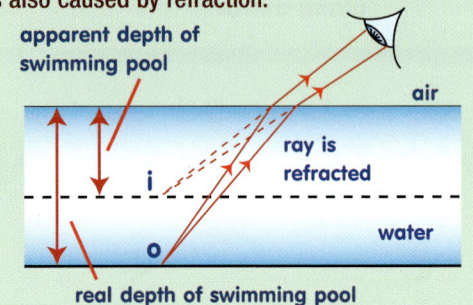

- apparent depth of swimming pool
- ray is refracted
- real depth of swimming pool
- pencil / water / beaker

LENSES

Lenses are specially shaped pieces of glass or plastic which are used to refract light in a particular direction.

- A converging lens refracts the light so that rays of light are brought together (converge).
- A diverging lens refracts light so that rays of light are made to spread out or diverge.

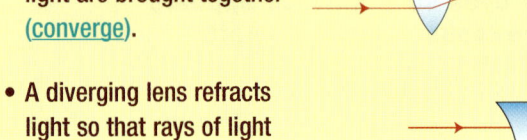

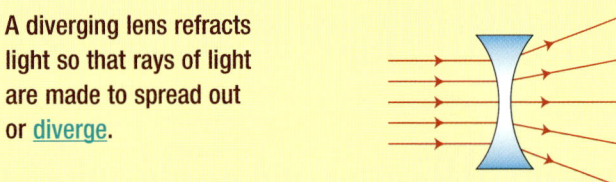

DISPERSION

- White light is a mixture of coloured lights.
- When white light travels through a prism, the different colours are refracted by different amounts. This is called dispersion.
- A band of colours called a spectrum is produced.
- The colours of the spectrum are always in the same order: red, orange, yellow, green, blue, indigo and violet.

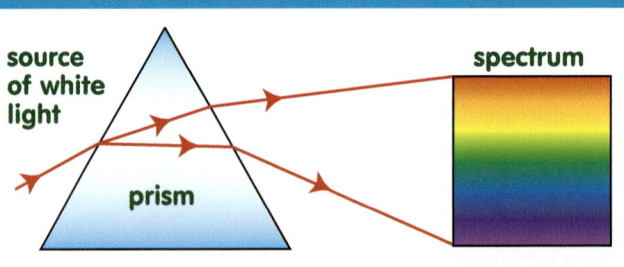

source of white light → prism → spectrum: red, orange, yellow, green, blue, indigo, violet

Easy to remember: Richard Of York Gave Battle In Vain.

COLOURED OBJECTS IN WHITE LIGHT

- Coloured objects contain a chemical called a <u>dye</u>.
- When white light hits a coloured object all the colours of the spectrum are <u>absorbed</u> by the dye <u>except for its own colour</u>. This is reflected into the eye of the observer.
- White objects reflect all colours.
- Black objects reflect no light.

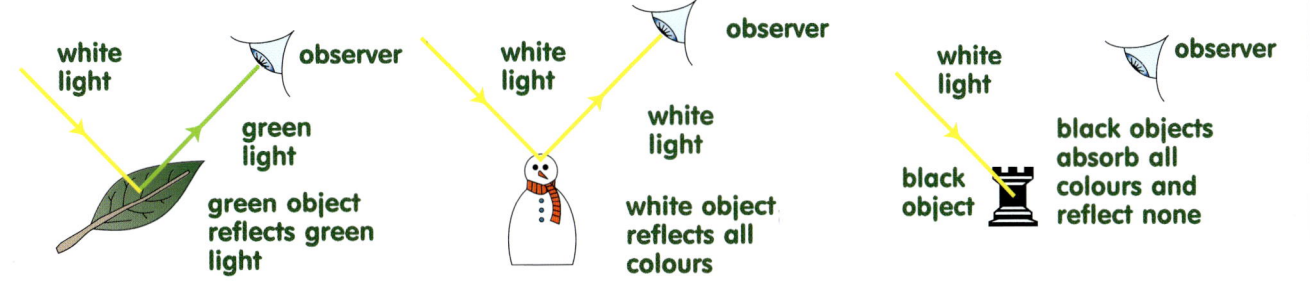

white light → green object reflects green light → green light → observer

white light → white object reflects all colours → white light → observer

white light → black object → black objects absorb all colours and reflect none → observer

COLOURED OBJECTS IN COLOURED LIGHT

- When coloured light strikes a coloured object only light common to both the object and the incident light is reflected.

red light → red object reflects red light → red light → observer

red light → no light reflected → object appears to be black

COLOURED FILTERS

<u>Filters</u> are <u>coloured pieces of transparent plastic or glass</u> which <u>only allow light of the same colour to pass through</u>. For example, green light can pass through a green filter but red or blue light will be absorbed.

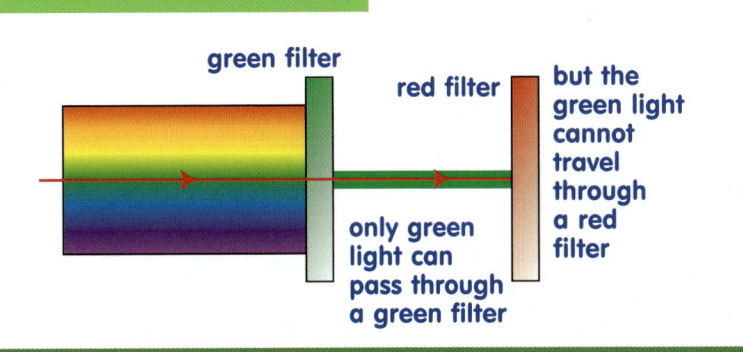

green filter — only green light can pass through a green filter

red filter — but the green light cannot travel through a red filter

QUICK TEST

1. What is the bending of a ray of light as it enters a glass block called?
2. Which way does a ray bend as it travels from air into glass?
3. Name one device that makes use of refraction.
4. What is a spectrum?
5. How is a spectrum produced?
6. Explain how an observer sees a green object in white light.
7. What is a green filter?

1. Refraction. 2. Towards the normal. 3. A lens. 4. Band of colours. 5. Dispersion. 6. Only green light is reflected. 7. Transparent plastic that only allows green light through.

101

SOUNDS

All sounds begin with an <u>object</u> that is <u>vibrating</u>. These vibrations travel outwards from the source. If they strike someone's <u>eardrum</u>, they may be heard.

PITCH AND FREQUENCY

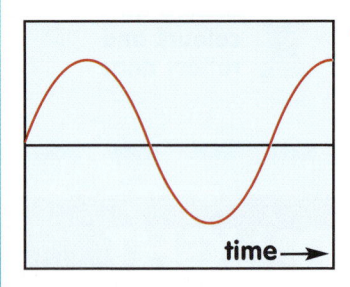

low-pitched sound

- Large objects <u>vibrate slowly</u> and produce just a few waves each second. These waves have a <u>low</u> <u>frequency</u> and produce <u>low-pitched</u> <u>sounds</u>.

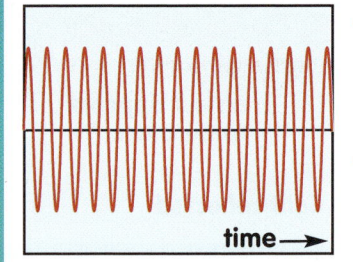

high-pitched sound

- Small objects vibrate quickly and produce lots of waves each second. These waves have a <u>high</u> <u>frequency</u> and produce <u>high-pitched</u> <u>sounds</u>.
- We measure the <u>frequency</u> of a wave or its source in <u>hertz</u> (<u>Hz</u>). An object which <u>vibrates</u> <u>once</u> <u>every</u> <u>second</u> and produces <u>one</u> <u>complete</u> <u>wave</u> <u>every</u> <u>second</u> has a <u>frequency</u> of <u>1</u> <u>Hz</u>.

LOUDNESS

- Objects that vibrate with <u>large</u> <u>amplitudes</u> produce <u>loud</u> <u>sounds</u>.
- Objects that have <u>small</u> <u>vibrations</u> produce <u>quiet</u> <u>sounds</u>.

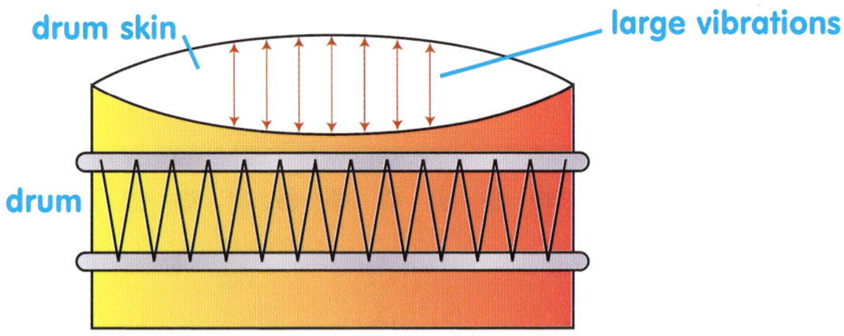

drum skin — large vibrations
drum

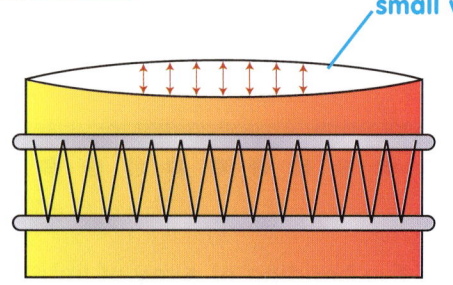

small vibrations

loud sound — large amplitude

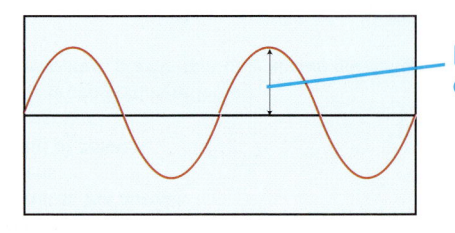

quiet sound — small amplitude

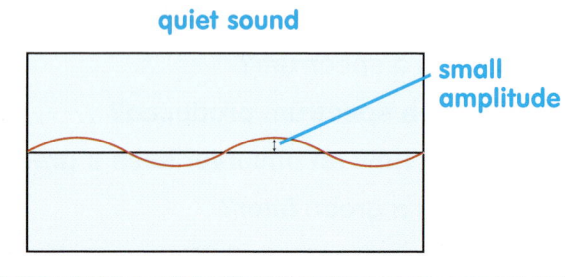

WHAT IS A SOUND WAVE?

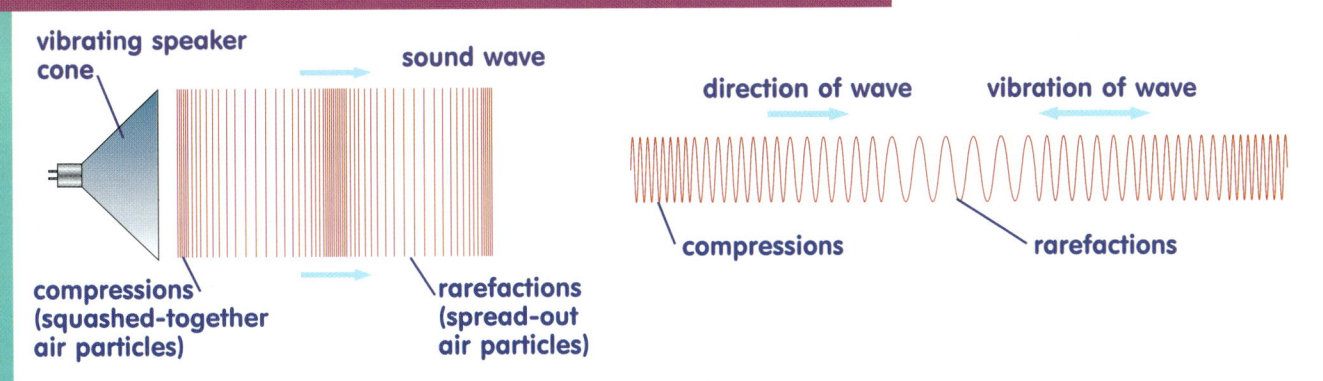

- A vibrating object pushes against air particles creating a compression.
- As it moves in the opposite direction, it creates a region of spread-out particles called a rarefaction.
- As the object continues to vibrate, it creates alternate regions of compressions and rarefactions travelling out from the source. This is a sound wave.

SPEED OF SOUND
- This is the speed at which the waves move away from the source.
- In air, the speed of sound is approximately 340 m/s.
- This is much lower than the speed of light (approximately 300 000 000 m/s), which is why we often see an event before we hear it, e.g. thunder and lightning.
- A plane which travels faster than sound is described as being supersonic.
- The particles in solids and liquids are much closer together than those in gases, and sound travels through them more quickly, e.g. the speed of sound in water is approximately 1500 m/s.

THE BELL JAR EXPERIMENT
Is there anything a sound wave cannot travel through?
- When the bell (right) is turned on, it can be seen and heard to ring.
- When all the air has been removed from the jar by the vacuum pump, the bell can be seen to be ringing but it cannot be heard.
- Conclusion: light waves can travel through a vacuum but sound waves cannot.

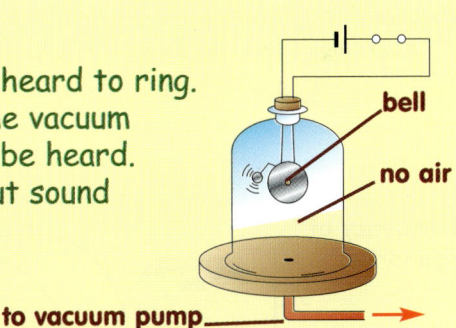

QUICK TEST

1. All sounds begin with an object that is ....
2. A large vibrating object will produce a .... sound.
3. A small vibrating object will produce a .... sound.
4. A sound wave consists of alternate regions where particles are packed close together or spread apart. These regions are called .... and ....
5. What does the word supersonic mean?
6. Is the speed of sound in a solid faster or slower than the speed of sound in air?
7. What can a sound wave not travel through? Explain your answer.

1. Vibrating. 2. Low-pitched. 3. High-pitched. 4. Compressions and rarefactions. 5. Faster than the speed of sound. 6. Faster. 7. A vacuum. It contains no particles to vibrate.

ECHOES AND HEARING

ECHOES

- When sound waves strike a hard surface they are <u>reflected</u>. This reflected sound is called an <u>echo</u>.
- Ships use echoes to find the depth of the ocean beneath them. An <u>echo-sounder</u> emits sound waves down towards the seabed. When the waves strike the seabed, they are reflected back up to the surface. A sound detector 'listens' for the echo.
- The deeper the ocean the longer it is before the echo is heard. Sound waves used in this way are called <u>SONAR</u>. This stands for <u>SO</u>und <u>N</u>avigation <u>A</u>nd <u>R</u>anging.
- Fishing boats often use sonar to detect shoals of fish. If an echo is heard sooner than expected it is likely that the wave has been reflected from a shoal of fish swimming beneath the boat.

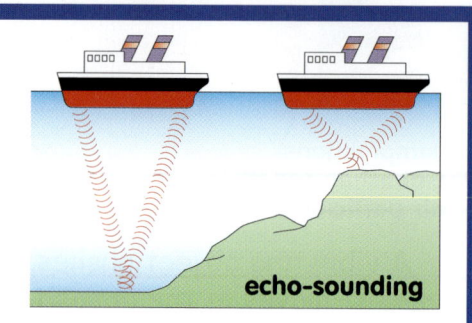

echo-sounding

HEARING RANGE (SOMETIMES CALLED AUDIBLE RANGE)

- An average person can only hear sounds that have a frequency above 20 Hz but below 20 000 Hz. This band of frequencies is called our <u>hearing range</u>.
- Hearing ranges do vary slightly from person to person but in general as we get older our hearing range becomes narrower.
- Sounds that have a frequency which is too high for the human ear to detect are called <u>ultrasounds</u>.

- Ultrasounds can be heard by some animals.
- <u>Dog whistles</u> produce notes we cannot detect but can be heard by a dog.

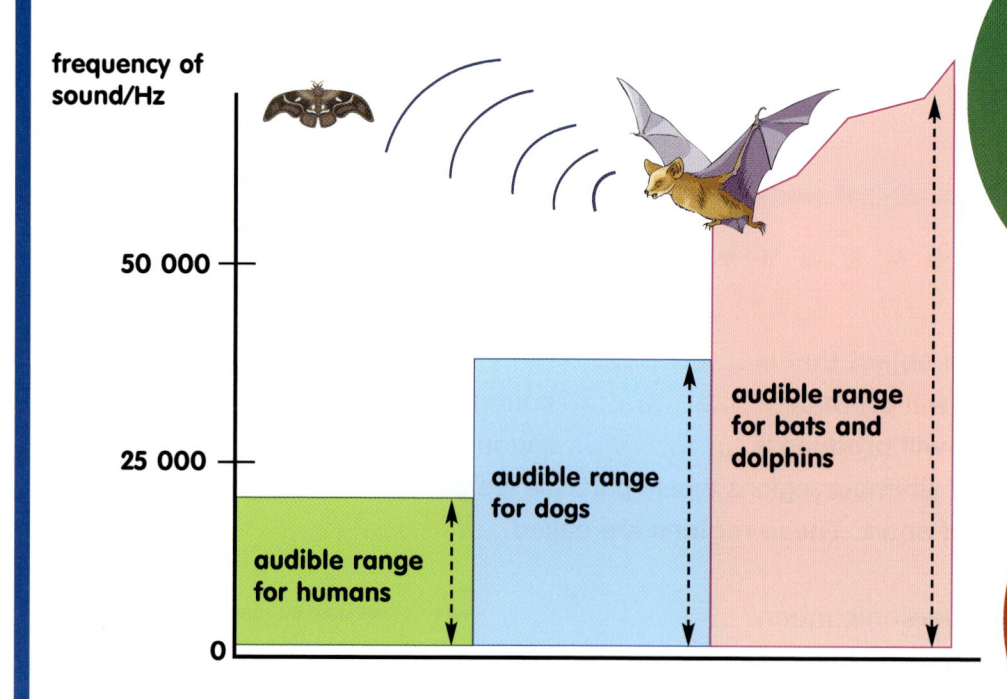

frequency of sound/Hz

50 000

25 000

audible range for humans

audible range for dogs

audible range for bats and dolphins

Examiner's Top Tip
Don't try to memorise any of the figures from this section but do try to understand that different people have different hearing ranges and that loud sounds can cause permanent hearing problems.

Examiner's Top Tip
When you read an exam question look at the number of marks it is worth. If it is worth three marks try to write three facts.

LOUDNESS AND THE DECIBEL SCALE

- Constant exposure to loud sounds can **damage your hearing**.
- People who work with noisy machinery should wear **ear defenders** to protect their hearing.
- People listening to music through earphones should be careful not to have the volume turned up too high. The **damage** caused to their hearing by persistent exposure to loud sounds could be permanent.  
- We measure loudness on the **decibel (dB) scale**.

HEARING

- Sound waves are gathered by the outer ear.
- Sound waves make the eardrum vibrate.
- The vibrations are amplified by small bones.
- The vibrations pass through a liquid causing hairs to vibrate.
- These hairs pass signals via the auditory nerve to the brain.
- Poor hearing might be caused by damage to the eardrum, bones, hairs or nerves.

QUICK TEST

1. What is an echo?
2. What is the hearing range of an average person?
3. What is an ultrasound?
4. Name two animals that can hear ultrasounds.
5. How can workers avoid damage to their hearing if they use noisy machinery in their work?
6. How can you avoid damaging your hearing when listening to your personal stereo?

1. Reflection of a sound wave.
2. 20 Hz to 20 000 Hz.
3. Frequency too high for humans to hear.
4. Dogs, bats.
5. Ear defenders.
6. Turn down the volume.

PHYSICS

ENERGY

We all need energy in order to be able to do things. As human beings we get this energy from the food we eat. Food is a form of chemical energy. But there are other forms of energy.

DIFFERENT FORMS OF ENERGY

HEAT OR THERMAL ENERGY
Hot objects are sources of heat energy.

LIGHT ENERGY
The Sun, light bulbs and lamps are luminous objects. They give off light energy.

SOUND ENERGY
Vibrating objects give off sound energy.

ELECTRICAL ENERGY
Electrical energy is available every time a current flows. The electrical energy from this battery is being used to make the bulb glow.

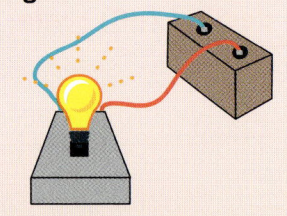

CHEMICAL ENERGY
Food, fuels and batteries all contain chemical energy.

KINETIC ENERGY
This is the energy an object has because it is moving. Wind (moving air) and flowing water have kinetic energy.

ELASTIC POTENTIAL ENERGY
Objects such as springs and rubber bands that are stretched or twisted or bent contain elastic potential energy.

GRAVITATIONAL POTENTIAL ENERGY
Objects that have a high position and are able to fall have gravitational potential energy.

NUCLEAR ENERGY
Reactions in the centre or nucleus of an atom are the source of nuclear energy.

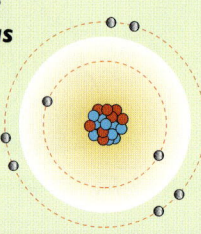

STORED ENERGY
- Chemical energy, elastic potential energy and gravitational potential energy are often referred to as forms of stored energy.
- They are forms of energy that are waiting to be used.

chemical energy in the wax

106

ENERGY TRANSFERS

When energy is used it does not disappear. It is transferred into other different forms of energy.

A light bulb changes electrical energy into heat and light energy.

A log fire changes chemical energy into heat and light energy.

A loudspeaker changes electrical energy into sound.

Other examples of energy changes:

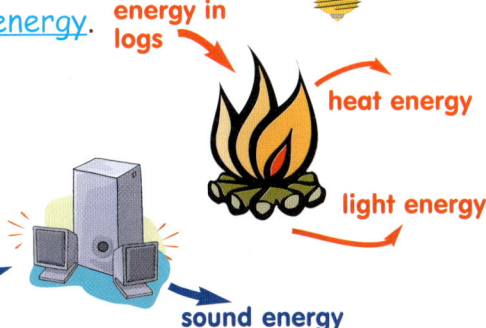

Energy in	Energy changer	Energy out
Chemical (food)	Animal	Heat, kinetic, chemical
Light	Solar cell	Electrical
Kinetic	Wind turbine	Electrical
Strain potential energy	Bow and arrow	Kinetic
Chemical	Battery	Electrical
Electrical	Battery charger	Chemical
Sound	Microphone	Electrical
Electrical	Electric motor	Kinetic
Kinetic energy	Generator	Electrical
Gravitational potential energy	Falling object	Kinetic
Elastic potential energy	Clockwork car	Kinetic

QUICK TEST

1. Name five different types of energy.
2. Name three types of stored energy.
3. What kind of energy does a crate gain as it is lifted by a crane?
4. What kind of energy does water gain as it travels down a waterfall?
5. Write down the energy transfer that takes place when using a hair drier.
6. Write down the energy transfer that takes place when you speak into a microphone.

Examiner's Top Tip
This is another topic that crops up nearly every year in all the exams. Make sure you know lots of examples of energy changes. Write down the names of some machines and devices, then try to describe the energy transfers that take place when they are used.

1. Heat, light, sound, electricity, chemical.
2. Chemical, elastic and gravitational potential energy.
3. Gravitational potential energy.
4. Kinetic energy.
5. Electrical to heat, kinetic and sound.
6. Sound to electrical energy.

USING ENERGY RESOURCES

electrical energy ⇨ sound

Electrical energy is one of the most convenient forms of energy. It is easily converted into other forms of energy.

FOSSIL FUELS

Coal, oil and gas are called fossil fuels. They are concentrated sources of energy.

- Fossil fuels are formed from plants and animals that died over 100 million years ago.
- When they died they became covered with many layers of mud and earth.
- The resulting large pressures and high temperatures changed them into fossil fuels.
- Because they take millions of years to form these fuels are called non-renewable fuels.
- Once they have been used up they cannot be replaced.

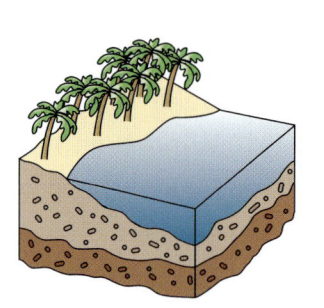

Dead plants and animals being covered with mud and earth.

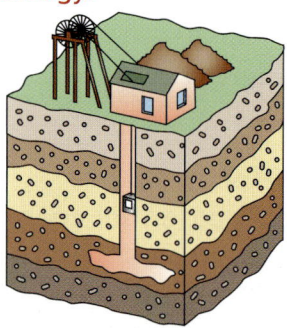

After hundreds of millions of years they have changed into fossil fuels such as coal.

THE PROBLEMS WITH NON-RENEWABLE FUELS
- When any of the fossil fuels are burned they produce carbon dioxide. Increasing the amount of carbon dioxide in the atmosphere will tend to cause the temperature of the Earth's atmosphere to rise. This is called the Greenhouse Effect.
- When coal and oil are burned they also produce gases that cause acid rain.
- Environmental problems are created by mining and spillage of oil during transport.
- We are using up fossil fuels very quickly and will soon have to find other sources of energy but we need to start looking now.

THE SOLUTIONS
- We need to slow down the rate at which we are using fossil fuels so that they will last longer. There are several ways in which we can do this.
- Reduce petrol consumption by driving smaller cars, using public transport or walking or cycling. We should also develop more efficient car engines.
- Improve the insulation to our homes and factories so less energy is wasted heating them.
- Increase public awareness of how people are wasting energy so that they turn off lights and turn down heating where possible.

- We need to make greater use of other sources of energy.
- In the UK some of our electricity is generated by nuclear power stations, but these produce waste disposal problems.
- Renewable sources of energy such as wind, waves, tidal, solar, geothermal, biomass and hydroelectric need to be developed. Each of these sources has some advantages and disadvantages. These are described in more detail on pages (110-111).

electrical energy ⇨ light

electrical energy ⇨ heat

electrical energy ⇨ kinetic energy

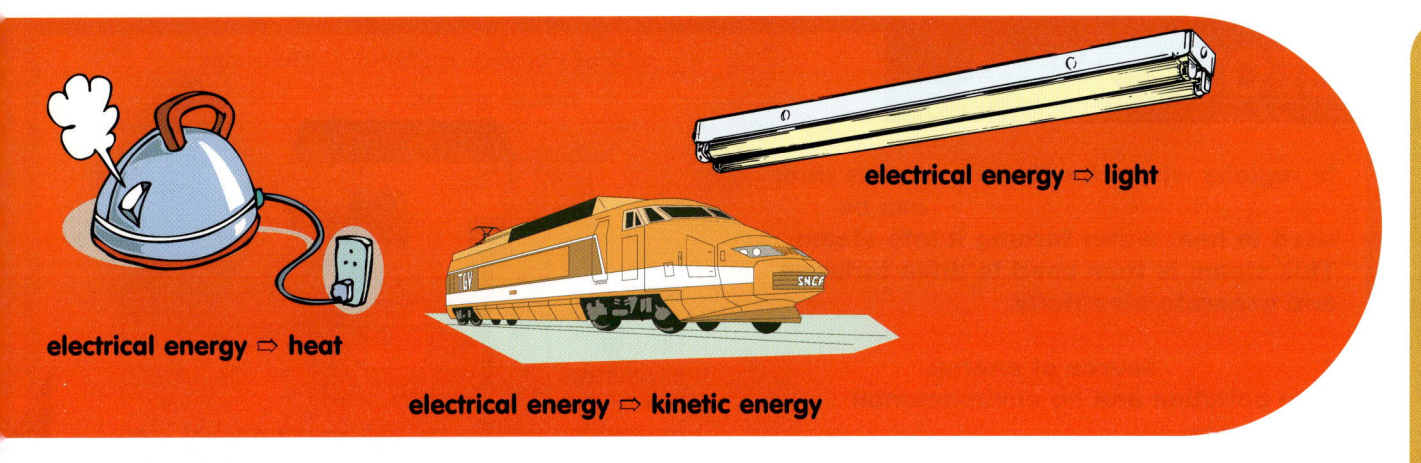

POWER STATIONS

Most of the electrical energy we use at home is generated at <u>power</u> <u>stations</u>. There are several different types of power station but the most common in the UK use <u>coal</u> <u>or</u> <u>gas</u> <u>as</u> <u>their</u> <u>source</u> <u>of</u> <u>energy</u> <u>(fuel)</u>.

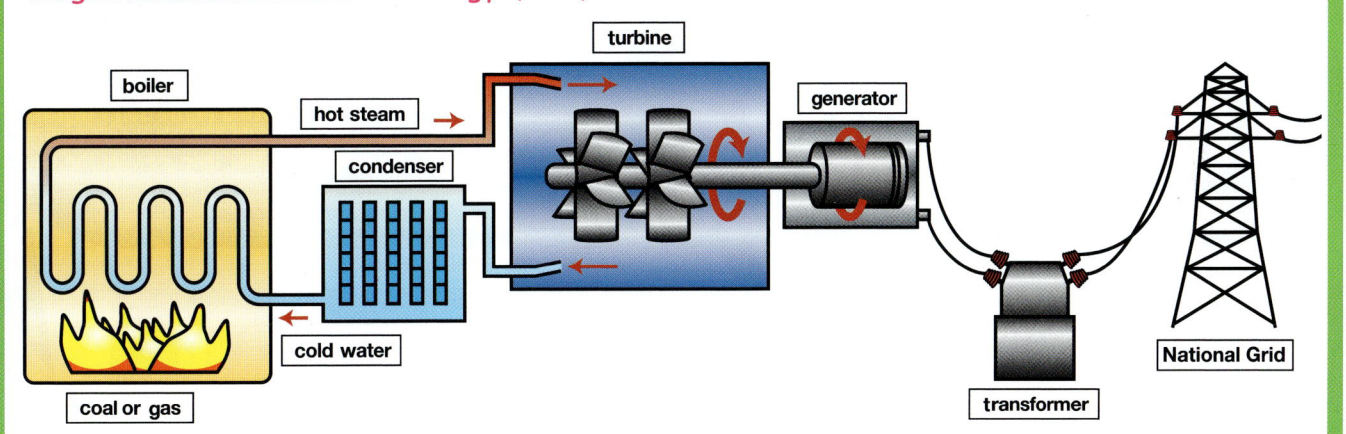

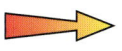

(Diagram: boiler with coal or gas → hot steam → turbine → generator → transformer → National Grid; condenser with cold water)

CHEMICAL ENERGY ⇨ HEAT ENERGY ⇨ KINETIC ENERGY ⇨ ELECTRICAL ENERGY

- The fuel is burned to release its <u>chemical energy</u>.
- The <u>heat energy released</u> is used to heat water and turn it into <u>steam</u>.
- The steam <u>turns turbines</u>.
- The turbines <u>turn large generators</u>.
- The <u>generators produce electrical energy</u>.
- The electrical energy is carried to our homes through the <u>National Grid</u>.

Examiner's Top Tip
This is another very popular topic and appears regularly on exam papers. Make sure that you understand the energy changes that take place when electricity is generated at the power station. Also learn the problems that burning fossil fuels create for the atmosphere and the environment.

QUICK TEST

1. Name three fossil fuels.
2. What gas causes the greenhouse effect?
3. Which fossil fuels when burned cause acid rain?
4. Name one type of environmental damage that might be caused as a result of using fossil fuels in our power stations.
5. Why are fossil fuels called non-renewable sources of energy?
6. Suggest three ways in which we could make fossil fuels last longer.

1. Coal, oil and gas.
2. Carbon dioxide.
3. Coal and oil.
4. Oil spillage.
5. Cannot be replaced.
6. More efficient insulation and engines. Make more use of alternative sources of energy.

USING ENERGY RESOURCES

GEOTHERMAL

In regions where the Earth's crust is thin, hot rocks beneath the ground can be used to heat water turning it into steam. This steam is then used to drive turbines and generate electricity.

+ Renewable source of energy.
+ No pollution and no environmental problems.

− Very few suitable sites.
− High cost of drilling deep into the ground.

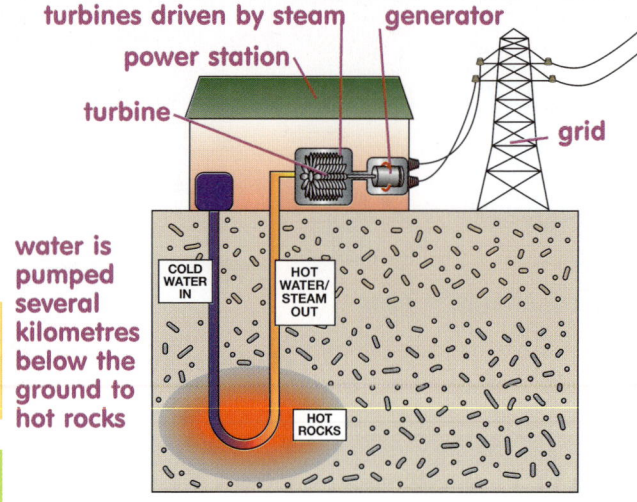

turbines driven by steam — generator
power station
turbine — grid
water is pumped several kilometres below the ground to hot rocks
COLD WATER IN — HOT WATER/STEAM OUT — HOT ROCKS
natural radioactive decay produces heat to warm the rocks

ALTERNATIVE SOURCES OF ENERGY

+ = advantages   − = disadvantages

The energy carried in the Sun's rays is converted directly into electrical energy by solar cells. This then powers the car.

TIDAL POWER

At high tide, water is trapped behind a barrage or dam. When it is released at low tide the gravitational potential energy of the water changes into kinetic energy which then drives turbines and generates electricity.

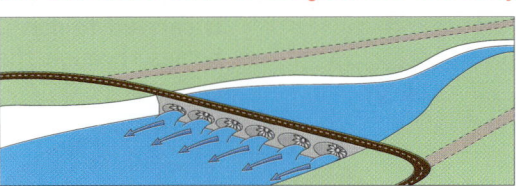

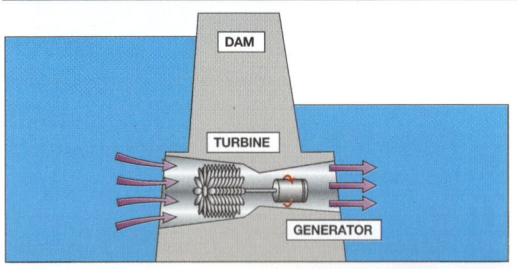

+ Renewable source.
+ Reliable: two tides per day.
+ No atmospheric pollution.
+ Low running costs.

− High initial cost.
− Possible damage to environment, e.g. flooding.
− Obstacle to water transport.

Examiner's Top Tip
Don't waste time memorising the diagrams. Do look at them and remember the advantages and disadvantages of each resource.

SOLAR ENERGY

The energy carried in the Sun's rays can be converted directly into electricity using solar cells.

sunlight → solar cell → electric current → electrical components

OR

The energy carried in the Sun's rays can be absorbed by dark coloured panels and used to heat water.

matt black solar panels on roof, cold water in, hot water out

+ No pollution.

− Initially quite expensive.
− May not be so useful in regions where there is limited sunshine.

ALTERNATIVE SOURCES OF ENERGY

BIOMASS

The chemical energy stored in 'things that have grown', e.g. wood, can be released by burning it. This energy source can be maintained by growing a succession of trees and then cropping them when they mature.

+ Renewable source of energy.
+ Low-level technology, therefore useful in developing countries.
+ Does not add to the greenhouse effect as the carbon dioxide plants release when burned was taken from the atmosphere as they grew.

− Large areas of land needed to grow sufficient numbers of trees.
− Can produce harmful fumes.

WIND POWER

The kinetic energy of the wind is used to drive turbines and generators.

+ It is a renewable source of energy and therefore will not be exhausted.
+ Has low-level technology and therefore can be used in developing countries.
+ No atmospheric pollution.

− Visual and noise pollution.
− Limited to windy sites.
− No wind, no energy.

HYDROELECTRICITY

The kinetic energy of flowing water is used to drive turbines and generators.

Diagram: high lake, dam, station generator, turbine, low lake, National Grid

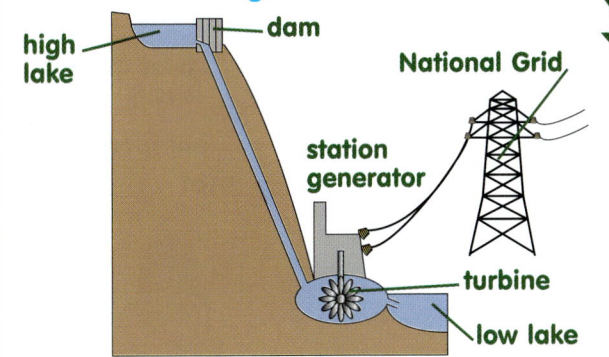

+ Renewable source.
+ Energy can be stored until required.
+ No atmospheric pollution.

− High initial cost.
− High cost to environment, e.g. flooding, loss of habitat.

WAVE POWER

The rocking motion of the waves is used to generate electricity.

Diagram: simple wave machine — the energy in the water waves make this machine rock; this motion is then used to generate electricity

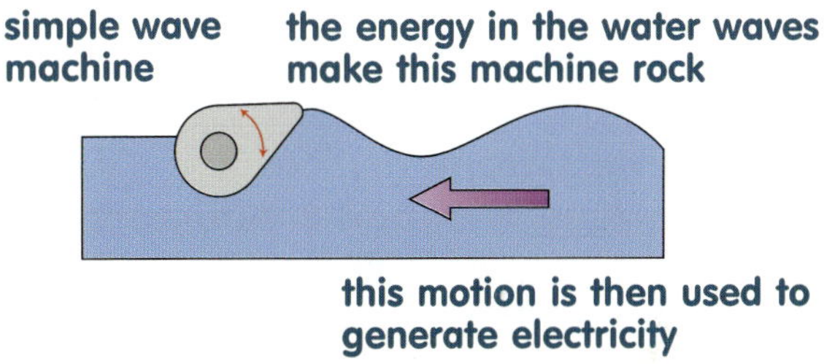

+ Renewable source.
+ No atmospheric pollution.
+ Useful for isolated islands.

− High initial cost.
− Visual pollution.
− Poor energy capture. Large area of machines needed even for small energy return.
− Subject to storm damage.

QUICK TEST

1. Name three ways in which water could be used as an energy resource.
2. Name two energy resources whose use may pollute the environment visually.
3. Name two energy resources which could be easily used and maintained in developing countries.
4. Name two energy resources whose capture requires a suitable site that might be rare.
5. Name one energy resource whose capture might cause an audible pollution.

Answers: 1. Hydroelectricity, tidal, wave. 2. Wind, waves. 3. Wind, biomass. 4. Geothermal, tidal. 5. Wind.

HEAT TRANSFER

Heat will flow when there is a temperature difference between two places. It will flow from the hotter to the cooler place. There are three methods by which it can do this. These are <u>conduction</u>, <u>convection</u> and <u>radiation</u>.

CONDUCTION

<u>Heat</u> is being <u>transferred</u> along this rod by <u>conduction</u>.

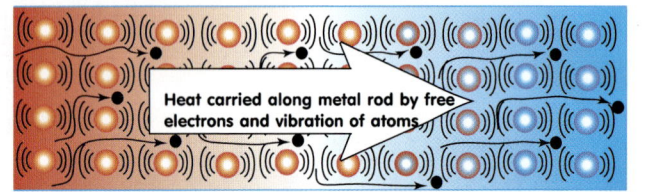

hot — Heat carried along metal rod by free electrons and vibration of atoms — cold

- Particles at the hot end <u>vibrate</u> and move around <u>more</u> <u>vigorously</u>.
- This additional motion is <u>passed</u> <u>on</u> <u>to</u> <u>neighbouring</u> <u>particles</u> causing them to move more vigorously.
- As a result the cold end of the rod gradually becomes warmer.
- All <u>metals</u> are <u>good</u> <u>conductors</u> of heat.
- Most <u>non-metals</u> are <u>poor</u> <u>conductors</u> of heat.
- Most liquids are poor conductors.
- <u>Gases</u> (air) are <u>excellent</u> <u>insulators</u>.
- They do no allow heat to pass through them easily by conduction.
- Woven materials, e.g. wool and cotton, contain trapped air and are excellent insulators.

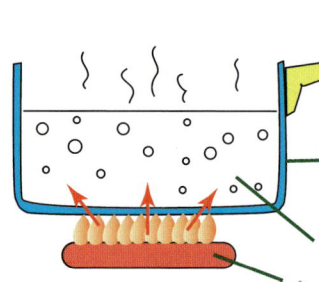

insulated handle
metal pan allows heat to pass through easily
hot food
heat

CONVECTION

Takes place in liquids and gases.

Heat is carried to all parts of the tube by convection current.

3. Fluid cools, becomes more dense and falls.

2. Fluid expands, becomes less dense and rises.

1. Liquid/gas is warmed.

Examiner's Top Tip
Most of our energy comes from the Sun. It must travel by radiation because there are no particles between the Sun and the Earth.

Examiner's Top Tip
Remember that the hottest region of a liquid or a gas is usually near the top.

RADIATION

Heat travelling in straight lines.

- Objects with <u>dark</u>, <u>rough surfaces absorb most of the radiation</u> and become warm/hot.

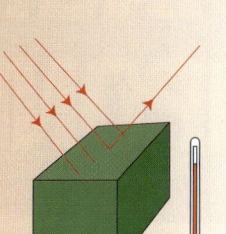

- Objects with light <u>coloured</u>, <u>shiny surfaces reflect most of the radiation</u> and will remain cooler.

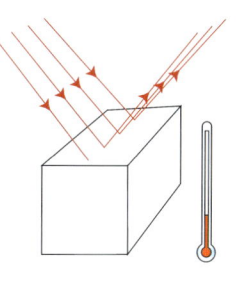

- Houses in hot countries are often painted white so they <u>reflect the radiation</u> and <u>stay cool</u>.

INSULATING THE HOME

This diagram shows how heat may escape from a house that has not been insulated.

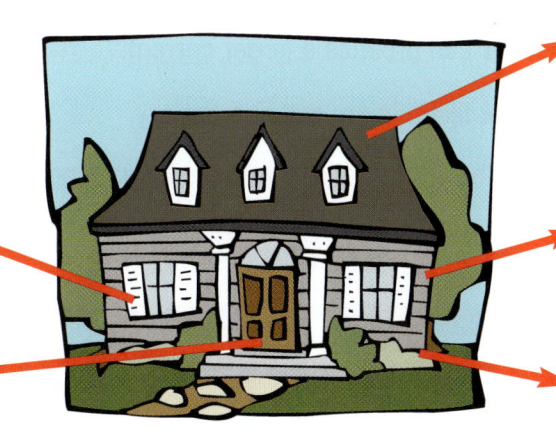

- 25% through roof, cured by putting insulation into loft.
- 10% through windows, cured by installing double glazing.
- 25% through walls, cured by having cavity wall insulation.
- 25% through gaps and cracks around doors and windows, cured by fitting draught excluders.
- 15% through floor, cured by fitting carpets and underlay.

QUICK TEST

1. Name three methods by which heat can travel.
2. Give one example and one use of a good conductor.
3. Give one example and one use of an insulator.
4. Why do metals always feel cold?
5. What is double glazing?
6. Suggest five methods by which you could reduce the heat escaping from your house.
7. How does heat travel from the Sun to the Earth?
8. What two things might happen when heat radiation strikes an object?
9. How is the heat from a radiator transferred to all parts of a room?

Examiner's Top Tip
Try to remember several uses for conductors and insulators especially around the home.

1. Conduction, convection and radiation.
2. Metal, saucepan.
3. Plastic, tablemat.
4. Conduct heat from body quickly.
5. Two panes of glass with air in between.
6. Fibreglass in loft, double glazing, draught excluders, cavity wall insulation, carpets and underlay.
7. Radiation.
8. Absorbed or reflected.
9. Convection current.

CIRCUIT DIAGRAMS AND COMPONENTS

ELECTRIC CURRENT

- An electric current is a flow of charge.
- Charges can be made to flow using a cell or a battery.
- Cells and batteries act as charge pumps.
- They give charges energy.
- Several cells connected together can produce a larger current.
- Several cells connected together like this are called a battery.
- Care must be taken to connect the cells so that they are all pumping in the same direction.

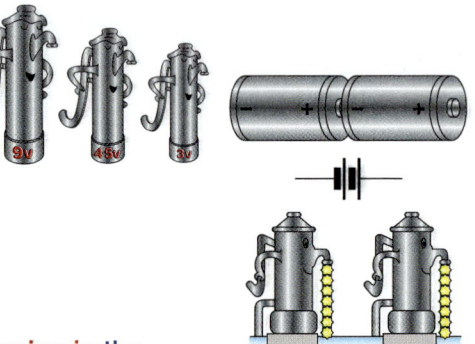

SIMPLE CIRCUITS

- **Charges can flow through wires in the same way that pumped water flows through pipes.**
- **The wires, cells, bulbs etc must be connected to form a complete loop (or circuit).**
- **If there are gaps the circuit will be incomplete and no current will flow.**

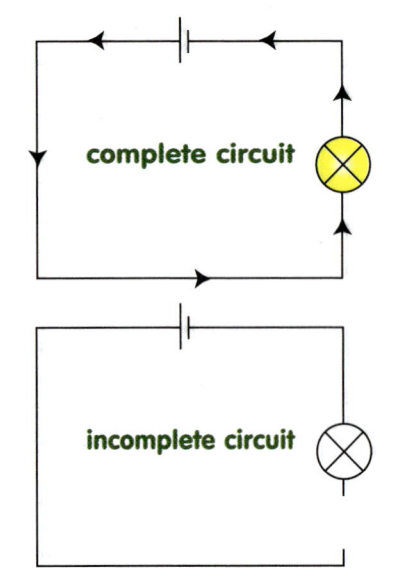

complete circuit

incomplete circuit

CIRCUIT DIAGRAMS

Instead of trying to draw diagrams of the actual components in a circuit we use circuit diagrams containing easy-to-draw symbols for the components, as shown in the diagram below.

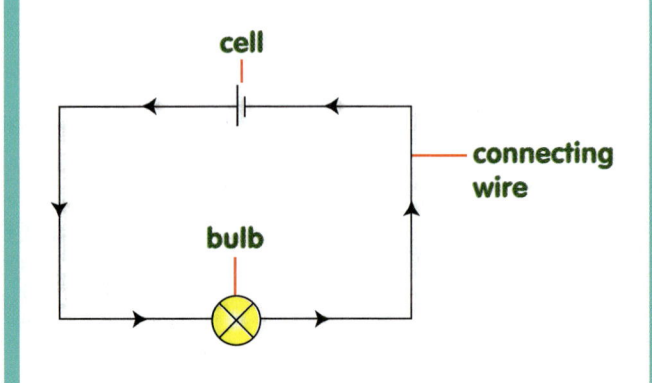

cell

connecting wire

bulb

CIRCUIT SYMBOLS YOU SHOULD KNOW

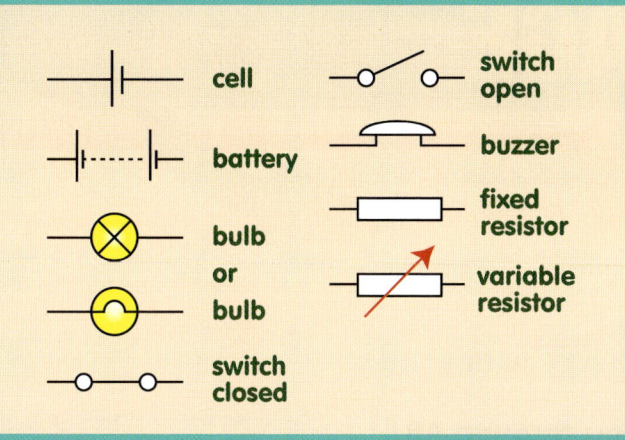

- cell
- battery
- bulb or bulb
- switch closed
- switch open
- buzzer
- fixed resistor
- variable resistor

SWITCHES

- Switches behave like <u>drawbridges</u>, making a circuit complete when they are closed and incomplete when they are open.

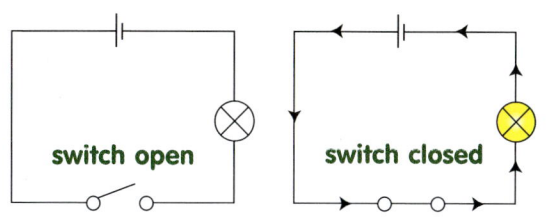

switch open   switch closed

- When the switch is <u>open</u> the circuit is <u>incomplete</u>, current will not flow and the bulb is turned <u>off</u>.
- When the switch is <u>closed</u> the circuit is <u>complete</u>, current will flow and the bulb is turned <u>on</u>.

CONDUCTORS AND INSULATORS

- <u>Metals</u> are <u>good</u> <u>conductors</u> of electricity.
- They allow charges to move through them easily.
- Non-metals are mainly <u>poor</u> <u>conductors</u> (or <u>insulators</u>).
- They do not allow charges to move through them easily.

an object made from an insulating material will not complete the circuit

an object made from a conducting material completes the circuit

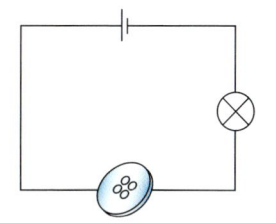

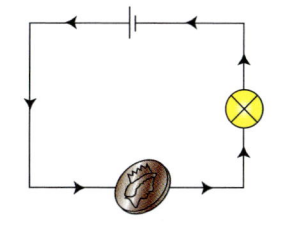

RESISTANCE

All components in a circuit offer <u>resistance</u> to the flow of current.
If the resistance in a circuit is low a large current will flow.
If the resistance in a circuit is high a smaller current will flow.

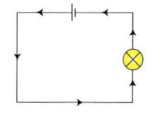

Circuit with low resistance. Bulb glows brightly.

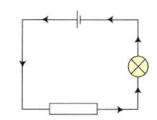

With a resistor in the circuit the current is smaller and the bulb dimmer.

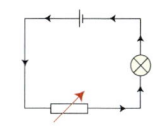

Altering the variable resistor changes the resistance in the circuit and so alters the brightness of the bulb.

CIRCUIT DIAGRAMS AND COMPONENTS

QUICK TEST

1. What is a battery?
2. What does a battery do in a circuit?
3. In order that a current will flow a circuit must be ....
4. Name one material that is a) a conductor and b) an insulator.
5. What do all components in a circuit offer to the flow of current?
6. What is a variable resistor?

1. Several cells connected together.
2. Push charge around.
3. Complete.
4. a) Any metal, b) plastic.
5. Resistance.
6. A resistor whose resistance can be changed.

CIRCUITS – CURRENT AND VOLTAGE

MEASURING CURRENT

- We <u>measure</u> <u>current</u> with an <u>ammeter</u>.
- We measure current in <u>amperes</u> <u>or</u> <u>amps (A)</u>.
- The size of a current is the <u>rate</u> at which <u>charge</u> is <u>flowing</u>.

- Ammeter 1 is measuring the current flowing through AB.
- Ammeter 2 is measuring the current flowing through BC.
- Ammeter 3 is measuring the current flowing through CD.
- All three ammeters show that the same current is flowing in all parts of the circuit.
- This proves that <u>current</u> <u>is</u> <u>not</u> <u>used</u> <u>up</u> <u>as</u> <u>it</u> <u>flows</u> <u>around</u> <u>a</u> <u>circuit</u>.

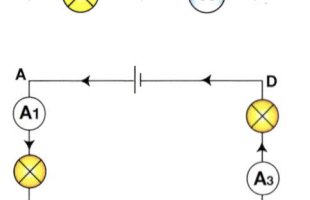

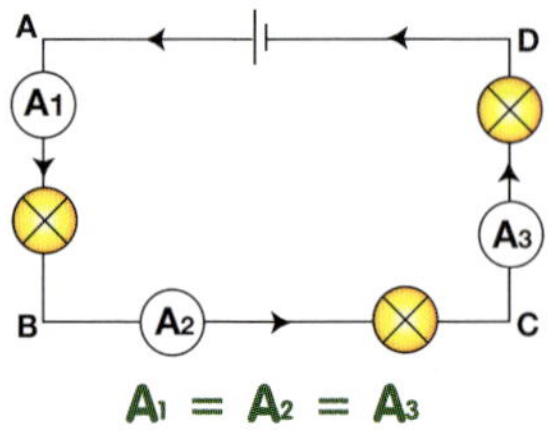

$A_1 = A_2 = A_3$

Examiner's Top Tip
Ammeters are connected in <u>series</u>. Voltmeters are connected in <u>parallel</u>.

ENERGY AND CIRCUITS

- Charges are given energy as they pass through a cell or battery.
- The higher the <u>voltage</u> of a cell or battery the greater the amount of <u>energy</u> given to the <u>charges</u>.
- We can <u>measure</u> the energy given to the charges by the cell or battery using a <u>voltmeter</u>.
- The voltmeter is connected across the cell.
- As charges flow around a circuit they <u>give</u> <u>away</u> <u>the</u> <u>energy</u> they were given by the cell/battery.
- This <u>energy</u> <u>is</u> <u>transferred</u> <u>into</u> <u>other</u> <u>forms</u> by the components in the circuit.

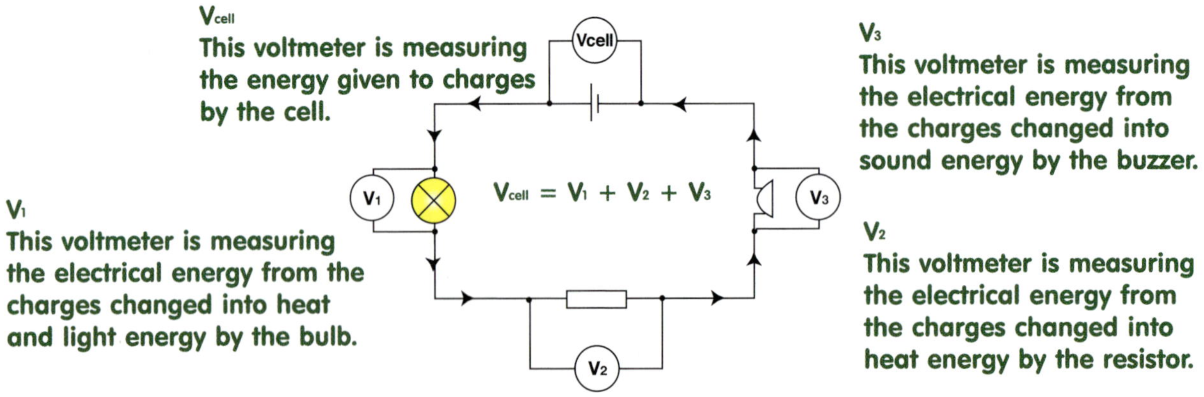

V_cell
This voltmeter is measuring the energy given to charges by the cell.

V_1
This voltmeter is measuring the electrical energy from the charges changed into heat and light energy by the bulb.

V_3
This voltmeter is measuring the electrical energy from the charges changed into sound energy by the buzzer.

V_2
This voltmeter is measuring the electrical energy from the charges changed into heat energy by the resistor.

$V_{cell} = V_1 + V_2 + V_3$

- A <u>bulb</u> <u>transfers</u> electrical energy into <u>heat</u> and <u>light</u> energy.
- A <u>resistor</u> <u>transfers</u> electrical energy into <u>heat</u> energy.
- A <u>buzzer</u> <u>transfers</u> electrical energy into <u>sound</u> energy, etc.
- The amount of electrical energy a component transfers each second is called its <u>power</u> <u>rating</u> and is measured in watts (W).
- A 200 W bulb transfers electrical energy into heat and light energy twice as quickly as a 100 W bulb and is so much brighter.

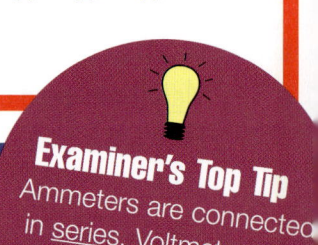

SERIES AND PARALLEL CIRCUITS

There are two types of circuit: series circuits and parallel circuits.

SERIES CIRCUITS

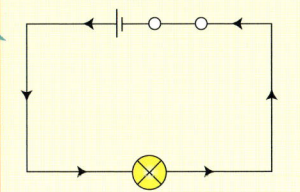

No branches only one path to follow.

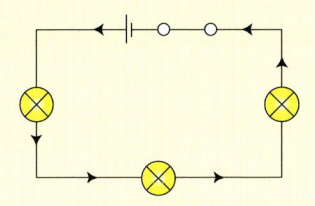

Same current in all parts.

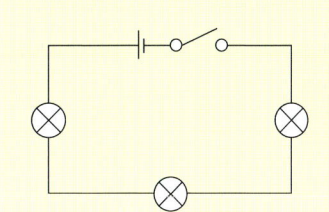

Switch open — no current anywhere in the circuit.

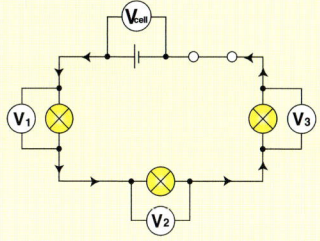

$V_{cell} = V_1 + V_2 + V_3$

- These have no branches or junctions.
- They only have one path for the current to follow.
- Can be turned on and off by a single switch anywhere in the circuit: 'one out all out'.
- They have the same current flowing in all parts of the circuit.
- The sum of the voltages across all the components is equal to the voltage across the cell or battery.

PARALLEL CIRCUITS

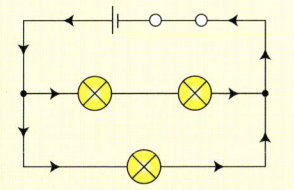

Parallel circuits have branches and more than one path to follow. Currents may be different in different parts of the circuit.

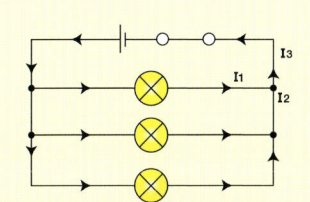

Different currents but currents flowing into junction = currents flowing out i.e. $I_1 + I_2 = I_3$

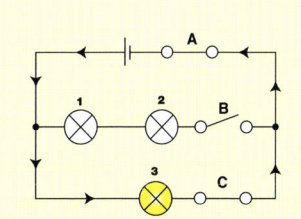

Opening switch B turns off bulbs 1 and 2 but current can still flow through bulb 3. Bulb 3 can be turned on and off with switch C. Switch A can turn all three bulbs on and off.

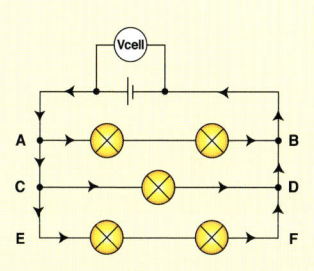

$V_{cell} = V_{AB} = V_{CD} = V_{EF}$

- These have branches and junctions.
- There is more than one path for the current to follow. There is choice.
- Switches can be put into the circuit to turn on and off all or just part of the circuit.
- The size of currents flowing in different parts of the circuit may be different.
- However, the current flowing into a junction must be equal to the current flowing out.

Examiner's Top Tip
It is really important to understand the properties and differences of series and parallel circuits and be able to draw examples of each. Practise drawing circuits containing five or six bulbs with lots of switches and then explaining which switches control which bulbs.

QUICK TEST

1. What is an electric current?
2. How do we measure the size of an electric current?
3. In what units do we measure electric current?
4. What is not used up in an electrical circuit?
5. What is carried around a circuit by the charges?
6. Which transfers electrical energy more quickly, a 500 W heater or a 200 W bulb?

1. Flow of charge. 2. Ammeter. 3. Amperes or amps. 4. Current. 5. Energy. 6. 500 W heater.

MAGNETISM AND ELECTROMAGNETISM

MAGNETS

- **Magnets** attract **magnetic materials**, e.g. iron, steel, nickel and cobalt.
- Magnets do not attract **non-magnetic materials**, e.g. wood, plastic, copper, aluminium, etc.

magnets do not attract non-magnetic materials e.g. plastic, paper, wood, etc.

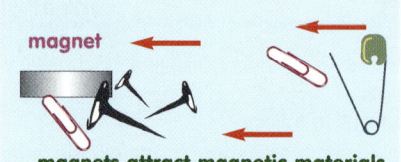

magnets attract magnetic materials e.g. iron, steel, nickel, cobalt

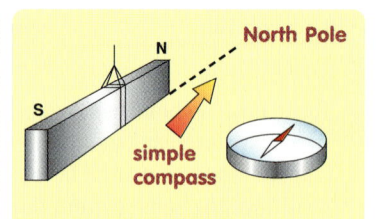

simple compass

similar poles repel

opposite poles attract

- The **strongest parts** of a magnet are its **poles**.
- Most magnets have **two poles**: a **North** pole and a **South** pole.
- A bar magnet suspended horizontally will align itself with the Earth's magnetic field so that its north pole points north and its south pole points south. The magnet behaves like **a compass**.

MAGNETIC DOMAINS

Inside all magnetic materials are tiny parts of crystals or domains containing mini-magnets.

In an unmagnetised piece of iron all the mini-magnets within a domain point in the same direction. But in neighbouring domains they point in different directions.

In a magnetised piece of iron all the mini-magnets in all the domains point in the same direction.

The domains can be made to line up by:
a) placing the iron inside a strong magnetic field
or
b) by stroking the iron with another magnet.

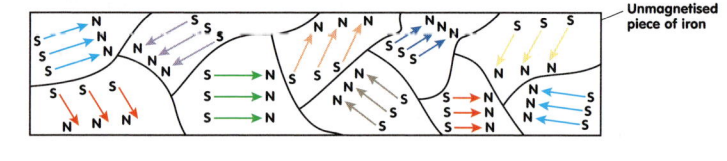

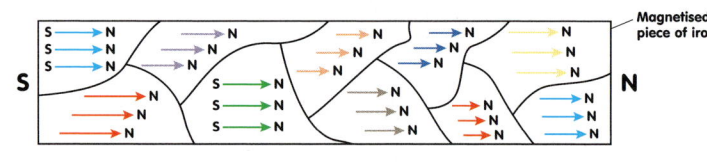

Unmagnetised piece of iron

Magnetised piece of iron

Heating a magnet or continually dropping it will disturb the domains and the magnet will lose its magnetism.

ELECTROMAGNETS

- If a current is passed through a wire which is wrapped around a piece of iron a <u>strong magnetic field</u> is created.
- This combination of <u>coil</u> and <u>core</u> is called an <u>electromagnet</u>.
- The <u>magnetic field</u> around this electromagnet is the <u>same shape</u> as that of a <u>bar magnet</u>.
- To make the magnetic <u>field stronger</u> we can:
  - <u>increase the current</u>
  - increase the <u>number of turns</u> on the coil.
- One of the main advantages of an electromagnet over a permanent magnet is that it can be turned on and off.

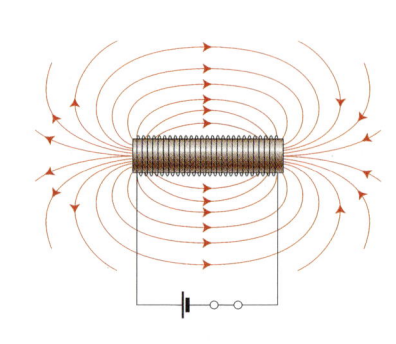

Examiner's Top Tip
Remember not all metals are magnetic, just iron, steel, nickel and cobalt.

MAGNETIC FIELDS

- A <u>magnetic</u> <u>field</u> is a <u>volume</u> <u>of</u> <u>space</u> where magnetic effects, e.g. attraction and repulsion, can be <u>detected</u>.
- The shape of the magnetic field around a bar magnet can be seen using iron filings or plotting compasses.

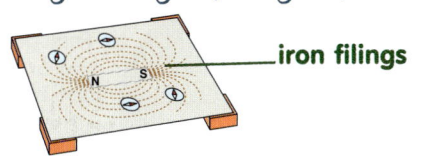

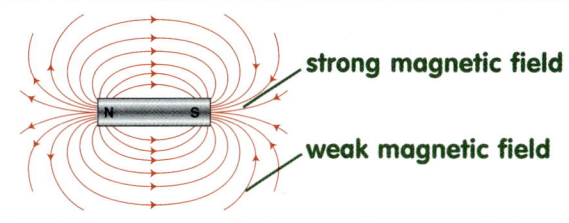

— iron filings

— strong magnetic field
— weak magnetic field

- The <u>shape</u>, strength and direction of magnetic fields is shown using <u>magnetic</u> <u>lines</u> <u>of</u> <u>force</u>.
- The lines are <u>close</u> <u>together</u> where the field is <u>strong</u>.
- The lines are <u>far</u> <u>apart</u> where the field is <u>weak</u>.
- The lines travel from <u>north</u> <u>to</u> <u>south</u>.

USES OF ELECTROMAGNETS

ELECTRIC BELL
- When the bell push is pressed the circuit is complete and the electromagnet is turned on.
- The <u>soft</u> <u>iron</u> <u>armature</u> is pulled towards the electromagnet and the <u>hammer</u> hits the <u>gong</u>.
- At the same time a gap is created at C and the electromagnet is turned off.
- The armature now springs back to its original position and the whole process starts again.
- As long as the bell push is pressed, the armature will vibrate back and forth striking the gong.

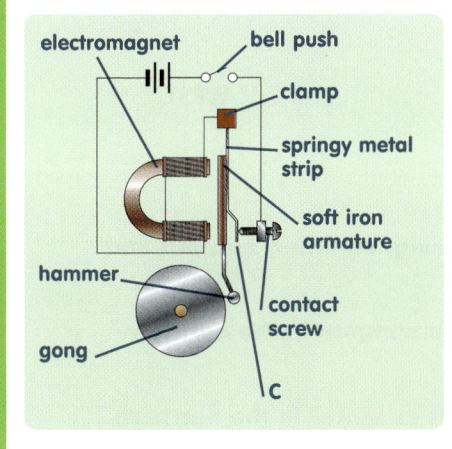

SCRAP-YARD ELECTROMAGNET

The soft iron core of this electromagnet is magnetised when the current is turned on but loses its magnetism when the current is turned off.

- When current flows through the coil, a very strong electromagnet is created which is able to pick up cars.
- When the magnet is <u>turned</u> <u>off</u> the <u>magnetic</u> <u>field</u> <u>collapses</u> and the car is <u>released</u>.

RELAY SWITCH

coil wound on iron core — pivot — L-shaped iron rocker — switch contacts — high voltage high current — machinery requiring large current e.g. car starter motor — low-voltage small current

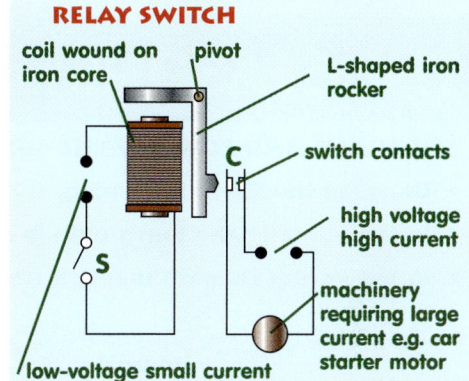

- This can be a safety device. It is often used to <u>turn</u> <u>on</u> <u>a</u> <u>circuit</u> through which a <u>large (potentially dangerous) current</u> flows using a circuit through which a <u>small</u> <u>current</u> <u>flows</u>.
- When the switch S is closed, a small current flows turning the electromagnet on.
- The <u>rocker</u> is pulled down and at the same time <u>the</u> <u>contacts</u> <u>at</u> <u>C</u> are pushed together.
- A large current now flows in the second circuit.
- When S is opened the <u>electromagnet</u> <u>is</u> <u>turned</u> <u>off</u>.
- The <u>rocker</u> <u>is</u> <u>released</u> and returns to its original position.
- The <u>contacts</u> <u>at</u> <u>C</u> <u>open</u> and <u>current</u> <u>ceases</u> <u>to</u> <u>flow</u> in the second circuit.

electromagnet — bell push — clamp — springy metal strip — soft iron armature — hammer — contact screw — gong — C

Examiner's Top Tip
Don't try to remember how to draw circuits for the electric bell, the relay switch and the circuit breaker. Just try to understand how they work.

QUICK TEST

1. What happens when similar poles are placed close to each other?
2. Describe the arrangement of mini-magnets and domains in a magnetised piece of steel.
3. Give two ways of increasing the strength of an electromagnet.
4. Give two uses of an electromagnet.
5. Compare the magnetic field around an electromagnet to that around a bar magnet.

1. They repel.
2. All point in the same direction.
3. Larger current, more turns in coil.
4. Electric bell, relay switch.
5. Both fields have the same shape.

MAGNETISM AND ELECTROMAGNETISM

THE SOLAR SYSTEM AND BEYOND I

We live on a planet called the Earth. Although we cannot feel it, the Earth is spinning. The Earth completes one turn every 24 hours (one day).

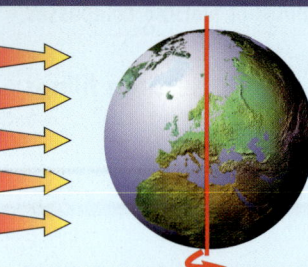

This part of the Earth is receiving sunlight – it is daytime here.

This part of the Earth is not receiving sunlight – it is nighttime here.

THE SEASONS

THE HIGHS AND LOWS OF THE SUN

- Because the Earth is turning, the Sun appears to travel across the sky from the East to the West.
- In the summer the Sun's path is high in the sky.
- In the winter its path is much lower.

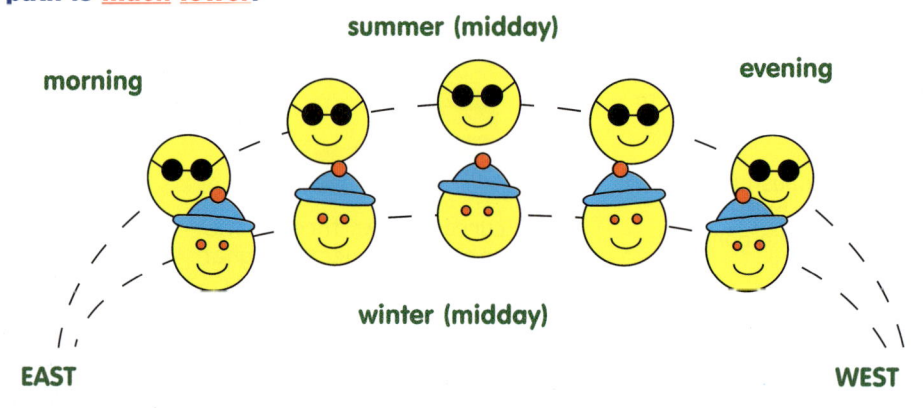

THE SEASONAL TILT

- The Earth orbits the Sun once every year.
- Because the Earth is tilted we experience different seasons – spring, summer, autumn and winter.
- When the northern part of the Earth is tilted towards the Sun it is summer in the northern hemisphere and winter in the southern hemisphere.
- When the northern part of the Earth is tilted away from the Sun it is winter in the northern hemisphere and summer in the southern hemisphere.

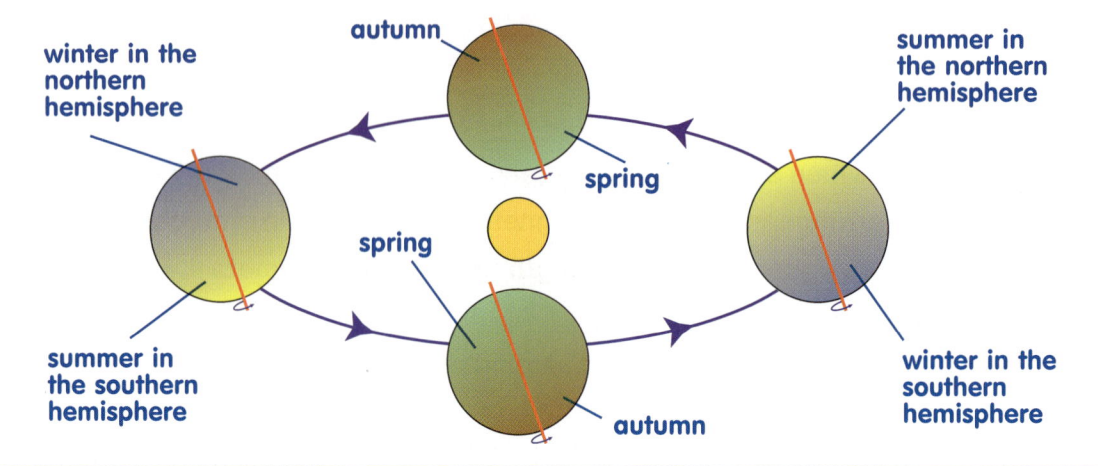

THE SOLAR SYSTEM

Our Solar System consists of a star, a number of planets, moons, asteroids and comets. We call our star the Sun. It contains over 99% of all the mass in our Solar System. The planets, their moons, the asteroids and the comets all orbit the Sun.

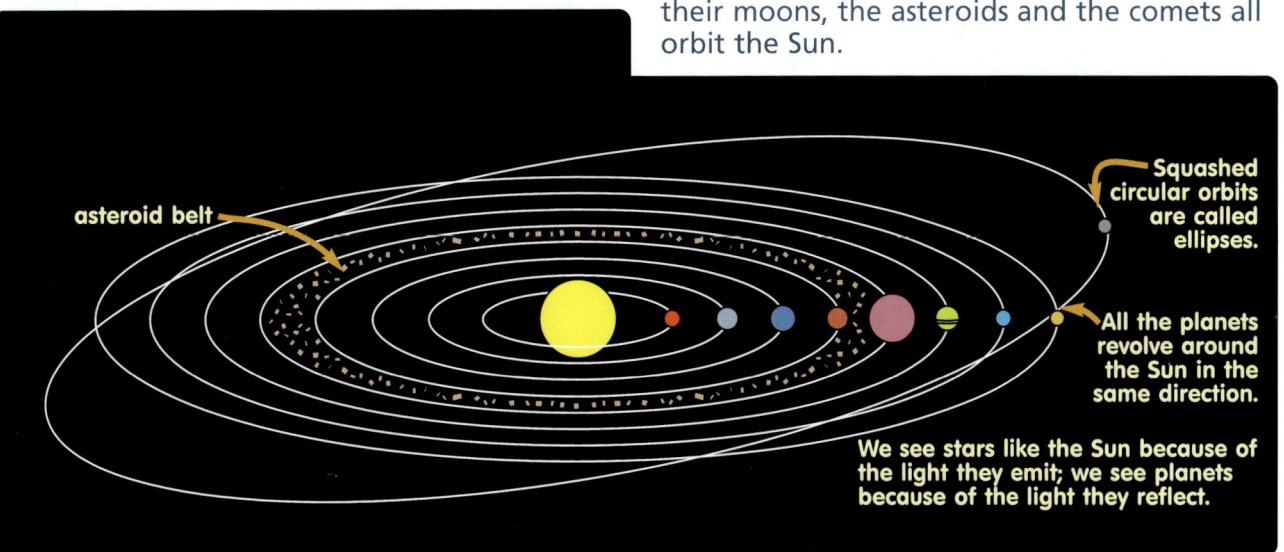

asteroid belt

Squashed circular orbits are called ellipses.

All the planets revolve around the Sun in the same direction.

We see stars like the Sun because of the light they emit; we see planets because of the light they reflect.

- The Earth is one of nine planets. In order from the planet nearest the Sun they are: Mercury, Venus, Earth, Mars, Jupiter, Saturn, Uranus, Neptune and Pluto.
- We can remember the order using the sentence: Many Very Energetic Men Jog Slowly Upto Newport Pagnell.
- We see stars like the Sun because of the light they emit. Stars are luminous objects.
- We see planets and moons because of the light they reflect. They are non-luminous objects.
- Asteroids are lumps of rock up to 1000 km across that orbit the Sun.

INTERESTING (BUT NOT TO BE MEMORISED)

Quite often in an examination you will be given a table of facts about the Solar System and then asked questions about it:

Planet	Distance from the Sun (millions of km)	Orbit time in Earth years	Mass compared with the Earth	Surface temperature in °C
Mercury	60	0.2	0.05	350
Venus	110	0.6	0.8	
Earth	150	1.0	1.0	22
Mars	230	1.9	0.1	−30
Jupiter	775	11.9	318	−150
Saturn	1450	29.5	95	
Uranus	2900	84	15	−210
Neptune	4500	165	17	
Pluto	5900	248	0.1	−230

Try these:

1. Name one planet that is closer to the Sun than the Earth.
2. Name two planets further away from the Sun than Jupiter.
3. Which is the largest planet in our Solar System?
4. Estimate the surface temperature of Saturn.

QUICK TEST

1. How long does it take for the Earth to complete one rotation about its axis?
2. How long does it take the Earth to make one complete orbit of the Sun?
3. What season is it in the southern hemisphere when the northern hemisphere is tilted towards the Sun?
4. Name one body in the sky which is a) luminous and b) non-luminous.
5. What shape are the orbits of the planets?
6. Where is the asteroid belt?

1. 1 day. 2. 1 year. 3. Winter. 4. a) The Sun, b) All planets and moons. 5. Ellipses. 6. Between the orbits of Mars and Jupiter.

THE SOLAR SYSTEM AND BEYOND II

GRAVITATIONAL FORCES

There is gravitational attraction between all objects.

- The greater the masses of the objects the greater the attractive forces between them.
- The closer the objects the greater the attraction between them.

THE PLANETS

The planets move in orbits because they are being 'pulled' by the gravitational attraction of the Sun.

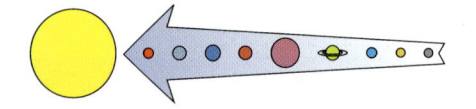

the gravitational pull of the Sun keeps the planets in their orbits

- Objects which are close to the Sun feel strong gravitational forces and so follow very curved paths.
- Objects that are a long way from the Sun feel weak gravitational forces and so follow less curved paths.
- An object on the surface of a planet will experience a gravitational force pulling it downwards. We call this force the **weight** of the object.
- The size of this force will be different on different planets: i.e. an object will have different weights on different planets (and moons). On Jupiter a man will weigh more than twice what he weighs on Earth. On the Moon he will weigh just 1/6th of what he weighs on Earth.

COMETS

- Comets are **large, rock-like pieces of ice** that orbit the Sun.
- They have very **elliptical** orbits.
- They **travel fastest** when they are **close to the Sun**, because the **gravitational forces here are large**.
- Close to the Sun, some of a **comet's ice vaporises, creating a long tail**.

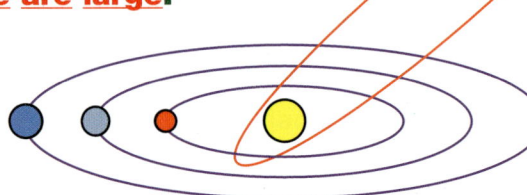

elongated comet orbit

SATELLITES

MOONS

- Moons are large natural satellites that orbit a planet.
- We have just one moon but some planets have several: e.g. Mars has two, Jupiter has 16 and Saturn has 21.

Our Moon is approximately 380,000 km from Earth. Its gravity is 1/6th that on Earth. It orbits the Earth once every 28 days. This is called a lunar month.

PHASES OF THE MOON

As the Moon orbits the Earth it appears to change shape. These shapes are called the phases of the Moon. This happens because we only see the part of the Moon's surface which reflects light from the Sun.

How the Moon is seen from the Earth

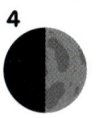

1. Full Moon
2. Third quarter
3. New Moon
4. First quarter

light from the Sun

ECLIPSES

- If the Moon passes between the Sun and the Earth and blocks off the sunlight it is called a solar eclipse.
- If the Moon passes behind the Earth so that the Earth prevents the sunlight from reaching the Moon it is called a lunar eclipse.

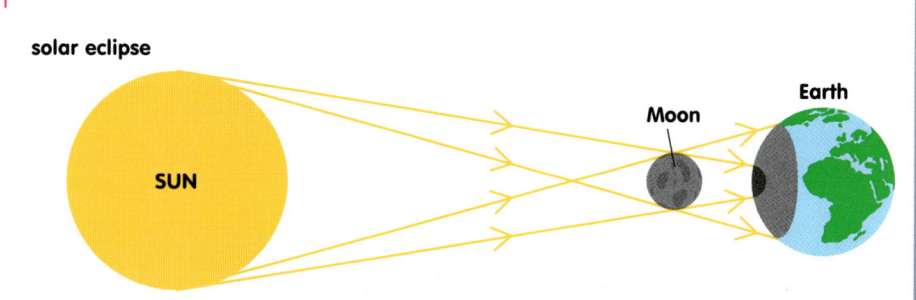

solar eclipse

THE SOLAR SYSTEM AND BEYOND II

QUICK TEST

1. What forces keep all the planets in orbit around the Sun?
2. Name two quantities that affect the size of the attractive forces between the Sun and one of the planets.
3. On which planet will you weigh the most?
4. What is a moon?
5. What is a lunar month?
6. What are the apparent changes in the shape of the Moon more usually called?
7. What kind of eclipse takes place when the Moon passes between the Sun and the Earth?

1. Gravitational forces. 2. The masses of the Sun and planet and their distance apart. 3. Jupiter. 4. A natural satellite. 5. The time for the Moon to orbit the Earth once (approx 28 days). 6. Phases of the Moon. 7. Solar eclipse.

123

EXAM QUESTIONS – Use the questions to test your progress. Check your answers on page 127.

1. A car travels 200 km in 4 hours. Calculate the speed of the car.

2. A train travels for 6 hours at an average speed of 120 km/h. Calculate the distance travelled by the train in this time.

3. A racing car averages 200 km/h in a race which is 600 km long. How long does it take for the car to complete the race?

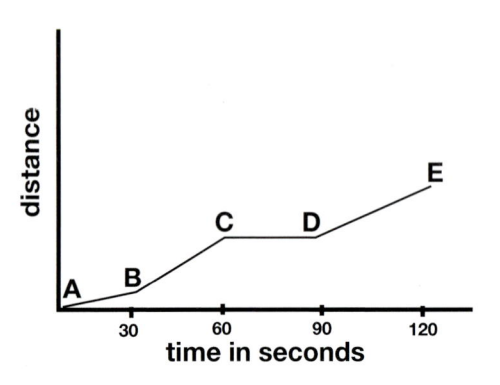

4. The graph below shows the journey of a cyclist.
    (i) During which part of the journey is the cyclist not moving?
    ....
    (ii) During which part of the journey is the cyclist travelling fastest?
    ....
    (iii) How long did the whole journey take?
    ....

5. The diagram below shows two tug of war teams pulling on a rope. At the moment neither of the teams is moving.
    (i) What is the size of the force being applied to the rope by team B?
    ....
    (ii) Explain your answer.
    ....

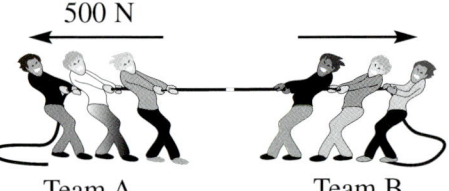

6. A man weighing 90 N floats in a swimming pool.
    (a) What is the name of the force which keeps him afloat?
    (b) What is the size of this force?

7. (a) What force causes an object to fall?
    (b) What force tries to prevent a falling object from accelerating?
    (c) Under what conditions does an object fall at a constant velocity called the terminal velocity?

8. The diagram below shows a piece of wood labelled A being spun quickly whilst in contact with another piece of wood labelled B. There is a large amount of friction between the two pieces of wood.
    (i) Name two possible effects of this friction.
    ....
    (ii) Suggest one way in which this friction could be reduced.
    ....
    (iii) Suggest two ways in which the friction between a car tyre and a road may be reduced.
    ....

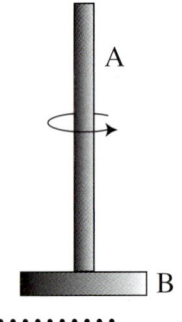

9. Explain the phrase 'an object has a streamlined shape'.

10. The diagram opposite shows a spanner being used to undo a nut.
    (i) Calculate the moment created by the force. ....
    (ii) Suggest two ways in which the size of the moment could be increased.
    ....

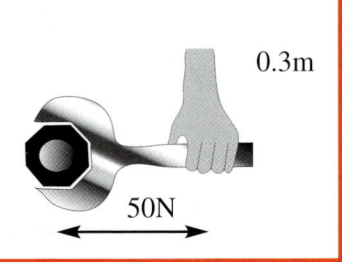

11. A man weighing 80 N sits 3 m from the centre of a see-saw. Where must a 60 N woman sit if the see-saw is to balance?

12. Explain why the base of a dam wall is always much thicker than the rest of the dam.

13. The diagram opposite shows a crowd of people watching a firework display.
    (i) Name one object in the diagram which is luminous.
    ....
    (ii) Name one object in the diagram which is non-luminous.
    ....
    (iii) Explain why during the display there is a delay between seeing and then hearing the fireworks explode.
    ....

14. The table below shows what happens when light hits a coloured object. Fill in the empty spaces.

Colour of incident light	Actual colour of object	Colour of object seen by observer
White	Green	
Green	Green	
Red	Green	

15. If a bee flies close by we can hear its buzzing.
    (i) Which part of the bee creates these sounds?..
    (ii) Explain in your own words how these sounds travel to our ears..

16. (i) Name three fossil fuels. ....
    (ii) Name two environmental problems caused by burning fossil fuels. ....
    ....
    (iii) Name three alternative sources of energy. ....
    ....

17. Complete the table shown below.

Energy in	Energy changer	Energy out
Electrical	Light bulb	Heat and A ....
Elastic	Catapult	B ....
C	Radio	Sound
D	Candle	E .... and F ....

How did you do?

1 – 4	correct	....start again
5 – 8	correct	....getting there
9 – 12	correct	....good work
12 – 17	correct	....excellent

ANSWERS

Biology

1. a) Nucleus b) Cytoplasm c) Cell membrane d) Mitochondria.
2. The chloroplasts.
3. A red blood cell, haemoglobin, transports oxygen around the body.
4. 1b, 2d, 3c, 4a
5. Flower, root, root hair, leaf, stem.
6. The circulatory system.
7. Male sex cells are in the anther, female in the ovary.
8. a) Water b) Chlorophyll c) Oxygen.
9. Reptiles.
10. Gets churned up and mixed with gastric juices containing protease enzymes and hydrochloric acid.
11. In the nucleus of cells.
12. Absorption.
13. Thin lining, lots of them (large surface area), and good blood supply.
14. The flow of energy from one organism to another.
15. Emphysema, bronchitis and lung cancer.
16. a) Oxygen b) Water c) Energy.
17. Plasma, platelets, red blood cells, white blood cells.
18. An artery carries blood away from the heart at high pressure and has much thicker walls; a vein carries blood back to the heart at low pressure and has thinner walls.
19. 1. Produce antibodies. 2. Produces antitoxins 3. Engulf some bacteria and viruses.
20. The thick lining of the womb, the placenta and the amniotic fluid surrounding the baby.
21. Muscles that oppose each other's movement e.g. the biceps and triceps.
22. a) Trachea b) Bronchus c) Bronchioles d) Alveoli e) Diaphragm f) Intercostal muscles.
23. Where the immune system has a memory for a particular microbe and can produce antibodies much more quickly to fight the disease.
24. Nitrates, phosphates and potassium.
25. The female part of a flowering plant, made up of a stigma, style and an ovary containing ovules.
26. Selective breeding.
27. The air we breathe out is cleaner, warmer, contains more water vapour, and more carbon dioxide.
28. 46.
29. The transfer of pollen from an anther to a stigma.
30. Carbohyrates, protein, fat, vitamins, minerals, fibre and water.

Chemistry

1. c).
2. a) green
   b) blue and yellow.
3. a) iodine
   b) bromine
   c) fluorine/chlorine.
4. a) magnesium + oxygen ➡ magnesium oxide
   b) The magnesium combines with oxygen.
5. a) iron oxide, carbon monoxide, carbon dioxide
   b) iron.
6. calcium carbonate ➡ calcium oxide + carbon dioxide.
7. a) magnesium, zinc, iron, copper
   b) magnesium + zinc sulphate ➡ zinc + magnesium sulphate.
8. methane + oxygen ➡ water and carbon dioxide.
9. magma cooled faster at T
10. oxygen.
11. 3.
12. a) neutralisation/exothermic
    b) $H_2SO_4 + 2NaOH \rightarrow Na_2SO_4 + 2H_2O$.
13. a) oxygen
    b) water vapour and carbon dioxide.
14. a) hydrogen
    b) zinc + hydrochloric acid ➡ zinc chloride + hydrogen.
15. purple/blue.

Physics

1. 50 km/h.
2. 720 km.
3. 3 h.
4. (i) CD, (ii) BC, (iii) 120 s.
5. (i) 500 N, (ii) If there is no motion the forces must be balanced.
6. a) Upthrust, b) 90 N.
7. a) Gravity, b) Friction or air resistance, c) Frictional force equals gravitational force.
8. (i) Wearing away of surface and heat,
   (ii) Use a lubricant such as oil or water,
   (iii) Worn tyre (lack of tread), smooth road surface or wet/greasy road surface.
9. It has a shape which keeps frictional forces to a minimum as it moves.
10. (i) 15 Nm, (ii) Increase size of force or use a longer spanner.
11. 4 m from centre of see-saw.
12. The pressure from the water is greatest at the base of the dam.
13. (i) Exploding rockets, (iii) People, ground, rug etc, (iii) Light waves travel much faster than sound waves.
14. Green, Green, Black.
15. (i) Its wings, (ii) Vibrating wings create a series of compressions and rarefactions in the air which travel outwards to our ears.
16. (i) Coal, oil and gas, (ii) Acid rain and greenhouse effect, (iii) Wind, wave tidal, solar, etc.
17. A Light, B Kinetic energy, C Electrical energy, D Chemical energy, E Heat, F Light.

INDEX

absorption 10
acceleration 87, 89, 91
acids 10-11, 46, 68-71
    dilute acids 65
    tests 68
acid rain 46, 48
adrenal 7
adaptation 40
air 18-19, 63-4, 75
air pollution 48-9
air resistance 92
alcohol 23, 77
alkalis 68-9
alkaline solutions 61
    tests 68
alloys 58
aluminium 67
alveoli 18
amps 116
animals and humans 4-27, 32-3, 40-1, 104
    classification of 32
    variation in 34
antibodies 14, 25
argon 75
arteries 13-15
astronomy 120-1
atoms 56-7, 60, 74, 80-1, 83
atomic mass 56
    electric charges 57
    nuclei 57

bacteria 5, 24-5, 30-1
bases 68, 70
Benedicts solution 8
biconcave discs 5
biology 4-43
biomass energy 111
biomass pyramids 39
bladder 7
blood 5, 7, 10-15, 18
    oxygenated and deoxygenated 12-15, 18, 25
    red blood cells 14-15
    white blood cells 14-15, 25
brain 7, 22
breathing 18-19, 23
bromine 60, 80
burning 62-4, 73

calcium 9, 64-6
calcium carbonate 44, 48, 69
calcium chloride 62, 69
    see also salts
capillaries 12, 14, 18
carbohydrates 8-9
carbon 60, 64, 80
carbon cycle 30
carbon dioxide 6, 14-15, 19, 26-7, 30, 46, 48-49, 63, 73, 75, 80, 108
    tests 72
cells 4-5, 9, 12, 14
    ciliated cells 5
    division 4
    membranes 4-5, 8
    nuclei 4-5, 14, 21, 36, 57
    plant cells 4-5
    specialised cells 4-5
    walls 4, 24

    see also palisade cells, red blood cells, white blood cells
central nervous system 7, 17, 23
chalk 46, 48
chemical energy 106-7
chemistry 44-85
chemical apparatus 72
chemical reactions 4, 8, 19, 46, 48, 62-5, 70, 76-8, 80
    balancing equations 82-3
    tests and hazards 72-3
chlorine 80
chlorophyll 4, 6, 26
chloroplasts 4-6, 26
chromatography 77
chromosomes 36
cilia 5
circulatory system 5, 7, 12-15
colours 100-1
compounds 74-5, 78-81
    naming 80-1
conduction 112
convection 112
copper 64-6
copper carbonate 70
copper chloride 70
copper oxide 70
copper sulphate 9, 66, 71, 78, 81
cytoplasm 14, 19
cytoplasts 4-5

death and decay 30-1
decibels 105
diabetes 7
diamonds 60
diet 9
diffusion 54
digestive system 7, 10-11, 15
disease and ill-health 9, 12, 14, 19, 24-5, 36, 48, 69, 73, 105
displacement reactions 66-7
dissolving 52-3
distance/time calculations and graphs 86-8
distillation 77
DNA 37
drugs 22-3
dyes 77, 101

ears 7, 17, 102-5
echoes 104
electricity 106-11, 114-17
    circuits 114-17
        series and parallel 117
    insulators and conductors 115
    resistors 115
    switches 115
electrolysis 64
electromagnetism 118-19
electrons 56-7
elements 56-7, 74, 79
emulsification 11
endocrine system 7
energy 8-9, 19, 26, 38, 106-11
energy transfers 107, 116
    renewable 108, 110-11
    see also electricity, energy, heat, kinetic energy, light, nuclear energy,
sound

environment 34, 38, 48-9, 108
enzymes 10-11, 24
erosion 47
ethanol 8, 27
evaporation 76
excretion (waste) 4, 7-8, 10-11, 19, 39
excretory system 7, 19
expansion 50, 55, 61
eyes 7, 17, 98-9, 101

fats 8-11, 17
    tests 8
feldspar 75
fertilisation 20-1
    in plants 28-9
fibre 9
filtration 76
flowers 6, 28
fluorine 80
food chains and webs 38-9
    see also nutrition
forces 90-4, 96-7
fossil fuels 49, 108
fossils 44
friction 92
fungi 24

gases 19, 30, 50-1, 54-5, 61, 73-5, 78, 112
gas exchange 18-19
genes 36
germs see microbes
glands 7, 11
glucose 6-8, 10, 19, 26
    tests 8
gneiss 45
gold 64-6
granite 44, 75
graphite 59-60
graphs of motion 88-9
gravitation 122
greenhouse effect 49
growth 4, 6, 9, 29

hair 17
heart 12-15, 18, 23
heat (thermal energy) and temperature 46, 51-2, 54-5, 58-9, 77, 106-7, 109
heat transfer 58-9, 112-13
    melting and boiling points 51, 58-9, 74-5, 77
hormones 7, 14, 20
hydrochloric acid 69-70
hydroelectricity 111
hydrogen 61, 65, 73, 81-3
    tests 72

igneous rocks 44, 47, 75
immune system 24-5
insulin 7
insulation 113
iodine 8, 27, 80
iron 9, 62-7, 78

joints 16-17

kidneys 7, 15, 23
kinetic energy 106-7, 111

INDEX

large intestine 11
lava 44
lead 64-6
leaves 6, 26-7
lenses 100
life 4
ligaments 16
light 6, 98-101, 107
    dispersion 100
    refraction 100
    speed of 98
limestone 44, 48
liquids 50-3, 54-5, 60-1, 77, 96, 112
liver 11, 15, 23
lungs 12-13, 15, 18-19

magma 44-5, 47
magnesium 62-6, 73, 80
magnetism 58-9, 78, 118-19
marble 46, 48
mass 51-2, 83, 91
meiosis 4
menstruation 7, 20-1
mercury 50, 61
metals 58-67, 70, 112
metal carbonates 70
metal hydroxides 71
metal oxides 70
metamorphic rocks 45, 47
methane 63
mica 75
microbes 24-5
minerals 6, 9, 26
mirrors 99
mitochondria 4
mitosis 4
mixtures 74-7
    separating 76-7
molecules 10-11, 75, 79
moments 94-5
mouth 11
movement 4, 16-17
mucus 5
muscles 5, 7, 16-18

neon 75
nerve cells 5
nervous system 7, 17, 22
neutralisation 69-70
neutrons 57
nitrates 27, 31
nitrogen 19, 75
nitrogen cycle 31
non-metals 48, 59, 60, 112
nose 7, 17, 54
nuclear energy 106, 108
nuclei see under cells
nutrition 4-6, 8-9

oesophagus (gut) 11
organs 4-7
organisms 4
ova (eggs) 5, 20-1, 36
ovaries 7
oxygen 6, 14, 19, 26, 36, 62, 73, 75, 80-3
    tests 72

palisade cells 5-6, 26
pancreas 7, 11

particles 50-1, 53-5, 75, 96, 112
    diffusion of 54
periodic table 56, 58
phloem 6, 26
phosphates 27
photosynthesis 4-6, 26-7, 30
physics 86-125
pituitary 7
plants 4-6, 27-35, 38, 40, 48
    classification of 33
    growth 26-7, 68
    reproduction 28-9
    roots 6, 26-7
    variation in 34
plasma 14
platelets 14
pollination 28
pollution 48
population sizes 40
potassium 27, 64-6
potassium nitrate 52
predators 40
pressure 54, 96-7
prey 40
prisms 100
proteins 9-10, 27, 31
    tests 9
protons 57
puberty 20
pulse 13

quartz 75

radiation 113
reactants 78
rectum 11
reflection 98-9
refraction 100
reproduction 4, 6-7, 20-1
respiration 4, 6-7, 19, 30
rocks 44-8, 75
    crystals 44
    igneous 44, 47, 75
    metamorphic 45, 47
    sedimentary 44, 47
    transportation 47
    weathering 46-7
root hairs 5-6
rusting and corrosion 62-3
    tests 62

safety hazards 73, 105
salts 14, 53, 65, 69-71, 74, 76
sand 76
sandstone 44
schist 45
seasons 120
sedimentary rocks 44, 47
seeds 28-9
sensitivity 4, 6-7, 16-17
sight 7, 17, 98-9
skeletal system 7, 16
skin 7, 17, 24, 27, 73
small intestine 11
smell 7, 17, 54
smoking 19
sodium 61, 64-6, 80
sodium hydroxide 9, 61, 65
sodium nitrate 52
solar system 120-3

solids 50-1, 53, 55, 75
solubility 52-3, 68, 70
solutes 52-3, 76
solutions 52, 77
solvents 23, 52-3, 76-7
sound 7, 17, 102-7
    amplitude 102
    vibrations 102
speed 86-9
sperm 4-5, 20-1
starch 8, 10, 27
    tests 8
states of matter, changing 50-5
steel 62-3
stems 6
stomach 11
stomata 6, 26
sugar 52
sulphur 48, 78, 80
    sulphur dioxide 46
    sulphuric acid 73
symbols 56
synovial fluid 16
synovial joints 16

taste 7, 17
teeth 10-11
tendons 16-17
testes 7, 20
thermit reactions 67
thyroid 7
tidal energy 110
tin 63
tissues 5
tongue 7, 17, 35
toxins 24-5
touch 7, 17
twins 21, 34

ultrasound 104

vacuoles 4
variation 34-5
veins 12-15, 26
velocity 86, 89
    terminal velocity 93
villi 11
viruses 24-5
vitamins 9
volts 116

waste see excretion
water 6-9, 27, 41, 44, 46, 51, 61, 65, 69-71, 74-7, 81-3
wave power 111

xylem 6, 26

zinc 64-6, 70
zinc carbonate 70
zinc chloride 70
zinc sulphate 66, 70